Walt Coburn: western word wrangler;
MT. B COB   20043

Coburn, Walt,

PHILLIPS COUNTY LIBRARY

Coburn, Walt

Walt Coburn: Western word wrangler

DATE DUE

MR 1 4 '14			
FE 1 0 '15			
OC 0 5 '16			
FE 1 7 '17			
SE 2 5 '17			
JY 1 4 '21			
DE 2 1 '21			
SEP 2 5 2024			

PHILLIPS-COUNTY LIBRARY

WALT COBURN: Western Word Wrangler

WALT COBURN

Western Word Wrangler

An Autobiography

With a foreword by
Walter Brennan

NORTHLAND PRESS

Appreciation is expressed to Ramon F. Adams
for his editorial contributions.

Copyright © 1973 by Mrs. Walt Coburn

All Rights Reserved

FIRST EDITION

ISBN 0-87358-122-9

Library of Congress Catalog Card Number 73-87458

Composed and Printed in the United States of America

Contents

ix		Foreword
1	CHAPTER 1:	The Circle C Ranch
16	CHAPTER 2:	Early Days in Montana
32	CHAPTER 3:	Santa Claus School Days
48	CHAPTER 4:	Bowse, Beer and Barrooms
63	CHAPTER 5:	Stanford meets Bowse
83	CHAPTER 6:	Cowboy in Prep School
96	CHAPTER 7:	John Barleycorn's Revenge
111	CHAPTER 8:	Farewell Palo Alto
122	CHAPTER 9:	A Well-burned Bridge
139	CHAPTER 10:	Pancho Villa's Army
155	CHAPTER 11:	From Saddle to Cockpit
183	CHAPTER 12:	$25 for the First One
192	CHAPTER 13:	More Money — Good Advice
202	CHAPTER 14:	Carmel and Calamity
226	CHAPTER 15:	Cold Sober and Married
237	CHAPTER 16:	King of the Western Pulps
253	Walt Coburn — 1889–1971	
255	Bibliographical Note	

Illustrations

23	Robert and Mary B. Coburn
37	House in White Sulphur Springs, Montana where Walt was born
59	Walt Coburn, age eight
79	Walt in Prescott
115	Walt ready for rugby
135	Will James illustration
159	Walt Coburn, Air Cadet
179	Walt on survey crew
231	Pat Coburn
233	Walt and Jack Dempsey
235	Walt as a young writer
241	Cover of *Walt Coburn's Action Novels*
245	Walt in Del Mar
249	Coburn home in Tucson
251	Walt on Peanuts

Foreword

IF MY FRIEND, WALT COBURN, looks down and sees me writing this foreword to his autobiography, he'll probably say, "They sure take advantage of a man when he's dead."

Walt could write this better than I can. But I'm honored and privileged that I've been asked. Still, I don't feel adequate. Walt's span of time covered so much ground, involved so many people, that in this life story I'm not much more than a bookmark.

But I place myself second to no one in the warmth, affection and admiration I felt for Walt Coburn. I miss him.

I miss him, not so much for the things he said, because I can read them in a thousand stories and books he wrote. But I miss him for the things he didn't live to say. I miss him for his keen mind and eye as to what was truly western. His cowboy background made his writing original and accurate. He refused to read western stories written by anyone else. "Heck," he told me, "those writers sitting in New York with their heels up on the desk looking out at skyscrapers — why they know as much about the west as I do about New York."

This was not ego. Walt was a gentle, shy man. I met him in 1939 when I went down to Tucson to play Judge Roy Bean in Gary Cooper's picture. Walt had seen me in a few movies and had someone arrange for him to meet me. He came over to the hotel wearing the cowboy hat and the pants with one leg in and one leg out of his western boots. He was so quiet I tried to break the ice by saying,

"I read an awfully good book you wrote, *Sky Pilot Cowboy*." Walt looked at me surprised and obviously flattered. After a moment he said, "You paid for that one — the next one's on me."

I have played in many western movies, but when, like a small boy, I sat at the knee of Walt Coburn and listened to yet unwritten tales of his experiences as a cowboy, I realized that as good as it was, my west was celluloid, Walt's was real. He had lived it and breathed it and though I too have loved the west, all the living and breathing of it I can do, won't get me caught up with Walt. He was at a time and place in the west which doesn't exist anymore.

I miss Walt for his sly humor. After some years I returned to Tucson to shoot "Red River" and Walt came to see me. He looked me over skeptically, squinted up at me and said, "You mean to tell me that I'm older than *you?*"

And I miss his brand of sentimentality. On his eightieth birthday I telephoned him in Prescott, Arizona to wish him a happy birthday. I heard him clear his throat once or twice and then he said, "You've got me crying."

"That wasn't what I intended," I said.

"Well," he answered, "this'll teach you — don't go around trying to make an old man happy."

I miss Walt's odd bits of philosophy. When he heard writers were using some of his material, I tried to console him by asking if he wasn't flattered at being imitated. He shrugged, "Imitation is the sincerest form of plagiarism."

I miss him for his opinions on anything and everything, including religion. Two months before Walt died I received a letter from him telling about going to Mass in a new church. He said, in part, "The latest mod innovation is a group of teenagers, the boys with long hair and the girls in mini-skirts, who play the guitar and sing rock music. So with the rock music and the good-looking teenage gals singing Beatle songs, not the beautiful old hymns in Latin, and the new Mass in English, it is hard for this old reprobate to gain any measure of the old Catholic faith to keep his mind on God. So I sit on a long modern cushioned bench (I call it the mourner's bench) where the ushers sit, and try my best to say my rosary and repent my sins and communicate with God."

I don't know why Walt died the way he did. I don't think he really wanted to die that way. I think he'd have preferred to die in bed — from bad whiskey. But if he thought he was getting away from us, or whatever it was he was tired of, he fooled himself. He left us this book, so in a way he hasn't gone that far from us, or the earth, or the sky, or the sun — all of which he was part of. But still, I miss him.

Walter Brennan

CHAPTER 1

The Circle C Ranch

IN SETTING DOWN the chronicle of a man's life the biographer customarily starts at the beginning, with the date of birth, the birthplace, and the salient facts connected with the birth of a mortal. That holds doubly true if the chronicler has the foolish temerity to write his own autobiography, in order to beat some later date biographer from picking the meat off his bones like a vulture.

The man who writes the story of his own life before he follows the ghostly rider on the pale horse into the Sand Hills is strictly on his own, and if he has any degree of honesty he will tell both the evil and the good and that which goes in between, acting as his own Devil's Advocate.

According to the birth certificate this mortal was born on October 23, 1889, in White Sulphur Springs, Meagher County, Montana Territory, a month before Montana received statehood, under the Zodiac sign of Scorpio, with all the scorpion's venomous sting that was to shape my destiny. The attending physician was Doctor Kumpe, and when he slapped the new born babe on its bare red rump I let out my first squeal.

For the first six or eight months of my babyhood I was very puny, with my chance of survival in grave doubt. My father always added a teaspoon of whisky to my milk bottle to pacify me into slumber. In later years my mother attributed my fondness for booze to my baby days when my milk bottle was spiked. But at the time my father claimed he used whisky to cure an ailing newborn colt and if the whisky mixed with mare's milk had cured the colt, why not a human baby.

My father had sired four sons and three daughters by his first marriage to Mary Morrow, and when she died he married my mother, the former Mary Blessing, and they had two sons, Harold and me. A year or so before my father and mother were married, my eldest half sister, Jessie, was married to Fletcher Maddox, a young Great Falls attorney fresh out of law school. Their son, Coburn, was born a year before I came into the world, so that I had a nephew a year older than I.

My older half brothers, Will and Bob, were also married and that left my mother the task of raising my half sisters, Agnes and Edna, and my half brother, Wallace. The youngest half brother, Warren, had died of pneumonia before I was born. My full brother, Harold, was six years younger than I.

By the time I was born my father was a prosperous cattleman. He had met and married my mother when she had come from Independence, Ohio, to visit her sister Kate in White Sulphur Springs. Aunt Kate was married to John O'Marr who had a small stock farm and owned a butchershop. I was six years old when my parents moved to Great Falls so that my recollection of my birthplace is vague. But a few kid impressions remain stamped forever in my memory, although as I write this, I have passed my eightieth milestone as time is marked.

I have a clear memory of the large two-story brick house with a railed-in front porch, and white trim. A one-story brick room joined the kitchen at the rear, and was used as a storeroom for Mason jars of canned fruit, preserves and cases of dried fruit of all descriptions, and also as a laundry room. There was an acre-sized fenced-in horse pasture and a barn with a hayloft and carriage house at the rear of the house. On one side of the house were the bay windows of the parlor and the master bedroom directly above, where I was born.

In that era small boys up to the age of six were dressed in knee-length Scottish kilts with matching jacket, a cap or a jellybean hat, and their hair in shoulder-length curls. I have a clear and painful recollection of sitting on a high stool while my mother spent an endless time with the curling iron heated to the right temperature over the lamp chimney, with me chewing on a licorice stick as a pacifier to keep me from squirming. There were times when my kid instinct warned me in advance and I would slip out the back gate, accompanied by my big shaggy dog, Rover, and head for Uncle John O'Marr's farm, my haven of safety. It was a three or four mile journey along the wagon road with hay meadows and irrigation ditches to wade in along the way. I would arrive at the farm with my kilts mud-plastered and my yellow curls a sodden mess.

There were other times when I had gone through the curling iron ordeal when Rover and I would head for Uncle John's farm where I had cached an old curry comb in the barn, and I would spend an hour combing out those despised curls as best I could.

My boyhood chum was Johnny Badger, a black-haired boy my age. We were pals, sharing secrets and laughter and our fun. My cousin, Austin Blessing, son of Uncle John Blessing, was a year or two older, as were cousin Clifford O'Marr and Carlos Kumpe, son of Doctor Kumpe. Together we played our favorite game which, naturally, was cowboys and Indians, or we would re-enact Custer's Last Stand. Uncle John Blessing had made all of us wooden rifles and pistols and my brother Wallace had made me a bow from a willow stick and a half dozen blunt-feathered arrows. We rode stick horses and an empty lot became our battleground.

Because of my yellow curls I was always chosen to play General Custer, fated to be killed at the Battle of the Little Big Horn. The black-haired Johnny Badger was Chief Sitting Bull, stripped to breechclout and painted for war. He would grab my curls and whittle at my scalp lock with a dull paring knife. Cousin Cliff O'Marr was Rain-in-the-Face, so I would perforce loan Cliff my bow and arrows. Copper lids, swiped from wash boilers, served as shields for Sitting Bull and Rain-in-the-Face. Custer's Last Stand usually wound up in a free-for-all fight as the half dozen kids tangled in the melee, bawling and yelling bloody murder as tempers flared. There would be hair pulling, kicking, scratching and all the while wrestling around in a pile-up until our mothers or sisters arrived on the battleground to put an ignominious end to this regular Saturday afternoon replica of the famous Custer battle.

It was during one of those battles that my playmate, Johnny Badger, hit me in the eye with a thrown rock, and the other kids fled the battlefield, leaving me on the ground screaming and bawling, until my mother arrived, took me home and quickly summoned Doctor Kumpe. After my eye was bandaged and the doctor left I slipped out of the kitchen and headed for the barn with Rover, in order to escape my mother's nagging lecture on the evils of rock throwing and fighting.

My eye was aching with needle pains and I had heard Doctor Kumpe say that I had barely missed total blindness in my right eye, and I was still nursing a smoldering grudge against Johnny Badger when I caught sight of him slinking along outside the picket fence. I yelled at him to come over to the barn and I ducked inside and picked up a halter rope. As Johnny came into the barn I jumped him from behind and tied him up to one of the posts of a stall. By then I was bawling mad.

"Doctor Kumpe says," I sobbed angrily, "that I'll be blind in one eye from that rock you threw at me."

I got the buggy whip and started whipping Johnny across the back and legs, and the more he yelled the harder I laid it on. Our neighbors, F. C. (Frosty) Barker and his wife, were visiting my mother and when they heard Johnny screaming, Mr. Barker came running into the barn. He grabbed me from behind and took the whip away from me, then he untied Johnny, and it took a while to get the two of us calmed down. By that time I was sick and sorry and repentant, and when Frosty told us one of his comical stories he soon had us both laughing. We wound up shaking hands and eating supper together in the kitchen with Becky, the fat, good-natured, colored hired girl, making a fuss over us. Becky was as black as soot with a double chin and ivory white teeth and a chuckling laugh. She had a brood of children of her own and knew how to handle youngsters. Her Bible stories of Daniel in the Lion's Den, David and his slingshot, Noah and the animals on the Ark, along with her ghost stories, made an indelible impression on my young mind.

To the best of my recollection I was close to six years old when the quarrel between Johnny and me took place, but the memory still remains clear after long years. Perhaps it was because this was my first act of hot-tempered violence that it sticks in my subconscious mind. This quick-tempered strain was destined to be part of me for the remainder of my life.

During the era of pioneer days in Montana there was lawlessness and violence. The blood-spattered Indian wars still lingered, with the hanging of road agents, cattle rustlers and horse thieves by the vigilantes. It was but natural that boys born in that era were duly impressed and had a reckless spirit of adventure in their young blood. Our pioneer fathers had endured untold hardships and dangers and we were proud of our heritage. At the tender age of six I had my heart set on being a cowboy, my future destiny. I distinctly recall my first pair of brass-toed, red-topped boots that had once belonged to my deceased half brother Warren, that were a trifle large and had cotton batting stuffed into the toes to make them fit better. Even so, I had painful blisters on both heels that I would rub with horse liniment and carbolic salve I found in the barn, and not wanting my mother to notice my limping gait, I somehow managed to cover up with a kid's swagger.

I had long since discarded the kilts for a pair of tight-fitting knee britches and a boy's blouse with a draw string on the brief shirttails, and a long pair of black stockings with elastic garters. But in spite of all my kid tantrums my mother insisted on keeping the long yellow curls. On Sunday she made me wear the hated Lord Fauntleroy suit of black velvet with frilly white lace collar and long frilly lace cuffs when I went to Sunday School.

The passage of time has faded the memory of our departure from

White Sulphur Springs. The knowledge that we were moving to the city of Great Falls had little meaning for a six-year-old. My father had bought a ranch forty miles south of Malta, Montana, and a home in Great Falls where we would live during the winters so that I could go to school. When my father told me I could spend every summer at the ranch in the Little Rockies, it was the big event of my young life and the main topic of conversation for days. His promise of a cowpony all my own and a new saddle conjured up wild dreams of actual cowboy life. There would be no more stick horses made of broom handles and old mops. My only regret in leaving White Sulphur Springs was having to leave Rover behind. That big dog had been my constant companion since I was old enough to walk, and when I was told I couldn't take him with me, I did the next best thing. I gave him to Johnny Badger the day we took our departure. It was in the cards of fate that I was destined never to return to my birthplace.

I still retain the memory of my first ride in a stagecoach, with my mother and sisters, Agnes and Edna, occupying the inside seats while I sat perched alongside the stage driver on his high seat as he drove the four-horse team. At the stop for noon dinner at the halfway-house I gorged myself with cake covered with rich whipped cream and up-chucked along the way.

There is the vague memory of the train ride on the old Jaw Bone railway, and a two weeks stay at the Park Hotel in Great Falls while my father completed the purchase of the three-storied, white frame house on the corner of Fourth Avenue North and Tenth Street. My older half sister, Jessie, now the wife of Attorney Fletcher Maddox, lived on Third Avenue, a block away.

The Park Hotel, with its wide verandas, was a block's walk through the park from the Great Northern Railway depot and the terminal of the streetcar line. I wore my new suit of knee pants and matching jacket, long stockings and red-topped, brass-toed boots, and a round jellybean hat on top of my despised yellow curls. I sat straddle of the low railing of the wide veranda watching the town kids peddle newspapers and the messenger boys, with their visored blue caps, from the American District Telegraph Office delivering telegrams. The A.D.T. and the newspaper kids looked mean and tough, all of them with trim haircuts.

Then came the memorable day when a small group of these tough kids stopped in front of the hotel where I sat straddle of the railing.

"Get a look at the curly-headed girl dressed in boy's clothes and girl's red-topped boots," they yelled and began calling me girlish names. That gang of tough kids sure had me scared and buffaloed for the first time in my young life, with their chorus of insults and dirty words. When I yelled back at them that I was no girl, they challenged me to prove it by telling me to pee over the rail. A couple of tough paper kids challenged me to fight, but I was too scared to move or speak. It was too late to quit my perch and make a run for the front door, so I sat there like a scared cottontail rabbit with a fearful shame I had never before experienced.

It was then that a blue-coated policeman, a big red-faced man, came walking down the board sidewalk, scattering the tough gang in all directions, so I quit my precarious perch and headed for the door at a high run and into our hotel room on the ground floor. Once inside I slammed the door and headed for the bathroom. I was not aware that I had peed in my pants until I quit vomiting in the toilet bowl. Luckily my new suit had come with an extra pair of pants and I changed quickly, but I was still too scared to leave the safety of the hotel room. But one thing I knew for certain, I was getting rid of those yellow curls. I found my mother's scissors and gathering a handful of curls I scissored them off as close to my scalp as I could. I was still cutting away when my father came in. I fully expected to receive a bawling out, not a whipping, because my father had never once raised his hand to spank me, but he could lay me out with a few words and that was what I expected now. He was a stern looking man with an iron gray mustache and short trimmed beard, Irish blue eyes deep-set under shaggy gray brows. He was fifty-two years old when I was born and nearing sixty now, and I was always a little in awe of his stern ways. But when I saw the slow grin on his bearded lips and a sparkle in his eyes, I knew he was on my side. He told me to put the curls in a paper bag for my mother who would want to save them, and then he took me to the barbershop for a real haircut. Ben Piper, the barber, sat me down in a chair and fastened a white apron around my neck and proceeded to give me what he called a lion tamer's roach, a Jim Corbett short pompador that stood up in front. When he finished the haircut and turned the chair around, I had to blink twice to recognize my reflection in the mirror. My tanned face was flushed with an inner excitement as I rubbed the palm of my hand over the close-clipped hair. Shorn of the curls, the tow-headed kid in the mirror cast a brand new, strange and brave image. It was a complete transformation and had by some trick of magic changed my whole life. I recalled my recent cowardly guilt, and right then I made up my mind to get even with those tough kids that peddled newspapers and delivered telegrams. I might add that I wore that same crew-cut all through my school years.

Smokey Jones, the Negro bellhop at the Park Hotel, had told me about two of the tough West Side kids who were known as the Katzenjammer Kids, whose real names were Carl and Fred Busse. Their widowed mother did the laundry for the hotel guests. According to the bellhop the two kids always traveled together for self-protection when they peddled their papers because a feud existed between the A.D.T. messengers and the newsboys. As I viewed my new image in the mirror, forewarned by Smokey Jones' tale of the fighting ability of Carl and Fred, I made my plan of action. I would lay low until the sign was right, wait until I made a lot of friends on the North Side, and with their backing I would tackle these tough kids from the West Side. I could well afford to wait and when the sign was right I would lick them one at a time.

After the family settled in our new home in Great Falls, we left for the Circle C Ranch, an overnight train ride to Malta, and a forty mile trip by stage or buggy to the ranch.

I still vividly remember my first train ride over the Great Northern Railroad on Jim Hill's Oriental Limited, known locally as the Flyer. The upper berth in the Pullman car was plush, with a swinging hammock to hold your clothes; the meals served by colored waiters in the luxurious dining car with its highly polished silver and glassware; and the observation lounge and rear open platform where I spent most of my time in a folding canvas chair despite the cinders.

At that time the cowtown of Malta was situated north of the railroad tracks. Main Street consisted of a wide dirt road which extended about two city blocks, with a wide plank sidewalk. The livery stable and blacksmith shop marked the east end of Main Street which boasted half a dozen saloons, the Mercantile, a barbershop and the Malta Hotel, with hitchracks along the entire street.

When we descended from the train, there was a jerkline freight outfit loading supplies at the Malta Mercantile. Cowpunchers rode up and down the street and horses were tied to the hitchracks. Horace Brewster, foreman of the Circle C Ranch, was in town and took me in hand while my mother and sisters went to the Malta Hotel to stay overnight. Brewster took me to the white frame house he called the White House, the property being enclosed by a white picket fence. Beyond the house with its outside privy was a barbwire fenced horse pasture extending to the banks of Milk River with its giant cottonwood trees and high willows. The White House and horse pasture belonged to the Circle C and was used by the outfit as a place to change clothes when in town. It was littered with discarded clothing, ropes, chaps, pack saddles, harness, guns of all descriptions, shaving mugs and open razors. A potbellied stove kept the place warm during the winter months. The walls and ceiling were bullet scarred. Tarp-covered bedrolls held together with ropes or wide buckled straps stood on end in a front room corner. The two bedrooms held two brass beds each and cluttered chests of drawers. There were blankets, quilts and clean pillow cases but no sheets. The small kitchen had a four-hole range with a large reservoir of water; a round, oilcloth-covered table and iron skillets on the walls.

No one had ever given the White House a thorough cleaning and Brewster said it would take a team and a slip-scraper to dig it out. He showed me the bloodstained spot on the littered pineboard floor where a tinhorn gambler had been killed in a gun duel between the tinhorn and a cowpuncher over a woman.

There was a man's atmosphere about the White House that penetrated my six-year-old mind with a strange excitement and a longing for adventure. I wanted to stay here with Horace Brewster that night and he saw no reason to refuse. He told me that when I grew up I would be staying at the White House like the rest of Robert Coburn's sons, Will, Bob and Wallace. While Brewster laid no claim as a latter day prophet during the passing years, the words he spoke that day came to pass in many and sometimes devious and unforeseen ways.

It was a warm June night and Brewster decided we would sleep outdoors in tarp-covered roundup beds, the first time I had ever slept outside. We spread our beds out in the tall bluejoint and timothy grass of the front yard under a star-filled sky and the pale glow of a lopsided moon. Horace built a sagebrush smudge to ward off the swarms of pesky mosquitos, the sage giving off with its pungent fragrance. Giant cottonwood trees were skylined along the banks of Milk River and there was the sweet odor of blooming alfalfa and wild roses, the chirping of crickets, the eerie sound of hoot owls in the trees, and the distant howl of the coyotes in the hills. Coming down wind in the soft warm breeze the smells and sounds conjured up strange dreams for this six-year-old whose heart's desire was to be a cowboy. As I lay wide awake, I saw the vastness of the star-filled sky and the far flung horizon of the open prairie rangeland of the immense Montana country. This was my homeland, my native land, my birthright, and no man could ever take it away from me. A boy's dreams were destined to be retained and deeply treasured throughout my life.

I was sound asleep at daybreak when Brewster shook me awake. After an early breakfast at the Malta Hotel we left for the ranch. Agnes and Edna traveled by stage and I went with my parents in the spring wagon, sitting between them on the wide cushioned seat, with my father driving a matched team of spirited trotting horses. We left Malta in a cloud of dust and once we crossed Alkali Creek the roan team settled down to a steady trot that ate up the miles. In the distance we could see the Little Rockies about sixty miles away, and the two timbered Coburn Buttes that marked the east end of the Circle C Ranch which joined the Fort Belknap Indian Reservation.

We stopped at noon for dinner at the Half-Way House, known as the Hog Ranch, along the Malta-Zortman-Landusky stage route. The stage tender unhooked the team, watered and grained them, while we ate in the large sod-roofed log cabin. It was country style food served on large platters, all you could eat and the time to eat it.

We were within five miles of the home ranch on the stage road that circled Little Warm Lake when we sighted an Indian camp. There were several tall canvas-covered tepees, Indian women tending the iron kettles cooking over outside open fires, a lot of naked children playing games, and the male Indians sitting in front of the tepees smoking and talking. Just as we neared the camp a dozen or more mongrel dogs charged out barking and yelping, spooking the roan team, and in a split second my father had a runaway on his hands. He sawed on the lines to circle the horses over the sagebrush-covered prairie, while my mother and I held on to the seat for dear life.

One rear wheel struck a large boulder half hidden in the high swamp grass along the lake with such a sudden force that it shattered the spokes and sent them flying in all directions. Then the iron tire came loose and rolled like a steel hoop to scatter the yelling children and screaming women. With one steel axle and a wooden hub dragging deep into the ground acting as a brake, my father stopped the winded team right in the middle of the Indian camp. Three buck Indians approached the spring wagon, being careful not to again spook the horses. They shook hands with all of us and I learned that they were Black Dog, Iron Horn and Watch His Walking, all three Assiniboine Chiefs.

Under my father's directions they rigged a long pole under the rear axle, lifting it up to where it was level and roping it solid. When the subdued team got their second wind we got under way for the final stretch to the home ranch, the lodge pole leaving a trail of dust as it dragged in the dirt. My mother was badly frightened and a little shaken up, but once I got over my first scare I was filled with excitement. I had seen my first Indian camp, had shaken hands with three tribal chiefs, and had been in my first runaway. What more could a fellow ask?

With the family unharmed, my father's concern now was the condition of the horses. He cocked his ear and listened closely to their breathing, and said aloud that they showed no signs of being wind broken, and I knew that his anxiety was relieved. He explained that it was the "Injun stink" that had spooked the horses in the first place, and the charging of the mongrel dogs was all they needed for an excuse to run. He cautioned me that if I ever rode a horse that spooked at anything to head it straight for whatever had boogered him and to keep at it until he stood tracked, and was no longer spooked. He went on to describe what he meant by "Injun stink." It was the peculiar odor of Indian tanned buckskin clothing and moccasins, and the pungent smoke from the small fires burning inside the lodges.

The Circle C Ranch, located on Beaver Creek in the long shadow of the twin timbered Coburn Buttes, with its scattered log buildings and pole corrals, looked for all the world like some pioneer settlement. The near proximity of the Fort Belknap Indian Reservation with small villages of tall tepees along the upper creek in the foothills of the Little Rockies to the west lent a certain atmosphere to the place.

The banks along Beaver Creek were lined with tall willows, wild roses and berry bushes, red currants, Buffalo berries, gooseberries, thickets of tall chokeberry and sarvis berries, and tall cottonwood trees and thickets of tall willows.

On the rolling prairies we had crossed there were large prairie dog towns with high mounds built around the holes that were above the water level of the heavy rains. The prairie dogs perched on their haunches like picket pins and barked a loud chorus audible for quite a distance. Each prairie dog town had its large quota of screech owls whose large yellow eyes peered in all directions as they twisted their heads from motionless bodies.

There were badger holes scattered on the outskirts of the flats, partly concealed by high clumps of sagebrush and greasewood. This was the habitat of the large sage hens, small prairie chicken, and the long-legged, long-beaked curlews, which built their nests under the brush. Mallards and smaller teal ducks bred and nested on the creek banks, lakes and swampy sloughs. Ducks and helldiver mud hens filled the lakes. Cottontail and jack rabbits were everywhere.

The freight road followed the ridges, skirted the cut coulees, long draws and cutbanks that were flooded during the rainy season and in the winter contained snowdrifts ten feet high. The stage road doubtlessly had been mapped by the grizzled jerkline freighters, a hardy breed of Montana pioneers, who would naturally follow the line of least resistance, taking the shortest route possible over the gumbo flats which, during the rainy season, would bog a loaded freight wagon hub deep.

The stage road approached the ranch to the north along a high benchland, leaving the home ranch unseen until the road slanted down a long hill. Then there it was spread out directly below, the log buildings and pole corrals comprising the Circle C home ranch. The Circle C range extended from the Little Rockies east to the Larb Hills, south to the banks of the Missouri River, including the rolling prairie and the badlands from the mouth of the Musselshell to Cow Island, and north to Milk River, the cattle drifting on the open range as far as the Canadian border. This was to be my heritage, the wishful dream of a young cowboy who had not yet straddled his first cowpony.

For a city-raised boy the big event of his boyhood was to own his first bicycle. To me, the crowning event was to own my first cowpony and saddle. My father had his old saddlemaker friend, Jerry Sullivan, at Fort Benton make my saddle on a boy-sized tree, a single cinch, center fire, round-skirted saddle. It came to the ranch by stage in a gunnysack, with the bridle and saddle blanket. I took it to the barn and my brother Wallace placed it on an empty manger in a stall and told me to climb aboard to try out the stirrups for length. When he had adjusted them to my size he had me stand up in them to make sure. I was horrified when Wallace dunked the stirrups in the horse trough, but he reassured me that when the sun dried the leather the polish would return, that a cowhand's saddle was made to withstand countless rains and snows over long years.

Wallace placed the saddle on the top of the corral and shoved a stout stick through the turned back stirrups and left it there for a few hours. He then told me to sit up on the corral rail, that he had a surprise for me. He went into the barn and came out leading a snow-white, fat cowpony which he had named Snowflake, and told me that he was mine to keep. Wallace went on to explain that Snowflake was no two-bit Indian cayuse, that he was a three-year-old gelding, gentle broke for an all around cowpony. He later told me that an outlaw named Kid Curry had picked the pony up along the Outlaw Trail and brought him to the neighboring ranch of Jim Thornhill as a gift for Jim's oldest son. But the son already had a pony of his own and Thornhill had given the pony to Wallace as a present to me.

For the next few days Wallace taught me how to sit my saddle with natural balance, how to hold the bridle reins with just enough slack, and how to neck rein. When we hit a lope Wallace taught me how to sit tight in the saddle, carry my weight in the stirrups without bouncing like a greenhorn, and how to lean forward to ease the strain on my legs. When we rode along at a slow trot Wallace told me that was the cowpuncher's gait when traveling a long distance. He also taught me how to tell the time of day by the sun.

That memorable first day's ride on Snowflake marked a red letter day on my calendar. There was an unforgettable pride which filled my heart in the ownership of my first cowpony, marking the beginning of my life as a cowhand. During that first summer at the Circle C Ranch there were many things that marked a gradual change in my identity during these formative years of early boyhood.

Wallace kept a hound pack at the ranch to rid the range of prairie wolves and coyotes that were killing stock, and every time I got the chance I played with the big overgrown hound pups. Dog fleas never seemed to bother me, but my mother and sisters were always after me, handing me a whiskbroom before they would let me in the house. When my father turned me over to his foreman, Horace Brewster, to make a cowhand of me, I moved into the small whitewashed log cabin occupied by Brewster. I seldom went to my father's house, and kept clear of the womenfolks, eating my meals with the cowhands at the mess hall. After supper I would spend a few hours in the bunkhouse listening to the tall tales, often ribald, told by the cowhands, and to the endless dirty verses of the old song, "The Chisholm Trail," sung by some puncher.

From the very beginning, my father laid down the strict rule that I was to speak only when spoken to, not to interrupt or butt in when grownups were talking, that there was no place on a cow ranch for a smart-aleck kid, and I was warned never to use cuss words or any sort of profanity around him or the womenfolks. Therefore, when anyone spoke to me I learned to say, "Yes, sir! No, sir!" and "Yes, ma'am! No, ma'am!" as the case may be. But around the bunkhouse it was a different story. I called the cowpunchers and ranch hands by their first names, and cussed when I felt like it. But I always kept in the background and never acted smart-alecky, and I kept my mouth shut about the conversations I heard in the bunkhouse and around the ranch. That close-mouthed reputation established at an early age was destined to remain inviolate the rest of my long life.

CHAPTER 2

Early Days in Montana

MY FIRST SUMMER at the Circle C Ranch ended and my mother took me back to Great Falls to enter school the day following Labor Day. My sisters, Agnes and Edna, had already left for St. Paul, Minnesota, to enter boarding school at the Vistacian Convent.

Another new horizon had spread its wide vista for me. A new life to be explored, at first a little bewildering and strange. Coburn Maddox, son of my married half sister, Jessie, a year older than myself, took me around to meet every kid in the neighborhood, so that by the time school opened I was part of the North Side Gang. No girls were allowed when we played Shinny on Your Own Side, Run Sheep, Run, marbles and tops.

The L. H. Hamiltons lived on the corner of Fourth Avenue and 11th Street and their son, Henry, referred to as Hen, was my age. Hen's father owned a large sheep ranch at Utica in the Judith Basin and our families were close friends. Like me, Hen was going to first grade at Whittier School two blocks away. Coburn Maddox and Will Goodwin, who lived across the street, and Harry Wallenstein, who lived on Third Avenue North, said that any first grader who had his mother bring him to school on his first day was a sissy. So it was Coburn and Bill and Harry and fat Herb Nathan who took Hen and me to school that first day. At morning recess Coburn, who was a head taller than I, made it known to one and all that I was his Uncle Walt. Being a year older than I, Coburn got a big laugh out of it which made me sore, so I tied into him, but he held me off with his longer arms until I ducked under those long skinny arms and butted him in the belly. It turned into a wrestling match until the teachers broke it up, making us shake hands. But for a few weeks the kids called me Uncle to get a rise out of me. I got into a few fights, but they were soon forgotten.

The North Side of Great Falls was supposed to be the elite of society. The well-to-do people like bankers, merchants, doctors and lawyers lived there. Cattlemen and sheepmen lived next door to each other. Charlie Russell, the cowboy artist, lived three blocks from us on Fourth Avenue North.

There was a stigma attached to the South Side, namely the Red Light District, and the famous, or infamous, Stockholm Beer Hall with its stage and can-can dancers. The ground floor was sprinkled with sawdust and the burly waiters also acted as bouncers. The Stockholm Beer Hall was the burlesque honkeytonk of Great Falls and was owned by Ben Steele, formerly Chief of Police, a tall, handsome man with iron gray hair. "No women or minors allowed" read the sign over the door.

To the West were the railroad sidings, where the freight cars were unloaded of cumbersome farm machinery, wagons and lumber on the platform of the large warehouses. Here, too, was the wool house, a long, shed-like structure where huge sacks of sheep fleece were stored at lamb shearing time. A hobo jungle was located under the railroad bridge, and there was a row of saloons along the track sidings where the hoboes could purchase a gallon lard pail of beer for a dime. A bucket of beer was called a "growler" for the reason that the inside of the pail was greased to reduce the foam.

The West Side across the wide Missouri River was the location of the railroad yards and the roundhouse turntable, where the locomotives and Pullman cars were serviced. The freight cars, gondolas and coal cars had a separate siding where the freights were assembled. There were long coal chutes and water tanks. The West Side was where the railroad people lived, engineers, firemen, conductors, brakemen and superintendents. The section hands lived in quarters built by the Great Northern Railway. And so the West Side had its own community, with stores, saloons, and a grammar school.

The East Side, where the B & M (Boston & Montana) Smelter was located, was still another separate community. Located directly across the 13th Street Suspension Bridge, a combination streetcar, wagon and foot bridge, was the community called "Little Chicago." The smelter employees, the laboring class who were mostly foreigners, lived in Little Chicago with their large families. For the most part it was a shanty town, with a couple of small grocery stores and saloons.

The streetcar service over the suspension bridge extended to another settlement of finer and better homes, where the white collar executives for the B & M Smelter lived, including the graduate engineers from Boston Tech. There was a bachelor clubhouse on the banks of the Missouri River overlooking the enclosed waters of the mill race that was divided into three sections, first, second and tail, with its swift current that fed water into the mill. The first race with its slow moving current served as a swimming pool.

The kids from Smelter Town attended the North Side Whittier Grammar School and traveled by streetcar. They also attended the Great Falls High School on the North Side, and residents of this section were included in the North Side elite society.

Several of the North Side residents kept their own milk cows. During the summer months they were herded to green grass and water every morning in the vicinity of Box Elder Park, and returned in late afternoon for the evening milking. The Bodkin boys, Dick and Johnny, had the exclusive herding concession and the owners of the cows footed the nominal bill. Dick Bodkin, the eldest of the two brothers, worked as a cowhand for the Great Falls Meat Company and in later years was destined to become one of the best stunt men in Hollywood movie history.

My father had purchased a big bay gelding, a standardbred trotter, from John Paul, who owned a feed and livery barn in Great Falls. Big Ned came from the famous Huntley & Clark breed of trotting horses. Our hired man was Tom Austin, a halfbreed Negro who had served with the famous Tenth Cavalry during the Indian wars. Tom was our coachman and his pride and joy was Big Ned and the horse loved Tom with everything a horse had to give. Tom called Big Ned "an honest horse." Besides giving Big Ned all his loving care, Tom took the same care of the two-seated carriage and the harness. He kept the lawn mowed and watered and kept the corral and cow barn clean, as well as helping with the flower beds and berry bushes. Let a bunch of kids start playing on the lawn and Tom would run them off the place. During the summer he lived in a room at the barn and in winter he had a room in the basement of our house where he tended the coal furnace.

Louise Beckstrum, the hired girl, was a tall, broad-shouldered, rosy-cheeked, blonde, good-natured, Swedish girl about twenty years of age. She had come over from the old country a few years earlier, completely without knowledge of the English language, and now spoke with a strong Swedish accent, at times getting her words mixed. One thing old Tom hated was milking the cow so Louise took over the milking chores. Tom ate his meals in the kitchen and it was comical to listen to their conversation, his a Southern Negro dialect and hers broken English.

One end of the large basement was the laundry room, and one room was the furnace room with two coal bins, each holding a ton of coal. Another room was used for jellies and preserves, crocks of homemade mincemeat and pickles. Another room held empty trunks and other baggage. Except on washdays, the larger open space of the laundry room was used as a playroom for the kids I invited over on cold, rainy days to play marbles or tops.

When my brother Wallace came to town from the ranch, he would buy me sacks of marbles, flints and moss agates, tiger eyes of petrified wood, and spinning tops. We would mark a wide circle on the floor, or in the dirt outside in the summertime, and take turns by numbers at spinning the tops. Like in marbles, a line was drawn and the spinning top closest to the line won, followed by second, third and fourth place. The loser spun his top in the circle and the winner tried to knock it clear of the circle, and if successful he picked up the loser's top. A kid's wealth was measured by the number of tops and agates he possessed. The agates and tiger eyes were used for shooters, the common glass or china eyes used like a gambler uses poker chips. Every kid's pockets bulged with glass and china eye marbles. Often on Saturdays the marble games lasted for hours, until the losers' marble sacks were empty.

There was always a shinny game going on a vacant lot. The kids chose sides with two older kids for leaders. Each had his own shinny stick, usually a sawed-off broom handle, and an empty can served as a puck. The object of the game was to get the tin can to the opposite goal line. Another game of shinny was for each player to dig a deep hole in a wide circle twelve feet in diameter. The can was tossed in the middle and each player tried to hit it into another player's hole. The general mix-up in the center of the ring, with sticks flying in all directions, sent every kid home with bleeding and scabbed shins. "Shinny on Your Own Side," that shrill kid war cry, could be heard for blocks.

The grammar school days, from the First Grade until the Eighth, could well be described as the Santa Claus school years, when most of us still believed in Santa Claus. The two week school vacation at Christmas was something to look forward to when we kids visited the toy shops. Large department stores such as Strain Brothers, put on extra clerks and floorwalkers to ride herd on the gang of kids who came to look at toys. Somewhere, sometime, some worldly-wise adult proclaimed the undisputed fact that all kids were potential thieves, while the kids simply called it swiping. In those memorable days of my early youth the hiring of store detectives was unknown in the city of Great Falls. But the shop owners and clerks were wise to the swiping and kept an eagle eye on every one of us who came in the store.

Those were the good old days when every grocery store had open barrels of gingersnaps, crackers and apples sitting on the floor alongside the counters, and it was always a temptation for a kid to cast a weather eye out for unwary clerks, and when sooner or later they had to wait upon an adult customer, the kid would make a quick dip of his hand into the open barrel and quickly transfer whatever he took to his pocket.

At Weigand's Music Store there was one counter at the back which held dime novels. When the store door opened a small bell sounded and at the tell-tale tinkle Old Man Weigand would look over his specs to see who entered. If it happened to be kids, the old man would motion his fat wife, sitting in her rocking chair doing embroidery, to keep an eye on the group, for we traveled in pairs or threes when we went into the music store, usually once a week on Saturdays.

The dime novels were stacked in neat piles on the long back counter, so that Buffalo Bill, Diamond Dick, Nick Carter, King Brady, Jesse James and numerous other dime novel heroes had their own separate piles. As a rule each of us had a dime in his pants pocket and all of us wore loose fitting turtleneck sweaters like the ones worn by the different university students, orange and black for Princeton, crimson and white for Harvard, or blue and white for Yale. Our game was to browse around looking at the gaudy magazine covers, discussing the merits of the outlaws and the detectives, arguing good-naturedly. I always took the part of the outlaw, as did Hen Hamilton and Steve Doyle, while Jimmy Murray, whose uncle was a cop, sided with the law, as did Pete Cooper, whose father was an attorney, and Frankie McDonnell, whose father was also a lawyer. During the arguments each of us would swipe one dime novel, shoving it up underneath our sweaters, and we could always tell when old man Weigand's nervousness meant we had worn out our welcome, so we would take one dime novel in one hand and a dime in the other and head for the cash register. When we had paid for the dime novel we would leave the warmth of the store for the frosty winter air outside with one swiped dime novel under our sweaters.

One day during the winter on a Saturday afternoon, half a dozen kids from the North Side went on what we called our dime novel raid, seeking a little excitement. On this particular day there was a young, sportily dressed musician in the store playing the mandolin and fiddle and jabbering in German to the Weigands. When it came time for us to leave the store with a dime novel concealed under our sweaters, and one dime novel in our hand, we lined up at the cash register and then headed for the door where we found this young musician blocking our way.

"Line up, kids!" he ordered. "Let's have a look at what you have under your sweaters." He began lifting each kid's sweater to let the swiped dime novel fall to the floor, and I can tell you we were a lot of scared kids. We were ordered to pick up the novels, put them on the counter and pay for them, or he would call the cops. Peter Cooper happened to have a silver dollar in his pocket and he used it to pay for the novels. When the musician demanded to know our names and threatened to notify our parents, we were a badly scared bunch of kids and it was a long time before we dared enter the place again. The news of our being caught red-handed traveled to the other kids by word of mouth and it frightened them enough that all agreed that Weigand's Music Store now had our names on its blacklist so it was a place from which to stay away.

This racket of swiping dime novels from the only store in town that stocked them came to a sad end. When the news leaked out in our kid underground that Weigand's nephew, who belonged to a mandolin club, was only a week-end visitor and had long since departed, we were tempted to try again, but the dire threat of the police and being taken to task by our parents kept us away, and the swiping of dime novels was over for keeps.

Grove's store was the neighborhood grocery, a typical old-fashioned country store. On the end of the long counter was a large coffee mill where Mr. Grove ground the Arbuckle coffee beans into pound paper sacks. Beside the red coffee mill was a grocer's scale used to weigh sugar, flour, white beans, cheese, dried fruit and such. Next to the scales was a large, round, yellow cheese with a cheese cutter.

Walt's Father, Robert Coburn

Walt's Mother, Mary B. Coburn

Inside the glass-covered counter there were assorted candies, horehound, peppermint, lemon, wintergreen, lollipops, all-day suckers, long limber licorice sticks, hard candies and chocolate bars, and the usual barrels of gingersnaps, crackers and apples. On the opposite side of the store was the drygoods counter, with bolts of cloth on the back shelves. The store was heated in winter by a large pot-bellied stove with isinglass doors set in a sandbox in the center of the room.

Grove's Store was the hangout for the neighborhood kids who left their sleds outside in winter and bellied up to the stove to thaw out cold hands and feet. Mr. Grove was a kindly man and did not mind us dipping into the barrels of gingersnaps and apples. Usually the kids had a nickle or a dime to spend and our mothers all traded there so what we did not pay for went on the monthly bill.

Above Grove's Store was a dance hall known as Grove's Hall, and it was there that a Miss Wallace held her dancing class every other Saturday afternoon. Miss Wallace was in her early thirties, a tall, slender lady with dark chestnut hair, a professional dance teacher. Every boy and girl in the neighborhood belonged to her dancing class, for which our parents footed the bill. That Saturday afternoon dancing lesson was a pain in the neck to us boys and it put a crimp in our skating and hockey games. We were scrubbed and bathed and dressed in our Sunday suits, carrying patent leather dancing pumps in velvet bags.

Miss Wallace had a small silver whistle hung around her neck by a blue silk ribbon, and when the piano player started a waltz or two-step, she would blow the whistle to signal the boys from the cloak room to choose their partners from the girls sitting on long benches, dressed up like Astor's pet poodles. The older boys always chose the best dancers, leaving the wall flowers for the younger ones. Any grammar school boy who liked girls and dancing was branded as a sissy, but if we dared play hookey from dancing class it was reported to our mothers and we were punished in various ways, because those dancing lessons did not come cheap.

Miss Wallace was a strict disciplinarian when it came to manners and social graces, guaranteeing to make us behave like perfect ladies and gentlemen. Making a perfect gentleman from a rowdy bunch of boys must have been a trying ordeal for her, but we soon learned to toe the mark. A smart-aleck boy might get by if he bumped into another dancing couple by politely saying, "Excuse me." But if he had done it on purpose he was kept after class and given a lecture on good behavior.

Every other Saturday the North Side gang of kids headed for the Missouri River with their skates and hockey sticks. We would skate as far as First Island near where Sun River empties into the Missouri, choose sides and play hockey all day. Usually it was ten to twenty-five below zero and snowing, or a cold, icy wind was blowing, and we would have to build a big bonfire on the ice. There was usually a gang of men from the ice company sawing cakes of ice they hauled off on long bobsleds hooked to teams of horses. We kids would take four or five broken ice blocks the men had shoved aside and use them for goal posts. We would station the kids with weak ankles for goal keepers, and it would be a rough and tumble game of hockey. Shinny on the ice would have been the proper name for our so-called hockey games. When a kid got winded or his ankles gave out, or his shin bone got skinned, he would skate over to the bonfire and rest.

When school let out at four in the afternoon, too late to play hockey, we got our sleds and hooked rides behind the delivery wagons with a length of clothesline fastened to the sled and the end of the wagon. The delivery team traveled at a slow trot, but if you wanted a fast ride behind a cutter with a team of fast trotters you chose such an outfit. On moonlight nights we went riding in a hay rack on bobsled runners, bundled up in overcoats, mittens and galoshes, and buffalo lap robes and blankets. After a two hour hay ride we would return to somebody's house for mugs of steaming hot cocoa. Sometimes we would have a taffy pull or duck for apples in water-filled galvanized tubs. Other times we would play at pinning on the donkey's tail, the post office kissing game, or musical chairs.

Christmas holidays were the big events of the year. Every boy was sure to get a new pair of skates and a hockey stick, and a new bobsled, besides various toys and many books. The Alger books were our favorites, as were *Jack Harkaway*, Mark Twain's *Tom Sawyer* and *Huck Finn*, Stevenson's *Treasure Island*, *Tom Brown's Schooldays*, Conan Doyle's *Sherlock Holmes*, and many others. Our toys were usually hook and ladder fire wagons, pioneer canvas-covered wagons, replicas of Sir Thomas Lipton's *Shamrock* sailboat, trick metal banks, and many others too numerous to mention.

The neighboring boys exchanged presents and visited back and forth to view the various Christmas trees in the homes. On the North Side there were the churches that handed out Christmas stockings made from red and green mosquito netting, and where all denominations were welcome. Howard Stanley, for instance, belonged to the Baptist church, Bill and Art Goodwin and Coburn Maddox were Espiscopalians. Frankie McDonnell, Steve Doyle, and the Fontana boys and I were Catholics. The Walensteins, the Nathan and Kaufman boys were of the Jewish faith, but there being no synagogue in Great Falls, they came along with us while we made the rounds of the different churches to get our stockings filled with Christmas loot.

In the spring when the frozen waters of the wide Missouri broke up in flood time it was a spectactlar sight to behold. Everybody, men, women and youngsters of all ages, gathered to watch at the railway bridge at the foot of Central Avenue or at the suspension bridge at Thirteenth Street. But the large dance pavilion on the high cliff above the river was the best place to get a panoramic view of the dam at Black Eagle Falls across from the B & M Smelter. For transportation there were streetcars, carriages, buggies, buckboards and spring wagons, but we boys traveled on foot or by bicycle with lunches for an all day stay. Another spectacular view was from Rainbow Falls, ten miles by wagon road, but a pleasant carriage drive.

The warm Chinook wind, the harbinger of spring in Montana, melted the winter drifts, leaving the ground bare. The melting snow in the mountains swelled the Missouri with flood waters over its banks. Huge cakes of ice, weighing tons, crashed like cannon as they piled up in choked floes fifty or more feet in height. Crews of workmen used dynamite to dislodge the ice jam in the narrows, and the crashing of ice and the ominous sound of the swift current was continuous thunder.

Uprooted giant cottonwoods and tall willows and underbrush floated downstream in foam-flecked, dirty debris. Half-submerged haystacks, chicken coops, backhouse privies, log cabins, and frame houses, fence posts with strands of barb wire, bloated carcasses of drowned cattle, horses and hogs, floated downstream on the swift muddy current. Crews of workmen with their long poles and ropes worked to clear the debris at Black Eagle Dam where the usual spillway of six or eight inches deep rose to fifteen or more feet. Other crews of workmen, mostly section hands, worked to clear the debris at the Great Northern Railway Bridge in day and night shifts. Freight trains were kept on sidings. Only passenger trains, slowed to a few miles per hour, were allowed to run. Traffic over the suspension bridge to Little Chicago and Smelter Town was limited. No streetcars, carriages, or wagons were allowed to cross, and foot traffic was cut down to smelter employees only.

The annual flood waters took their toll of human lives, despite the warnings of Nature and the newspapers to all farmers and ranchers to leave their river bottomlands days ahead of the high water. The old time river ranchers, for the most part, heeded the warnings and moved their livestock and household goods to high ground, living in tents until the flood waters subsided and the Missouri was back in its regular channel. Then they would return to repair their homes and barns that had somehow survived the flood, and to rebuild the barb wire fences and pole corrals that had been washed away, and to reseed their fields.

For the boys of all ages in Great Falls the warm days of summer were the time to go swimming. For the North Side gang the annual spring flood left swimming water on one side of the high willow thicket along Park Drive. The small-fry dog-paddled in the shallow end while the older boys swam out into neck-deep water, using driftwood planks that had floated down from the sawmill to support their weight while they dog-paddled and eventually learned to swim.

Old man Krantz, the park tender, kept a watchful eye on us and if he caught any kid without swimming trunks he bawled him out and sent him home. We changed clothes behind a tall willow thicket, stripped down to our bathing trunks and then headed along the sandbar to the water. Before we went into the water we lined up and peed on our legs, supposedly to prevent cramps.

I had better backtrack here to the Katzenjammer Kids and the grudge I still carried against them for too long. I had confided my grudge to Art Goodwin, one of the North Side gang about my age, who was better known as Winkie because he squinted both eyes shut when he talked. He had a paper route for the *Morning Tribune* and *Evening Leader*, and had had a few run-ins with the Katzenjammer Kids so was ready to tackle them when the sign was right.

One Saturday when Winkie and I, Frankie McDonnell and Pat Logan, and a tall Negro boy named Harry Johnson, were out on the sandbar in our bathing trunks peeing on our legs to prevent cramps, the Katzenjammer Kids showed up. I grinned at Winkie and he squinted both eyes and grinned back. When the Katzenjammer Kids, whose real names were Carl and Fred Busse, commenced peeing on their legs, Winkie and I slipped up behind them and turned loose, peeing all over them.

"So you won't get cramps!" we hollered at them as they jumped out of the way. Then we crowded them into the water and the fight was on. We shoved them down in the shallow water, holding their tow heads under by their hair, sitting straddle of them and yelling:

"Blow bubbles! Eat mud! Puke pollywogs! Blow bubbles! You stinkin' tough Katzenjammer Kids! Blow bubbles!" we kept yelling while we punched their noses until blood spurted and they were choking and hollering bloody murder.

The kids gathered on the sandbar kept yelling "Fight! Fight!"

"Jiggers! The cops!" yelled some kid, and they all ran.

Just then Old Man Krantz, the park tender, and Fat Gus Jones, the poundmaster, arrived and before Winkie and I could get away Krantz and the pot-bellied dogcatcher grabbed us.

"Them two kids peed all over us and beat us up!" Carl and Fred complained as they waded out of the water.

Gus Jones had his poundmaster's nickel-plated badge pinned to his vest in plain sight. He told the four of us to get into our clothes, that he was taking us to the police station in the dog wagon. He was a mean stinker and sure had us scared. Behind the high willows Winkie and I got dressed in a hurry and then made a run for it, both of us barefooted. We kept close to the willows along Park Drive for a mile, crouching and running as fast as our legs would carry us, and in no time we were long gone.

Aware of the fact that Krantz and Jones did not know the names of any of our gang, we felt safe once we got away and headed for home, keeping to the side streets and alleyways. If the Katzenjammer Kids were stupid enough to ride the paddy wagon to the police station that was their hard luck, but as it turned out they, too, made a clean getaway. I never learned if Carl and Fred knew why I peed on them and bloodied their noses. I doubt if they remembered me as the kid with the yellow curls.

Winkie and I became overnight heroes of the North Side Gang for a few weeks. Mr. Cooney, owner and editor of the *Great Falls Evening Leader*, whose fondness for youngsters was a sort of legend, wrote a humorous editorial about us in the Sunday edition of the paper when his son, Eugene (Gene for short), one of the North Side Gang, told his father the whole story.

Raiding the pound at night to free the impounded dogs was a frequent chore for the North Side Gang. The large pound shed was located on the river bank at the end of Park Drive, and it was easy to smash the padlock under cover of darkness when Fatty Gus Jones was guzzling beer at some saloon.

Opening the rear door of the pound wagon when Jones was

sneaking up with his large net fastened to a ten foot pole on some stray dog, was easy, and Fatty Gus would return to find his captured dogs set free. Every kid in town hated the poundmaster. His plump rear end made an easy target for a slingshot as the kids hid out behind a high fence or billboard. When the beer-bellied dog catcher chased us and had to pull up winded, he was greeted with catcalls, jeers and shouted insults.

As we grew older there were other and more dangerous swimming holes for the good swimmers on the North Side by way of Little Chicago. These could be reached by streetcar, bicycle, or on foot across the Thirteenth Street Suspension Bridge, or you could swim the wide Missouri behind a driftwood plank with your pants and shirt tied on. Any route we took our North Side Gang traveled in groups of half a dozen, with slingshots and rocks in our pockets in case the Little Chicago kids laid in ambush. By rights the swimming hole on the north bank of the river belonged to the Polak and Slav kids and they were a mean and tough gang to whip. Their favorite trick was to wait until we had swum out to a small sandbar island about two hundred feet away from the bank where we had left our clothes. Then the Little Chicago Gang would crawl through the underbrush, soak our clothes in the water and tie hard knots in the wet sleeves and pant legs, then throw them into the river to be carried downstream, pegging rocks and slingshot pebbles at us when we swam out to rescue them.

We found good swimming in Sun River about a half mile above where it emptied into the Missouri. Another place was Shirt-tail Canyon above Giant Springs below Black Eagle Falls. The older kids rode there on bikes, the younger ones walked the five or six miles, and all carried lunches in brown paper bags for an all-day swim on Saturdays.

In early spring, on cold Saturdays when the raw wind was too chilly for swimming, the North Side Gang packed lunches and headed for the Sand Hills, about five miles south of town. The Sand Hills was disputed ground between the North Side Gang and the

South Side Gang. Both gangs, armed with slingshots and air guns, would wage all day battles. Building forts from loose, coarse sand, yelling insults and defiance, they would charge the other's fort to knock it down. It was a kid guerrilla sort of battle which usually lasted until sundown.

CHAPTER 3

Santa Claus School Days

DURING MY GRAMMAR SCHOOL DAYS, my two half sisters, Agnes and Edna, graduated from finishing school at the Vistacian Convent in St. Paul, Minnesota, and proceeded to get married. Agnes married Carl Evans, a graduate mining engineer employed by the B & M Smelter in Great Falls. Edna married Doctor Leonard Ellis, a Spanish-American War veteran, with the retired rank of Colonel, now Chief of Staff at the large Government Hospital at Hot Springs, Arkansas. My older half sister, Jessie, had already married Attorney Fletcher Maddox of Great Falls. My half brothers Will, Bob and Wallace were also married, and about the time I was in the first grade my full brother, Harold, was born. By the time I was in the eighth grade Harold was eight years old and had his own playmates.

It was just before Agnes and Edna married that I saw a brand new Iver-Johnson .32 caliber double-action pistol in the hardware department of Strain Brothers Department Store. By dint of long persuasion I talked my sisters into buying the pistol for me, complete with holster, cartridge belt, and a box of cartridges. I promised to keep the gun in my room on the third floor and to never keep it loaded.

My bedroom was furnished with a four-poster birdseye maple bed and a matching dresser and chest of drawers. I proudly hung the cartridge belt and holstered gun from the high bedpost, along with a long corded light bulb in a wire cage I used for a reading lamp. My bedroom walls were covered with college pennants and western prints by Charlie Russell and a few rattlesnake skins. There were two Indian-tanned wolf skins on the floor and an Indian-tanned steerhide, the underside painted with a brightly colored Indian symbol, which I used for a bedspread. This was my own private bedroom and den, and it was forbidden territory for my brother Harold. I had repeatedly warned Harold never to bring any of his gang of playmates up to my room and to never touch the holstered gun.

My mother had laid down the law in no uncertain terms, often repeated. I was allowed to keep the Iver-Johnson pistol only on the condition that there were no cartridges in the gun or belt. So I hid the box of cartridges in the stable and once in a while I would take the gun into the Sand Hills where Hen Hamilton and Winkie Goodwin would set up a target and we would hold a shooting match. Then I would clean the gun with a willow ramrod and oiled rag before putting it back in its holster in the bedroom. I kept a few cartridges in my pants pocket to show off in front of the town kids, and I would put empty shells into the gun chambers to show off when my pals came up to my room to read dime novels on rainy days.

Of all the small kids who were Harold's friends there was only one I disliked. That was Fatty Golder who lived across the street from us. Time and again I had warned Harold to keep his friends out of my room, and I had put fear in all of them except Fatty Golder. Fatty was an only child, rotten-spoiled, bad-mannered, sassy and all-around obnoxious. One of his ill-mannered habits was to come in the kitchen door without knocking and wander through the house when none of the family was at home. If Louise tried to stop him he would sass her, calling her the big Swede hired girl and telling her to leave him alone. If Old Tom ever caught him picking the flowers and stuffing himself with red currants from the berry bushes which grew along the back fence, he would chase him away. But Fatty Golder was Harold's friend and they seemed to like each other.

One bright sunny Saturday morning in May Old Tom had taken my mother and sisters in the carriage to shop at the Paris Dry Goods

Store for their wedding trousseaus, and I was at Hamilton's house to see if Hen wanted to go swimming. When I returned home to pick up my swimming trunks while Hen got the gang together, Louise was ironing in the basement and I ran upstairs to my room. I found the bedroom door, which I always kept closed, standing open and there stood Fatty Golder on tiptoe trying to reach the holstered gun. He was about to climb on the bed when I yelled at him, asking him what he was doing in my room. He said he was hunting Harold, sassing me in his smart-aleck way which made me angry. When he asked me to show him how the pistol worked, I told him I would show him how it could make a bad-mannered kid like him dance.

When the double-action .32 in my hand, I was remembering how my brother Wallace had taught me never to aim an empty gun at anyone, so instead of pointing the gun at Fatty's feet, I aimed at the light bulb in the wire cage. Standing about ten feet away, I began pulling the triger as fast as I could. It made a loud clicking noise as the hammer hit the empty shells, click — click — click — click — bang! The hammer had hit a live cartridge, the recoil kicking the gun from my loose grip and sending it flying behind me. For a long moment I stood there thunderstruck by the sudden, unexpected explosion of the pistol I thought was empty, the acrid stench of burnt powder-smoke filling the small attic room. Somewhere in those tense, frightful moments I heard Fatty's shrill, terrified scream, and what I saw when I looked around was a picture which was to be indelibly stamped in my memory for all time.

Rolly-polly Fatty Golder lay motionless, sprawled flat on his belly, face down on the floor. In that death-like silence, as I stared, a realization came with a sudden shock which sent me into a panic. I had killed Fatty Golder and I had better move. I was out the door and down the three flights of stairs as fast as I could run, then downstairs to the basement. My voice sounded strange in my own ears as I yelled for Louise.

"Listen, Louise, when Hen Hamilton shows up tell him he'll find me at the roundhouse. I'll be hid out in a boxcar."

"Yah! Yah! Don't bother me," she answered.

"Tell Hen to bring along the five dollar gold piece he got for his birthday. Tell him I just shot Fatty Golder in my room and I have to make a fast getaway before the police arrive to arrest me. You understand, Louise?" I asked in a creaky voice.

"Yah! Yah! Pack your own lunch and don't bother me when I got ironing to do."

I was sure glad Louise reminded me about taking a lunch. I filled a paper bag with everything I could grab in a hurry and slipped out the back door. I took a quick look around to see if Hen and the gang were coming, but they were nowhere in sight so, keeping to the alleyways, I hit a jog trot. That I had killed the despised fat boy now filled me with remorse, and I had a dreaded fear of what would happen to me. The cops would arrest me for murder and lock me in jail, and I would be sent to reform school until I was old enough to go to the state penitentiary.

In spite of my panic, there came a cold clarity of a plan for escape as I trotted on. Those summers at the Circle C Ranch I had heard stories about Kid Curry and his gang traveling the Outlaw Trail. I made up my mind to hide in an empty boxcar of an eastbound freight, get off at Malta and head for the safety of the ranch where I would saddle Snowflake. I would then hide out at Jim Thornhill's ranch, and wait until his partner Kid Curry showed up to take me to the Hole-in-the-Wall outlaw country where I could throw in with the Wild Bunch. I was doing some fast thinking as I followed the railroad tracks to the roundhouse. This was familiar ground to us North Side kids, and we knew the engineer on the switch engine. His name was Spud Murphy, a big, red-faced Irishman, proud father of a dozen children of assorted ages, and whose foghorn voice always shouted profane warnings at the kids to get the goddamned hell away from the tracks or we would be killed. His son, Mike, was my age and I was remembering he invited Steve Doyle and myself one Sunday over to their home on the West Side where his father and some lodge brothers of the Ancient Order of

Hibernians were holding a beer bust. Spud Murphy let us kids have one schooner of beer each and then told us to get the hell out from underfoot, that one beer was our limit. But later that afternoon Mike swiped a clean five pound lard pail from the kitchen and while the lodge brothers were singing old Irish ballads, Mike "rushed the growler," filling the greased pail to the brim, and the three of us located an empty boxcar and got slightly tipsy.

The memory of that day came back to me now as I slipped alone down a sidetrack, there to keep a lonely vigil in an empty boxcar waiting for Hen Hamilton to show up. I could keep an eye on the switch engine as it made up the long freight that would pull out during the night. Kid wise to the railroad yards, I would know when the caboose was backed to the tail, and that the eastbound freight would move slowly to the high water tower to take on water after filling the coal tender at the coal chutes, and I would be riding the boxcar as far as Malta. I had no watch, only the sun to go by. When it was noon high, there still was no sign of Hen and the sudden blast of the roundhouse whistle at noon threw a quick scare into me.

As I waited my kid imagination conjured up all kinds of mixed thoughts. By now the cops had found Fatty Golder's dead body, and had nabbed Hen Hamilton, my friend. My mother and sisters were in a state of panic. Louise had told the police I had gone to the roundhouse and they were hot on my trail. I ducked back out of sight in the boxcar and became more panicky when the roundhouse whistle blasted one o'clock, and still no sign of Hen. When the switch engine coupled onto the caboose an hour later it was a sure sign that the freight train was made up and ready to go. Now I was really gripped in a cold sweat.

Just then I caught sight of Hen Hamilton, Pete Cooper, Frankie McDonnell and Winkie Goodwin picking up round sulphur balls the size of marbles for slingshot ammunition. I waited in a cold sweat until they came near enough, then I stuck two fingers in my mouth, gave the North Side Gang whistle, and began waving.

"You sure as heck took a long time getting here, Hen," I com-

The house in White Sulphur Springs, Montana, where Walt Coburn was born on October 23, 1889

plained. "Didn't you get the message I left with Louise that I had shot Fatty Golder in my room and for you to bring your five dollar gold piece? I'm quitting the country before the police catch me."

"What kind of a whopper lie you tellin'?" Hen asked, then added, "When I came by your house Louise said you'd gone to the roundhouse, so when I rounded up the gang we came to get you. I saw Fatty Golder running around playing with your brother and Harold Randall. Nothing was wrong with that fat greaseball."

"You sure, Hen?" I asked, still worried.

"Cross my heart and hope to die." Hen crossed himself with a big X.

I jumped out of the boxcar and told Hen and the others what had happened, saying I had no idea how that live cartridge got in the gun with the empty shells I kept in the chambers. I reached into the pocket of my pants and counted twice to make sure, but there were only five cartridges left of the six I usually carried to show the kids and brag that I owned a six-shooter. Later I questioned all my young pals who had been in my room, but not a single one acknowledged putting a live cartridge in the gun, so it remained a mystery.

Embedded in the birdseye maple bedpost was the .32 slug. I had aimed at the electric light bulb but had missed my target. I will say this much for Fatty Golder, he never breathed a word about what had happened. He probably did not want to admit that he was so scared he fainted, but he could not be bribed to climb the stairs to the third floor again, much less cross the threshold of my bedroom. But I had to hand over the pistol and cartridges to my mother, and that was the last I ever saw of the gun. For quite a spell I was in the doghouse as sure as God made little green apples. The slug in the bedpost was a constant reminder of that near tragedy.

Ever since I can remember I have had a love for dogs. Probably it began with my being raised from babyhood with that big shaggy dog, Rover, my constant companion until I was six years of age. To my way of thinking there is something radically wrong with a boy who does not love and want to own a dog.

Shortly after we moved to Great Falls, I brought home a stray dog. He was coal black and about a year old, a wire-haired terrier the size and conformation of an Airedale, with black whiskers and large, white teeth and a short, docked tail. I named him Whiskers and he loved horses. When he caught sight of Big Ned in his corral, the dog put on a grin and wagged his tail, whining as he walked slowly toward the big bay gelding. Big Ned lowered his head to muzzle the stray dog and it was love at first sight. When Old Tom hooked Big Ned to the carriage and drove off, Whiskers traveled close to the horse's shod hind feet. Old Tom, wise in the ways of horseflesh, told me a horse liked to have a dog around for companionship. Animal instinct, Old Tom called it.

Every youngster in the neighborhood liked Whiskers and he became part of the North Side Gang, as did Charlie, Coburn Maddox's big black, tan and white Shepherd dog. When Carl Evans, who married my sister Agnes, gave me a Great Dane called Tug, Whiskers and Tug became friends from the start.

I had seen photographs of Alaskan sled dogs wearing breast collars, and with the help of Old Tom I rigged a harness for Tug. It was made of soft leather straps and oiled whang leather reins fastened to a wide collar studded with brass spikes half an inch long to protect his neck when he got into a fight. When I first broke Tug into hauling my long sled, I used one of the lines hooked to his collar to lead him around the yard. Tug liked to haul the sled, but he never got bridle wise to the gee-haw reining, so I gave up on that. One kid would trot ahead holding the long leash fastened to the collar, with one or two others riding the sled. Everything would be fine until Tug caught sight of a stray cat and took off after him, upsetting the sled and kids in a wild chase until he treed the cat.

One winter during the Christmas holidays, Hen and myself hooked Tug to the sled and went downtown to look over the toy departments in the various stores. Strain Brothers Department Store was our first stop. The toy department was in the basement, as was the china department, where long, waist-high tables displayed sets of expensive china, crystal and cut glass. Beyond the chinaware were the toys and a sporting goods display.

Outside Strain Brothers was an insulated board storm shed extending part way across the wide plank sidewalk, with built-in benches along the sides where customers could remove their overshoes and hang overcoats on hooks along the wall. Portable kerosene stoves provided heat for the entrance shed. Strangely enough those were honest times. The theft of overcoats and galoshes was unheard of, yet to be on the safe side a high school boy was employed during the holidays to prevent theft and to attend the heaters and broom out the snow.

Percy Foster, one of the North Side Gang, and a freshman in high school, was working in the shed the day Hen and I visited the store. Percy promised to take good care of Tug, now lying down in his harness in a corner where dog and sled would be out of the way of customers. Hen and I took off our one-buckle overshoes and stowed them under the bench and went down the wide stairway to the basement. For us this was strictly a sight-seeing tour because neither of us had any money. The floorwalkers and clerks kept an eagle eye on the swarm of kids that crowded, shoved and elbowed one another, to prevent the winding up and breaking of toys. For Hen and myself the passing of time had lost all meaning, and we were now in the sporting goods department looking at ice skates, hockey sticks, punching bags, air rifles, shotguns and pistols, tennis rackets, boxing gloves and all other articles on display. I had it in mind to later buy my brother Wallace a hunting knife and was looking at the array of Bowie knives in the glassed case when I heard a commotion near the stairway, then a woman's scream. I looked up and here came Tug still hooked to the sled. That big, gentle Great Dane came down the long stairway dragging the red sled clattering and banging, his long tail wagging as he tried to find me. In nothing flat Tug's long wagging tail knocked the high piled chinaware, crystal and cut glass in a smashing heap to the floor. A woman screamed "Mad dog!" and the floorwalker came running, wanting to know who owned the dog, demanding he get the dog out of there. Once Tug caught sight of me there was no denying to whom he belonged for he had reared up on his hind legs and was swiping his tongue on my face, telling me how happy he was to have found me.

I gave him a bear hug and set him down on all fours, telling Hen to grab hold of his wagging tail. I picked up the leash and started leading him out, every step I took tromping the mess of broken glass and chinaware. I was being escorted by a red-faced, irate floorwalker muttering dire threats, yet frightened of gentle Tug who had never so much as snapped at a human. I'll tell a man that trip down the narrow littered aisle was the longest, sweatingest journey I ever hoped to travel, then up the stairway with the sled clumping every step to the main floor.

One of the Strain Brothers, father of my chums, Russ and Art, was there to greet us, scowling fiercely. He was a tall, handsome man, and a close friend of our parents, but just then he was a little pale around the gills and stern looking as he told me to get the dog and sled out of the store and be quick about it. In the storm shed we grabbed our overcoats and left in a hurry, wondering where Percy Foster was to have let Tug leave the shed.

"Man, oh mister," I grinned at Hen as we leaned against the outside wall to buckle our overshoes. "I was never so glad to get out of a place in my life, with that darn screeching woman."

"That isn't the half of it by a long shot," Hen said as we buttoned our winter jackets and let down the fur-lined ear-flaps on our caps. "Wait until your folks get the bill for the damage the first of the month. It's not going to be a Happy New Year for you. All that broken china and glass, Wow!"

"No need to rub it in, Hen," I said, rubbing Tug behind his long black ears. "What bothers me more is that I dare not go back to Strain's store the rest of vacation time, and that goes for you, too."

"Heck, we'll take our trade to Porter Brothers, or some other store," said Hen.

"But not today," I said. "Let's go home to Old Tom's basement room where it's warm. I got part of a package of cubebs hid out there."

On the way we stopped at the butchershop to get soup bones and meat scraps for Tug and Whiskers, and talked it over as we walked along and began laughing fit to kill over the whole deal. It would be something scary to tell the rest of the gang.

We got our cubebs from Bob Lepeyre whose father owned a drug store. The Lepeyres lived on Third Avenue North, their backyard fence across the alley from ours. Their oldest boy, Bob, was about my age, and once when Bob, Hen Hamilton, Winkie Goodwin and I were up in my room smoking cubebs, the pungent odor traveled down to the ground floor and my mother came running up stairs thinking the house was on fire. The cubebs had a horrible medicinal odor, but were supposed to ease minor nose and throat trouble, such as sniffles or a scratchy throat. While they were harmless, my mother forbid me to smoke them ever again, but Old Tom let us smoke in his room.

Occasionally we tried smoking brown cornsilk cigarettes. Other times we picked up driftwood when we went swimming, dry, porous willow sticks the size of a small cigar which we would puff, blowing pure wood smoke, and if by accident we inhaled we ended with a coughing fit. While my father never smoked, he always kept a box of cigars for guests, and when we reached our house I suggested we take one of his cigars to the basement and smoke it in the coal bin with the door shut. I grabbed a couple of red candles from the Christmas decorations because it would be pitch dark in the coal bin. We lit the candles and let the tallow drip on a large flat piece of hard anthracite coal to hold the candles upright. I cut the long cigar in two with my pocket knife, giving half to Hen, and when our cigars were lit we leaned back on the coal pile to enjoy our first cigar.

In a few minutes we both began to feel a little dizzy. When Hen asked me how I was doing, I said fine and dandy, nothing like a good cigar. But the inside of my head began spinning like a top and nausea began crawling inside my belly. My eyes had trouble focusing on Hen who sat a few feet away.

"I'm getting a little dizzy," I admitted. "How about you, Hen?"

But there was no reply and I saw Hen was lying down.

It was not long before we were both sick as poisoned pups and vomiting. I do not recollect how long we lay there with the sour stench of vomit mixed with the pungent smoke clogging our nostrils. The candles had gone out and when we were finally able to move we crawled to the door and over to Old Tom's room. When Tom came in he led a sick kid in each hand to the laundry tubs, shoved our heads under the faucet and sponged off our clothes as best he could, then bedded us down on his cot. It was Old Tom who turned the hose on the mess in the coal bin and disposed of the cigar butts. That ended our cigar smoking for some time.

The professional baseball season opened each spring sometime in April. The Montana League included Butte, Helena, Great Falls, Lewistown, Billings, and other towns. They had some very fine ball players who later were bought by the Major Leagues. Beginning at two P.M., the games were held at Black Eagle Park on Sunday afternoons.

No boy in Great Falls worthy of the name ever paid admission to get into the ball park. All were members of the Knot Hole Gang. When a hit ball went over the fence there was a battle royal to see who would get the ball, because whoever was lucky enough to glom onto it was admitted free and allowed to carry the ball to the bench and hand it to the Captain. It was then up to the rest of us to sneak in by a dug tunnel under the fence at some remote place where we would line up and crawl under. Another kid's dodge was to carry a player's glove or bat to get in free.

We bummed our way to the ball park on the open summer streetcar. The adult passengers riding the wide sides and hanging onto overhead straps paid no attention to the smallfry crouched around their legs. If a small kid was unable to hook a streetcar ride he went on foot.

For a few seasons a tall Negro high school boy, Harry Johnson, who had the making of a top pitcher, was the mascot of the Great Falls team. In later years he was destined to pitch in one of the big leagues. Even at an early age Harry attracted attention as a natural baseball player. He would play hookey from school to be Johnny-on-the-spot at Black Eagle Park when the team practiced on week days. We kids had a right to be proud of our Negro schoolmate. We were also proud of a Negro girl named Odessa, one of the prettiest girls in high school and in the top ten in scholastics.

While I am on the subject of Harry Johnson and Odessa let me say there were usually two or three colored boys and girls in most of the grammar school classes and in high school. Drawing the color line had no meaning at the North Side Whittier Grammar School. There was no racial color line between whites and blacks in the city of Great Falls. But, due perhaps to the Smelter Union, no Chinese were allowed in Great Falls. There used to be posted signs at the Great Northern Depot which read: "NO CHINAMEN ALLOWED IN THE CITY OF GREAT FALLS, MONTANA."

When a road show came to the Great Falls Opera House, such as the Primrose & Dockstatler Minstrels, or a stock company playing *Ole Olson*, *Yon Yonsen*, *Ten Nights in a Barroom*, and other stock plays too numerous to mention, or the famous Shakespearian plays, there would be a dozen or more kids gathered at Bill Steegy's office at the Opera House, waiting for him to give us our stack of handbills to be left on every front porch in our specified district. And always Bill Steegy would give us the usual spiel that he wanted every single handbill delivered. Any kid caught stuffing a bunch of handbills in culverts or garbage cans would be fired and put on the blacklist for all time. Steegy knew every one of us by name. The pay for distributing the handbills was a two-bit ticket to a seat in the last five rows of Nigger Heaven on the third balcony. The seats consisted of long benches with back rests. The ushers were stationed in the aisles at the sixth row and any kid with a two-bit seat attempting to climb over the sixth row was kicked out. The time to sneak down to the four-bit section was when the entire theater was in semi-darkness and the show began.

After the first act when all tickets were sold, if there were any vacant seats in the four-bit section the ushers allowed a few choice friends from Nigger Heaven to move down during intermission. If you were a real good friend of dapper Paddy Ryan, the head usher and ticket man on the lower floor and first balcony, and he had the tickets for the reserved seats in his coat pocket, he would slip his friend into a reserved seat for a four-bit tip, but you had to be dressed as befitted the ground floor audience, wearing your best suit, clean shirt and necktie, to crash the plush seat section.

The stock company shows could be viewed from Nigger Heaven with the same perspective as from a more expensive seat, but a minstrel show or musical comedy with a line of can-can dancers was something else, and then was when Paddy Ryan was worth knowing. When I attended grammar school I had no time for girls and was content with my seat in Nigger Heaven, but as a freshman in high school I commenced to take notice of girls in general, suddenly strangely aware of the feminine sex. It was then that I craved a reserved seat with a closeup of the chorus line.

Every year we kids would get the circus fever when it came to town. We would be up at the crack of dawn to meet the circus train which was always late, arriving about eight o'clock, long past sunrise. For a free pass we delivered handbills from house to house, then labored and sweated lugging endless buckets of water for the elephants, dragging the long board seats for the roustabouts to lay in tiers in the grandstand and then helped sprinkle the sawdust.

We were allowed to lead the Shetland ponies in the parade, with or without a monkey on their backs, and we would jockey for a place behind the clown band. We were given seats in the top row in the grandstand which commanded a view of all three sawdust rings, the clowns, the acrobats, the flying trapezes and tightrope walkers, the wild Cossack Riders, the four-horse stage and the Indian attacks. We took in all the sideshows and enjoyed the delicious aroma of popping corn and fresh roasted peanuts which we had money to buy.

After the last performance, when the circus was leaving town, we still hung around watching the caged animals being loaded, following the parade of elephants to the circus train on the railway siding and watched them loaded, all choked up inside as finally the circus train pulled out, with a gnawing hunger in our hearts to be aboard and traveling to unknown places. We dragged our weary legs homeward in the first gray light of the false dawn, tired and sore in every muscle and bone, and hungry for breakfast.

The old Great Northern Depot at Great Falls still holds nostalgic memories of the memorable departure of the Company A Volunteer Infantry Division leaving for the Spanish-American War, when our grammar school class marched in the long parade with each of us waving a small American flag. Captain Harry Athey lead his uniformed men down Central Avenue, accompanied by the Black Eagle Band in dress uniform, and on to the depot where the troop train waited. I have memories of the packed crowd of Great Falls citizens on the wide platform to say goodbye to their sons, the flag waving, the speeches, and the band playing "There'll Be a Hot Time in the Old Town Tonight," "Today Is the Day We Give Babies Away With Half a Pound of Tea," and "When Johnny Comes Marching Home."

Another memorable occasion and parade was when William Jennings Bryan, the silver-tongued orator, made his campaign speech at the old grandstand in the park near the depot, with the gray-haired, dignified Judge Benton, a staunch dyed-in-the-wool Democrat, perched high atop a tall telephone pole, cheering wildly and waving his plug hat.

I also remember the time the great herd of buffalo was rounded up near the Flat Head Indian Reservation and passed through Great Falls on their way to Canada, to be turned loose on a vast protected range in the Province of Alberta. The Canadian Government had out-bid Uncle Sam's lukewarm bid to keep the buffalo, and the old-time Montana pioneers called it a crying damn shame to allow the last of the big herd of bison to be shipped in the long train of cattle cars across the Canadian border, when the United States had vast grazing range at both Yellowstone and Glacier National Parks.

The departure of that long train of cattle cars loaded with buffalo bulls, cows and calves in slatted cars left the group that crowded the platform strangely silent, with bitterness in their hearts and tears in their eyes, blaming the politicians in Washington and the President of the United States for the shameful disgrace. The United States was allowing the Dominion of Canada to outbid Uncle Sam in the purchase of the vanishing breed of great shaggy beasts whose once vast herds roamed the Montana prairies, for want of a few thousand dollars from the bursting coffers of the wealthiest nation on the face of the earth.

It was a shameful disgrace, a black mark, and a wide band of black crepe for Uncle Sam's Star-spangled plug hat.

CHAPTER 4

Bowse, Beer and Barrooms

IN MY THIRD YEAR of high school (class of 1908), I was tagged with the nickname "Bowse" (also spelled Bouse). According to cowboy lingo a bowser was a cross between a sidehill gouger and a ringtailed albino warthog. Tracing the mythical pedigree back a generation, a sidehill gouger was a four-legged animal with the front and hind legs on the left side shorter than on the right side, enabling the animal to climb hills at a slant, anti-clockwise going up and clockwise coming down. The mythical sidehill gouger resembled a badger for size and appearance, digging deep caves in the steep sidehill for its den. The sidehill gouger was a cross between a cock-eyed Peruvian badger and a wall-eyed wallaby, a medium-sized kangaroo from Australia, while the ringtailed albino warthog was a cross between a ringtailed Argentine possum and a one-eyed, one-horned albino mountain goat imported from the Swiss Alps, the one eye in the middle of its forehead and the one long horn on top of its head.

The mythical bloodlines went back for many generations as the times the imagination of the cowboy teller of tall tales held out in endless detailed description, including minute ribald ways of breeding.

I had heard the cowhands at the Circle C Ranch rattle off the definition many times, and I remembered it all and had told the story of the bowser to a group of my North Side cronies one evening at a beer bust party, and they ganged up on me and spread the news throughout high school. The following day I was tagged with the nickname "Bowse" and I was stuck with it.

A month or so later my side-partner, Steve Doyle, happened on the word "Bowse" in Webster's dictionary during study period when the teacher, who kept a semblance of order in the classroom, was absent. Steve chalked the word on the blackboard for all the class to see, with the verbatim translation as found in the dictionary.

"BOWSE: TO DRINK ALCOHOL. TIPPLE. CAROUSE. BOOZER."

Steve Doyle, Bull Johnson, whose father owned the American Brewery, and myself, had all enjoyed the notoriety of being good beer drinkers. The students in the large assembly hall used for the study hour were aware of it and began whispering, and soon the girls were giggling and ribald laughter had the boys in stitches.

The whole class was in an uproar when Professor Largent, the high school superintendent, came in, accompanied by Miss Edgerton, the principal, and Miss Houliston, the mathematics teacher in charge of the study period. Then quite suddenly a pall of silence dropped like Doomsday.

From the superintendent and principal on down, all the teachers were aware of my nickname, but I doubt very much if any of them had ever taken the trouble to look up the word in the dictionary. Now they read its full meaning on the blackboard as I sat tight, red-faced and sweating with embarrassment.

Professor Largent, better known as Old Brocky, was a big, six-footer with a hard, fat paunch under his vest, a stern and dignified man as befitted his position as superintendent. I could not tell for certain if it was emotion or anger which caused his face to redden before he left the room with Miss Edgerton close at his heels, leaving Miss Houliston in charge. Houliston always called all the students, both boys and girls, by their last names. She had a sense of humor and sometimes a dry sarcastic wit which cut with razor sharpness. She now dismissed the class, telling Coburn and Doyle to remain seated. When the last student had left the room she picked up a piece of chalk and wrote in large letters Q.E.D. beneath Steve's chalked definition of the word "Bowse," telling us that when we were in our sophomore year in her geometry class we would understand the meaning of the Latin letters Q.E.D. *Quod erat Demonstendum* which translated into English meant "Which was to be demonstrated. The problem solved."

"Thanks to your friend Doyle, Coburn," she grinned down at me, "the true meaning of your nickname is hereby translated in its full meaning, a nickname that is bound to stick to you for the rest of your life, much to your embarrassment at times." Her green eyes sparkled with a glint of humor, her sardonic smile including both Doyle and myself when she added "The next time you two slip through the back door of the Montana Saloon to drink beer remember that if I turned the proprietor of the saloon in for selling liquor to minors he would lose his license. However, I am not the squealer type, so count your blessings. Wipe the blackboard, Doyle!" After this order she walked out, the tap-tap of her high heels echoing down the corridor.

Steve grabbed the eraser and chuckled as he wiped the board clean. We got our paper bag lunches and headed for the basement.

"How come that old maid schoolmarm got wise to our sneakin' into the Montana Saloon?" he muttered as we walked along.

"Miss Houliston rooms at the Henry Webster house near us," I said. "Besides owning part of the Churchill-Webster Grocery Store, Webster owns a cow outfit on the Canadian border which his son, Spike, runs. He was captain of the famous Black Horse Cavalry Troop and on graduation was appointed to West Point. He lasted two years, either he flunked or got kicked out."

"What's that got to do with Houliston seeing us sneak into the Montana Saloon?" Steve asked.

"She never saw us," I answered. "But Spike Webster did and he told her. You remember the night Spike and Harry Athey were getting a load on in the Montana bar when we sneaked in the back door?"

"It figures, Bowse. You hit the nail on the head," Steve agreed. "But I'm telling you for sure if that old maid thinks we're going to tell Bill Johnson that she threatened to get his license taken away she's talking through her bonnet. Bill Johnson has been good to us kids and we'll deny he ever sold us beer. His son Bull vouched for us keeping our traps shut and if his dad thinks we've had enough to drink he points to the back door and we slip into the alley."

While we were eating our lunch in the school basement, I told Steve I thought it was a low down dirty trick for him to write that stuff on the blackboard about Bowse meaning a drunk, and that he had made me the laughing stock of the whole school.

"Hold your horses," he said. "Would you rather be called Bowse the drunk or Bowser the cross between a sidehill gouger and a ringtailed albino warthog, with the long dirty word pedigree?"

"Only the boys know the story of Bowser," I said.

"Like heck they do!" Steve chuckled. "The girls know the dirty story. I could have written that definition on the blackboard and got a real laugh out of the assembly room. Give me credit for just writing the definition of Bowse I happened to run across."

"So from here on I'll be known as Bowse, the two-fisted drunk, thanks to Steve Doyle."

"Keep the change," said Steve.

And this is how I got the nickname Bowse which has stuck with me throughout my entire life.

The civic-minded men who belonged to the Great Falls Social and Athletic Club, declared at one of their meetings, by unanimous vote, that high school youths be admitted to the club. The name of a youth would be put up by an adult member, and by written vote would be passed on or blackballed as the case may be. The club was located on the second floor of a brick building occupied by the Great Falls Business College, the basement being occupied by the *Rocky Mountain Husbandman*, an old pioneer newspaper formerly established in White Sulphur Springs until the owner, Robert Sutherland, moved to Great Falls.

The entire second floor consisted of a large, modern equipped gymnasium, a spacious reading room, two separate card rooms and a billiard room. The list of house rules was thumbtacked to the blackboard in the hallway. No liquor allowed. No gambling. No rowdyism. All members should conduct themselves as gentlemen.

Albeit the Great Falls Club was financed and maintained by staid bankers, merchants, stockmen and professional men, who had homes in the city and were on the Board of Directors, those gray-haired men seldom visited the athletic club. They had their own Electric City Club, a plush, better furnished club with its bar and lounge rooms, card and billiard tables, while the athletic club was patronized for the most part by younger men, bank tellers, business and professional men, mining engineers working at the B & M Smelter, clerks in the court house and so on. They paid nominal monthly dues, while the dues of the high school youths were paid by our parents.

The main reason for allowing the teenagers to have membership in the club was to keep us out of pool rooms and saloons and off the streets after dark, and that was exactly what it did to a certain extent. For Steve Doyle, K. C. (Casey) Foster, Bull Johnson, Paddy O'Neil, Oshea Devine, Fred Andretta, myself and a few others, the Great Falls Athletic Club was the place to go after school, and those so inclined would strip down to trunks in the gym to play handball, punch the bag or exercise on the parallel bars and overhead rings.

Among the group Fred Andretta, a tall, well-built Italian lad with black hair and brown eyes who neither smoked nor drank, was by far the best athlete, boxer, wrestler and handball player. His widowed mother turned her three-story house on Third Avenue North into a lodging and boarding house. The best adult athlete at the club was Jimmy Madden, cashier at the First National Bank, a cousin of Frankie and Vince McDonnell. Jimmy was as well-muscled as a professional welterweight, a good boxer and wrestler who neither smoked nor drank.

Some evenings we played penny ante poker or pool or billiards, providing some adult members were not using the tables. Other evenings we enjoyed listening to Don Gibson play the piano. Don was the grandson of Paris Gibson, known as the founder of the city of Great Falls, and a senior to my freshman status. He was a born musician, a natural when it came to playing the piano. Often after a musical comedy or minstrel came to the Opera House, Don would sit at the piano and bang out the entire score of the musical comedy or the ragtime songs from the minstrel show, to the awed wonderment of the club audience. If he had the written music at home, we had no way of knowing.

During our high school years most of us smoked pipes, apeing the college students home for vacation. Our pipes were mostly bulldog, curved stem briar and an occasional meerschaum, with the flank pocket of our pants bulging with cans of Lucky Strike, Tuxedo, Prince Albert, or Edgeworth.

During my high school years the Montana Saloon was not the only barroom that Steve Doyle, myself and a few others frequented. Across the street on Central Avenue was a smaller barroom called The Hub, and a couple of smaller saloons on the South Side, one of them across the street from the Great Falls Hotel. It was Casey Foster, whose father was proprietor of the hotel, who first took me into the Black Eagle Bar owned and managed by Dutch Shroder, a short, red-faced, good-natured German who spoke broken English. In there we were allowed to play pool free of charge and buy nickel schooners of beer on the Q.T.

"When der cop comes in der front door," Dutch warned us, "you kids get the hell out der back door, lickety splitz!"

There was another club which I was welcome to frequent with any of my chums who had sense enough to keep their traps shut. It was called the Jockey Club and was on the South Side at the edge of the red light district, over the Stockholm Beer Hall, and was owned by Club Russell, a former jockey. It was a tough joint, with a lady's entrance at the back into a large room frequented by prostitutes, pimps, tinhorn gamblers, race track touts and former jockeys. Club

Russell was pint-sized, but tough, and married to a tall statuesque blonde prostitute named Goldie who ran a parlor house. There were times when Club would appear behind his bar with a black eye and scratched face after an argument with Goldie. Club hired a big Negro, Sam Jefferson, a meal ticket pug, for a bouncer.

A high school youth could learn a lot by listening to the grizzled Club Russell and from observing the different characters who hung out at the bar, the tinhorn gamblers who banked the games in the back card rooms, and the pimps in their double-breasted box-suits, coats, and patent leather button shoes with suede tops, a sort of uniform for that breed of men who lived off the earnings of prostitutes.

There was a very definite caste system among the prostitutes in the red light district. The parlor house girls who worked for Goldie and other madames such as Sylvia Bryant and Cricket Rockwell, were young, shapely and beautiful by any man's standards. It was common knowledge that the madames and the soiled doves got the first choice of expensive dresses that came into the Paris Dry Goods Store before the society women on the North Side had an opportunity to see them.

The dollar whores along Crib Row could not afford such luxuries, and they ate their meals at the Lunch Wagon, a long lunch counter across from the Jockey Club, and seldom went uptown. During warm weather the cheaper whores sat on kitchen chairs just inside their open doorways displaying their wares.

Because the Lunch Wagon was in the heart of the red light district, no minors were allowed except the A.D.T. messenger boys who delivered telegrams and packages to the parlor houses. Toad Nolan was the call boy for the Great Northern Railway who made the rounds to call some brakeman or freight conductor to get on the job. Toad was a black Irish teenager who enjoyed the reputation of being the toughest kid on the West Side. Besides being call boy he had a paper route for the *Morning Tribune* and *Evening Leader*, and when time permitted, Toad served as altar boy at the Catholic Church.

When any of our gang were in the vicinity of the red light district on a night's prowl we always looked around for Toad Nolan to take us to the Lunch Wagon for the best hamburgers in town. Toad was usually easy to find and because he had the two paper routes he knew every hooker on Crib Row and every parlor house madame by name.

Every parlor house had a young, good-looking Negro maid to answer the doorbell, usually recruited from the South Side Negro district. It was difficult for a Negro girl in Great Falls to get a job after finishing high school, so the next best thing was to hire out as a parlor house maid at a nominal wage, plus tips from the free spenders who frequented the houses. That some of the Negro maids, due to close familiarity, turned out to be prostitutes was a part of it, and this is what happened to the Negro girl, Odessa, of my high school class. Odessa was a quadroon with skin the color of thick cream. Her thick black hair was wavy rather than kinky and her eyes were dark gray, deep set under heavy black brows. She had no negroid thickness to her nose or lips, was tall and slender with long shapely legs, and was always quietly dressed. She was soft-spoken, her laughter quiet, and she ranked in the top ten in her class. There was no such thing then as a modern day beauty contest, but if there had been Odessa would have won hands down. She could have passed for a white girl in any other place except her home town. Her father was a Pullman conductor.

Odessa quit high school in her sophomore year to enroll in the Great Falls Business College and in order to pay her tuition she worked nights as a maid at Cricket Rockwell's parlor house, and managed to graduate with honors. That was about 1907.

I will have to skip a number of years to about 1924 when I was breaking into the writing game, living in Del Mar, California, a beach town twenty-five miles north of San Diego. I had driven my car down to Ensenada, Baja California, across the Mexican border, in order to obtain material first-hand on Chink and dope smuggling for a story I had in mind. While there I became acquainted with the

Negro piano player called Mac who played that instrument at Tom Quinlan's Green Front Bar. Mac told me that he had been born in Butte, Montana, and when I told him I had gone to school in Great Falls he asked me if I knew a colored girl named Odessa. I told him I did and he was strangely moved. He said Odessa was his wife, that he had killed a white man over her in the parlor house and had fled to Mexico, changing his name to MacDonald and that he did not dare write to Odessa for fear the law might track him down. When I was ready to leave Ensenada, he gave me three hundred dollars to send to Odessa. When I got back to Del Mar, I wrote her, wording it carefully, and got a prompt reply. I sent her the money, and about two months later I got a letter from her saying she had joined her husband, and they were working together in Guadalajara, Mexico.

The Great Falls High School was located on a high, sloping hill in a district called Boston Heights, the name Boston derived from the Boston & Montana Smelter. In the early 1900's Boston Heights was sparsely settled, so that the quarry-granite block school sat alone like some monument to higher learning. Graduates from the grammar schools went to the Great Falls High School and grammar school feuds were soon forgotten.

The High School was about a mile from our home and in good weather we rode our bikes there or took the Boston Heights streetcar. Winter, when the snowdrifts piled high, a horse-drawn, V-shaped, plank snowplow broke trail, and we walked the mile and thought nothing of it. It took a 30–40 below zero blizzard to keep us from attending school. The snowplow cleared the streetcar tracks in due time and the tracks were sanded by a gadget on the streetcar to prevent the wheels from slipping. In spite of the sand on the icy steel rails, there were times the streetcar went out of control and picked up runaway speed on the downgrade, and the motorman had his hands full trying to keep it from derailing. On the few occasions I remember the trolley car leaving the rails, the boys enjoyed the excitement while the girls got panicky, but there were no fatalities, just a few bruises.

On Halloween night, under the cover of darkness, one of the pranks played by the roving gang of kids was to grease the streetcar tracks on the long grade to Boston Heights with lard or axle grease. But the motorman and conductor, forewarned, would release the sand in the sand box and we were always disappointed that there was no runaway streetcar.

On Sunday afternoons during warm weather, Bull Johnson, who played on the football team, would gather a chosen few of his chums and we would ride our bicycles across the bridge to the Montana Brewery owned by his father. Bull explained to us that the keg of free beer on tap was chosen by the brew master. It was the special aged-in-the-keg beer the Montana Brewery brewed, similar to the Anheuser Busch Michelob draught beer which was supposed to be the finest keg beer in the country.

The brew master at the Montana Brewery was a big Swede who had formerly worked in a large brewery in Sweden, and he maintained that the Swedish beer was far better than the German beer, and that was the beer we kids drank, the formula brought over from Sweden by the aged brew master.

There were two breweries in Great Falls, the Montana Brewery and the American Brewery owned and operated by a Mr. Jensen. His son, Walt Jensen, was about the age of Bull Johnson, whose father owned the Montana Brewery. Mr. Johnson and Mr. Jensen were related by marriage and were very close friends, as were their sons, Walt and Bull. But it was only on rare occasions that Walt Jensen invited his close friends for free beer at the American Brewery. Walt traveled with the older crowd, Hartfield and Art Conrad and Lee and Shirley Ford. All of them worked in their father's banks and were more of the conservative society crowd, and that made a vast difference.

Walt Jensen was an athlete who kept in training, seldom smoked and never drank to amount to anything. He was destined to be a star football player at college, while Bull Johnson's aim in life was to learn the brewing trade and tour the country as a salesman for his father's brewery. As an only son he would someday inherit the Montana Brewery and all its many and varied responsibilities. Bull was a born mixer, a natural salesman, big and husky, stout as the proverbial bull which gave the big Swede his nickname. Good-natured and a poor student, he was always raising some kind of hell in high school. As Miss Edgerton, the high school principal, once remarked when she had Bull on the carpet, lecturing him: "You remind me of a big overgrown St. Bernard pup. Now get out of my sight before I have you expelled!"

Going back over the long bridge which spanned the wide Missouri River, beer tipsy, it was a little difficult to ride our bikes in a straight line, our grip on the handle bars being a little wobbly. Playing bike tag on the bridge we would ride into one another, piling up and laughing our heads off. But somehow we always managed to make it without falling into the river a hundred feet below.

Henry Hamilton and Pete Cooper never graduated from Great Falls High School. They quit after their junior year to go back East to Exeter Prep School and from there to some Ivy League university. I, too, wanted to quit after my junior year to go East with them and from prep school to enter Princeton University, but my father had different ideas. The same held true of Charlie Lowery, whose father owned the only wholesale produce company in the city. Both our fathers told us that after we graduated from high school it would be time enough to talk about college.

By that time, as I have said before, I began to sit up and take notice of the girls in my freshman year. Besides the regular high school dances and parties we attended with girls we were going with steady, there was the OAM (Once A Month) Club to which we all belonged. This club held monthly dances at Luther Hall in downtown Great Falls. It was much larger and more spacious than the neighborhood Grove's Hall and employed a full orchestra, usually Ed Pierce's.

Ed Pierce was five or six years older than our North Side Gang. He had taken violin lessons since he was old enough to hold a fiddle,

Walt Coburn, age eight, in Great Falls, Montana

and by the time I entered high school he had assembled his own orchestra.

Luther's Hall was where the various lodges, such as the Elks, the Ancient Order of Hibernians, the Sons of Luther, and the IOOF held their dances. There was a long, narrow hallway which led from the dancehall to several private rooms furnished with large round tables and chairs, and beyond was a long, narrow stairway leading to the Hoffman Bar. During the lodge dances there was a white-jacketed waiter serving the private rooms with drinks, and rather than climb back and forth on the stairway, he used a private telephone to order the drinks to be placed on a dumb waiter.

But there was no waiter upstairs during the OAM dances and it was one of the adult members who phoned the drink orders, cash on the line for the tab on the tray which went back down on the dumb waiter. Those were the days when no decent girl ever drank or smoked in public, and the girls we went with steady were treated with respect as befitted a young lady of social standing. No profanity or risqué stories were permitted. Holding hands and a mild goodnight kiss was the limit. But there were a few girls in high school who had the bad reputation of "putting out" and going the limit. They formed a clique of their own, aloof and apart from the majority. Those were the chosen few who smoked tailor-made cigarettes and took an occasional drink at the OAM dances in the ladies' cloak room. Those were the girls you held close during the moonlight waltz when the bright lights were turned off and a dark blue spotlight slowly crept over the heads of the dancers, but not enough to reach the balconies where young couples sat out the dances. All of which gave the OAM dances a bad name.

Let it be said that the parents of the elite North Side did not allow their teenage daughters to attend the OAM dances, and a North Side high school student going steady with a North Side girl stayed in the stag line.

It had long been the custom for any U.S. Congressman from a state to yearly appoint a high school graduate to West Point Military Academy, or to Annapolis Naval Academy. The entrance exams were tough and the candidate had to pass a strict physical. From the Great Falls High School in the year 1909, the graduate chosen was Arthur (Winkie) Goodwin, and he held the highest marks in the entrance exams and passed the physical without trouble. Winkie's father, who had a good position with the B & M Smelter, was a retired captain of a clipper sailing schooner, so of the two academies Winkie chose the Naval Academy when the news of the official appointment was received. All of us were highly elated for Winkie for he was popular with everybody in the neighborhood and in school. Winkie, a good athlete, would do front and back somersaults, cartwheels and handsprings on the way to school just to keep in practice. He was a natural all-around acrobat.

He was due to report to Annapolis on September 1, and in the meantime he and his older brother, Bill, had their regular summer jobs at the B & M Smelter. When school let out the first week in June, I headed for the Circle C Ranch to earn my forty-a-month wages which was my winter spending money. The daily Great Falls newspapers came to the ranch regularly by stage, and it was during the summer that I read the tragic news of the accident to Winkie Goodwin. There was always a long freight train of ore cars on the smelter sidings and rather than walk around the train the smelter employees would climb over the ore car couplings which were stationary for a limited time while the ore was being dumped into the ore pile. Somehow, in spite of Winkie's acrobatic ability, while climbing between two ore cars he was jolted from his precarious perch and the wheels of the heavily laden ore car ran over one of his legs and it had to be amputated at the knee joint.

I had graduated from high school and had persuaded my father to let me go to Stanford University at Palo Alto, California, and I was sitting sky high on cloud nine, but the tragic news of Winkie's accident which prevented him from going to Annapolis cast a black shadow on my cloud nine.

During that same summer another of my chums, Gene Cooney,

only son of the owner of the *Great Falls Leader* newspaper, drowned in a lake where he was spending his summer vacation. Such tragedies dimmed the sunny blue skies of Montana for me.

But despite the double tragedy I had my summer's work to do at the ranch. I would put in a full day in the saddle and was always dog tired and ready for bed when darkness came. It was only after the fall beef shipment that I returned to Great Falls, packed my suitcase and headed for Palo Alto, California. The year was 1909.

CHAPTER 5

Stanford meets Bowse

MR. THORNTON, president of the First National Bank, and his wife accompanied me as far as San Francisco. Mr. Thornton was a handsome, gray-haired man, a typical banker, and conducted himself as one. We checked in at the St. Francis Hotel, and the first night he telephoned his brother, Crittendon Thornton, a prominent San Francisco attorney. He told me that Crit, as he called his brother, would show me the high spots of the big city, winking at me when his wife was not looking.

We awaited Crittendon's coming in the famed Peacock Alley of the St. Francis, and I got the shock of my life when the prominent attorney-at-law appeared. Crit Thornton was a tall, handsome man, in well-tailored clothes and dove-gray spats with a dark red carnation in the buttonhole of his Harris tweed suit. He wore a clipped gray mustache and his broad smile crinkled crowsfeet at the corners of his eyes. Crit slapped his older brother between the shoulder blades and told him he was not in Great Falls now, that he could shed his banker's dignity, and he led him to the bar.

"If you figure on getting me drunk, Crit," John Thornton warned, "you're badly mistaken. I can still drink you under the table."

"That remains to be seen, John. I'll still be on my hind legs and rarin' to go at sunrise," Crit bragged.

"I'll stay with you drink for drink until my better half returns from the theater. That's when I quit, drunk or sober. Remember I'm a married man, Crit."

"And thanks to God I'm still a bachelor, and a man about town. It's Saturday night and my night to howl, John."

When we went into the plush barroom Crittendon Thornton promptly ordered Mum's champagne, naming the vintage date to the bartender. And it was on that momentous occasion I got my first taste of champagne. Despite all their joshing about drinking one another under the table, neither of the brothers got drunk.

When John took his departure to meet his wife, Crit took me to the Bismark and the Heidelberg, and he insisted upon me calling him Crit. At the Heidelberg we drank German beer in steins and ate plank steaks. From there we took a cab to the famous Barbary Coast and wound up at Spider Kelly's Black Cat Cabaret, where Crit introduced me to Spider Kelly, former lightweight champion in Great Falls where he knocked out Zubuck. I told Spider that when Ketchel was in training camp at Box Elder Park, I would ride my bike there every afternoon to watch him train. Spider Kelly told me I would always be welcome at the Black Cat when I entered Stanford, and that he would personally see that I never got a Mickey Finn at his place.

When we left the Black Cat to tour Chinatown, Crit told me Spider Kelly's cabaret was the toughest joint on the Barbary Coast, but that I would be as safe as in a church when there. From Chinatown Crit took me on a guided tour to visit a few parlor houses where he was known, and we finished up at the notorious House of All Nations.

The liquor we drank along the way was tempered by the cold, foggy air as we walked off our jags. We ate large bowls of noodles at a plush Chinese restaurant in Chinatown where we visited a few opium joints which had survived the 1906 earthquake. At sunrise we wound up at the plush Poodle Dog Café, where men in tuxedos and beautiful ladies in evening gowns were eating an early breakfast after an all night carousal. When a tall, distinguished-looking man, dressed in white tie and tails, came over to our table and greeted Crit tipsily, I was introduced to Earl Rogers, the famous California criminal attorney, second only to Clarence Darrow of Chicago. Rogers sat down at our table and promptly ordered Black Velvets, a potent mixture of champagne and Guinesses Stout, supposedly a sure cure for a night's hangover. After we got the Black Velvets down, Crit ordered a round of suissesse, a potent mixture of pernod, annisette, gin or vodka, simple syrup and raw egg white, chilled in silver shakers beaded with icy sweat. Instead of breakfast eggs we ate rare porterhouse steaks and drank Turkish coffee.

Instead of calling it a night Crit ordered a cab and told the driver to take us to Golden Gate Park where we could watch the sunrise, but when we got there the fog from the Pacific Ocean had drifted in, but we could see the Alcatraz Island Prison where Crit said Earl Rogers had a prisoner he was trying to save from the death chamber.

When we headed back for the St. Francis we were fairly sober, due to the raw wind and fog. Crit told me that on Monday morning we would board the train for Palo Alto where he knew the president of the bank and I could open a checking account. He kept his promise, telling the banker I was the son of a Montana cattleman and the sky was the limit.

This was some send-off for a forty-a-month cowhand, a stranger in a strange land, spending his first winter away from his Montana home. This big buildup probably had something to do with the spending spree I went on to use up a good part of the money I had in the Palo Alto Bank.

Crit Thornton had an important board meeting with the directors of some large corporation as their legal advisor at one P.M. at the St. Francis Hotel. We barely made it to the local San Francisco train after he had fixed me up at the bank. He wanted to accompany me to the registrar's office on the Stanford campus, but that was impossible. I told him I would make out easily — a white lie if there ever was one — because I was a rank stranger in a brand new environment. It was the first time I was ever within a hundred miles of any university and I was a little awed, gun shy, and apt to get buck fever when I entered the registrar's office alone. I stood on the wide plank platform and watched the train out of sight, a hollow feeling inside.

"You must be Bowse Coburn from Montana." The unexpected deep-toned voice behind me surely gave me a start, like dry lightning out of a clear sky. I turned quickly to see a rangy six-foot stranger in his early twenties standing there, a wide grin on his deeply tanned face. He wore a blue flannel shirt open at the collar, a pair of well-worn pegtop pants, brown brogues, and a flat-brimmed Stetson hat, its crown dented on four sides, and with a black leather hatband. I knew he was a Stanford student because Crit had pointed out a group of college boys in front of Larkin's Cigar and Coffee Shop and had explained the way they were dressed.

"I'm Courtney Moore, Court for short," the stranger introduced himself as we shook hands. "Don Gibson, a fraternity brother of mine, wrote the Chi Psi House to expect you, take you to the registrar's office and make you feel at home. Let's go over to Larkin's for a cup of coffe, then we'll get you registered. You're about two weeks early. The campus is deserted. I'm down here to open the Chi Psi Lodge, air it out and hire a Chink cook."

While we drank our coffee Court remarked that I sure traveled in high class company, that Crittendon Thornton was high man on the totem pole, one of the best corporation lawyers in San Francisco and something of a legendary figure around town.

I explained how I had come from Montana to San Francisco with Crit's brother John, president of the First National Bank in Great Falls, how Crit had shown me the high spots of San Francisco and the Barbary Coast, and how we had eaten breakfast at the Poodle Dog where I had met the famous lawyer, Earl Rogers.

"Judas in a wheelbarrow! Earl Rogers! Man, you don't realize!" Court went on to recite a few legendary stories of the fabulous Earl Rogers. "I'd give my eye teeth to have been in your boots, Bowse." Court said he was impressed because he was studying law at Stanford.

When we finished our coffee we went back to the depot where a couple of horse-drawn surreys were waiting for passengers. Court called the driver of one by name and we climbed in. He asked me if I had written the registrar in advance about my high school grades.

"Nope," I answered. "It was only a week ago that I persuaded my father to send me to Stanford. The Coburn Cattle Company is footing the bill. They have interests in gold mines in the Little Rockies and I'm supposed to take a mining engineer's course. I got my high school diploma by the skin of my teeth. My grades are nothing to brag about, especially mathematics."

To shorten a lengthy story, I got turned down flat by the registrar.

"Try the University of California at Berkeley," he suggested to let me down easy.

Court Moore took me over to the empty Chi Psi House and we talked it over at length that afternoon. I was in low spirits, but stubbornly held out for Stanford, not wanting any part of Berkeley, mainly because Leland Stanford was a horse lover, breeding and raising standardbred trotting horses on his large horse farm. Court was somewhat amused at my reasons for wanting to enter Stanford.

"The only thing for you to do, Bowse," he told me, "is to go to a prep school for the first semester, an accredited one recognized by Stanford University. There's Belmont Military prep school of Belmont, or there's Manzanita Hall here in Palo Alto. Dr. William Shedd, the headmaster at Manzanita, is one of the best educators in California. You want me to phone him for an appointment?"

"The sooner the better, Court." That glimmer of hope was like a ray of bright sunshine in an overcast cloudy sky.

After Court talked to Dr. Shedd and hung up the phone he said:

"Grab your hat, Bowse. Dr. Shedd is anxious to meet you."

Court hailed a surrey at the book store and we drove to town, then caught a streetcar that took us within a few blocks of the prep school at the other end of Palo Alto. Manzanita Hall's white two-storied building was situated in a grove of tall oak trees. Dr. Shedd came out on the porch to meet us with a welcoming smile on his deeply-tanned face. I took an instant liking to this tall, lean scholarly-looking man with the close-clipped gray mustache. It took only a brief half hour of friendly talk to sell me on Manzanita Hall and I said so. Dr. Shedd showed us through the dormitory which contained his office, and after showing us the two tennis courts and the gymnasium, he took us to his home to meet his wife, a handsome, slender woman with a gorgeous tan. I later learned that she was an expert tennis player.

I made out a check for the first semester. Dr. Shedd told me to have my trunk and suitcase sent out, and that my roommate would be a senior from Reno. His name was Raymond Quinn and he had spent the previous year at Manzanita Hall.

Mrs. Shedd invited us to stay for dinner, but Court declined, saying he wanted to show me around my first college town. But instead we boarded the local train for Menlo Park. Court told me that by a strict ruling no liquor of any kind was permitted within a mile of the vast Stanford campus, and that we would hoist a few beers at Charlie Myers' Tavern at Menlo, where Myers served the best cold lunch one could find anywhere.

I was to learn that Charlie Myers' Tavern was the hangout for Stanford students, and the gathering place of the TNE, a secret drinking fraternity which held beer busts over the weekends. The TNE (Tau Nu Epsilon) fraternity pin was the solid gold skull with ruby eyes and was worn concealed, pinned to a member's undershirt. Any suspected TNE member could be called on the carpet by the faculty and tried by what Court called the "benzine board." If a member admitted he was a TNE he could be suspended for a semester or a year, or expelled. But that was only if that particular student was found drunk and disorderly or obnoxious in any way on campus. Court said it was an open secret, known by some of the faculty, that every fraternity and the men's dormitory held its small quota of TNE's, especially among the athletes who were beer drinkers.

When Court asked me if I had gone in for athletics while in high school I told him I was too light for football and was not interested in the track team but had done a little boxing and lightweight wrestling and was above the average swimmer. He said the Stanford coach, Pop Warner, was one of the top athletic coaches in the country, that Stanford went in for English rugby, and that he had played rugby until he received a bad knee injury. I noticed that he walked with a slight limp.

Charlie Myers' Tavern was a typical college tavern. The main barroom walls were lined with framed pictures of Stanford's football teams over the past years and other athletic sports. Charlie Myers was behind the bar when we went in and he put on a wide grin as he shook hands with Court Moore, saying: "You got here early this year, Court."

"Came down to open the Chi Psi Lodge, and to meet this young cowboy from Montana. Shake hands with Bowse Coburn. Bowse, this is the famous Charlie Myers I've been telling you about."

At the far end of the bar there were a lot of brown beer mugs hanging by their handles on rows of wooden pegs. Above each mug was a printed number identifying the owner, and embossed on the glazed brown surface were the Greek letters TNE and below the insignia of the skull with the ruby eyes. Court took his mug from its peg and Charlie Myers took a bone-white mug with a crimson S embossed on one side and placed it in front of me, then filled our mugs with beer and poured a shot glass of whisky for himself.

"Welcome to the Tavern, Bowse," he said, and we drank to it, then Court and I carried our filled mugs down a narrow hallway which led to three drinking rooms. In the first room there was a large round table, a solid unvarnished pine plank bolted to a wide post standard, in the center of which was deep-branded the letters TNE. The sides and top were covered with carved initials and dates, some dating back about fifteen years.

Along the four sides of the room were old barroom chairs with deep notches carved on the arms, and Court told me to pull up a chair and carve my notch with the pocket knife on the table. When I offered to pay for the next round of beer, Court shook his head, saying it was on the Chi Psi House and came out of the rushing funds.

The term "rushing funds" was new to this old country boy fresh from the cow country, and as Greek as the then unknown lettering TNE. But I kept my mouth shut and later Court gave me my first inkling of what fraternity rushing of freshmen meant.

He took me into the other two rooms which held similar tables with carvings. He told me the tables were later auctioned off to TNE alumni and the money donated to the TNE treasury to be used for entertainment. When we had finished our tour of inspection we went back to our beer and there on the table was a large tray covered with a white napkin and filled with the cold lunch Court had mentioned, enough to make your mouth water. While we ate there were the sounds of members entering the next room, much talking and laughter, then the sound of a ukulele and barbershop harmony as they sang:

> For there's a road to Menlo
> As plain as plain could be!
> And if you want to see a wreck
> Just take a look at me!
> For I have been to Charlie Myers'
> And tasted of his beer
> And that's the reason
> Why my eyes are weak,
> And I had to rest for a year!

"That will be the one and only Charlie Brownell," Court informed me. "His family is loaded, related to the Pullmans of the Pullman Car Company, and lives in a mansion at Burlingame. Charlie's a wild one, sort of the black sheep. His old man built and furnished the Chi Psi House, the finest on the campus. Charlie's been suspended twice and the benzine board has decreed the next time he'll be expelled. He's an international playboy and has just returned from the French Riviera where his family owns another mansion. Yesterday he drove up to the Chi Psi House in a brand new fireman red Chalmers car. He was half-drunk as usual and wanted me to join him making the rounds of the roadhouses between the city and San Jose, but I declined."

Once again came the sound of the ukulele and the barbershop quartet singing:

> I was drunk last night,
> Drunk the night before,
> Going to get drunk tonight
> If I never get drunk anymore.
> 'Cause when I'm drunk,
> I'm as happy as can be
> For I am a member
> Of the TNE.

"Charlie's off to the races," Court said, "and may his patron saint look after him when he takes his drunken companions to the Chi Psi House. When the benzine board sights that red Chalmers with the throttle wide open that'll be the end of playboy Charlie. He'll be kicked out and good riddance."

Court explained that it was the likes of Charlie Brownell who caused the big scandal on the Stanford campus which resulted in the decree of no liquor allowed within a mile. It seems some drunken student got fouled up with a professor's young wife and got himself shot. The professor was tried for murder, and criminal attorney Earl Rogers got him off scot-free.

"The tragic affair was hushed up and is best forgotten so don't repeat it, Bowse," said Court. "I am just explaining what can happen when a student hits the booze too hard."

It was long after dark when we parted company that evening. Court returned to the campus and I boarded a streetcar for Palo Alto. Before we parted I told Court I felt a little guilty showing up at Manzanita Hall with a beery breath, but Court assured me I had no need to worry, that while Dr. Shedd ran his prep school with a headmaster's capabilities and a measure of dignity, he was an understanding man with whom a student could discuss his problems.

The three or four blocks from the streetcar to Manzanita Hall in the night air cleared my head and I could walk the chalkline without weaving. While my high school grades were a notch or two below average, I had learned to hold my liquor with the best of the youthful drinkers, and was head of the class when it came to that liberal education. I knew it was lights out at 10 P.M., and I still had fifteen minutes to go. In the glare of the arc light I noticed a motorcycle parked nearby. It had saddlebags strapped behind the seat, and it was dusty and mud-spattered. When I entered the hall, Dr. Shedd's door was open, and he was leaning back in his swivel chair talking to a tall kid in a dust-covered blue flannel shirt and pegtop corduroys. His face was long and lean, his straw-colored hair crewcut, and on the floor beside him was a pair of black gauntlet gloves, a Sherlock Holmes dusty linen cap and a pair of dark-colored goggles.

". . . About a mile outside of Palo Alto I had the first flat tire since I left Reno," he was saying. "The rear tire blew like a shotgun blast and there I was stranded on the last lap. . . ." It was then they looked up and saw me standing in the hall.

"Come right in, Bowse, and meet your roommate," Dr. Shedd invited. "Meet Ray Quinn, better known as Gimpy."

Gimpy got to his feet, a lanky, loose-jointed youth with a wide grin and laughter in his blue-gray eyes.

Together we went to our room to find it piled with my trunk and suitcase, and Gimpy's baggage as well. Both black enameled beds were made up. We stripped down, got into our pajamas and went down the hall with our bath towels to the showers.

"Ever ride a motorcycle, Bowse?" Gimpy asked.

"Nope. Just horses and bikes."

"We got a week–ten days before school opens," Gimpy said. "We'll tour the country on my motorcycle. First stop will be Charlie Myers' Tavern at Menlo for a few beers."

"I just came from there, Gimpy," I said. "I needed this cold shower to get shed of the beery effects."

"I'm sure as hell happy to get a roommate who likes a few beers, Bowse."

"That goes both ways, Gimpy."

We turned out the light and crawled into bed and talked for about an hour. Gimpy did most of the talking, bringing me up to date on our schoolmates. He said most of them were good scouts, only a few were stinkers. There was the big Swede, Henry Olsen, from San Francisco where his old man was a bank president. John Cookson, known as Cookie, was from Los Angeles, his father a real estate broker. Tom and Ab Couch were day dogs who lived in Palo Alto and were from Montana.

"Sun River?" I cut in.

"That's right. Sun River. You know them, Bowse?"

"Yep, their folks sold their big cattle ranch on Sun River and moved to California a few years ago. I'm glad they live in Palo Alto." That welcome news gave me a big lift.

"There's Charlie Arthur," Gimpy went on. "Charlie's from Portland, Oregon, where his father owns timberland and sawmills. Last year Charlie showed up driving a large green Fiat. Dr. Shedd made him send it back. He doesn't want Manzanita students driving expensive cars, or any car for that matter. You'll like Charlie, Bowse. He's a crack amateur tennis player, but he never brags about being a top player for the Multnomah Club in Portland. Last year he beat Mrs. Shedd and that took a lot of sweat and hard work. That lady is tops in tennis."

In Gimpy Quinn's book Dr. Shedd was the salt of the earth. A gentleman and a scholar. Gimpy said Shedd had taken a postgraduate course at Heidelberg University in Germany and spoke both German and French like a native. Let a student at Manzanita get into trouble and Dr. Shedd, with every degree known to a scholarly man tacked onto his name, would get him out of it, and stand behind him all the way.

Gimpy Quinn went on at great length describing the good-looking girls he called Queens at Miss Harker's School for Girls, and Miss Lockey's exclusive Castilleja Finishing School, both schools located within walking distance of Manzanita Hall. Gimpy said the best bet was to have a Queen at both schools. In that way you got invited to all the dances.

"You got a tux, Bowse?"

"Nope," I admitted.

"Tomorrow I'll take you to Thiel's Tailor Shop and get you measured for a tux and a couple of pairs of cords. You can buy the blue flannel shirts at the store. Lucky we came early before Thiel gets too busy to fit you out."

We were at Thiel's Tailor Shop when the doors opened at 8 A.M. and by 6 P.M. I was the proud possessor of my first tailored pegtop cords. I bought a couple of blue flannel shirts at the local store, and when dressed I felt like a real college student. That day we toured the nearby countryside on the Harley-Davidson, with me riding the baggage rack behind, making the rounds of the roadhouses from San Jose to the Cliff House on the outskirts of San Francisco, known as The City to the students. We wound up at Menlo Park and Charlie Myers' Tavern, getting home by ten o'clock curfew, glad to bed down for the night. For the next few days we repeated the performance, seeing new places each day.

In addition to the formal tux, I also ordered a Harris tweed suit to be made. I already had a tailor-made blue suit for informal evening wear. The following evening when the Shedds invited Gimpy and me for dinner, we accepted. Mrs. Shedd informed us beforehand that she had invited Miss Lockey of Castilleja and Miss Harker, of Harker's, and Gimpy said we would have to be on our best behavior, no beer smell to offend the guests. He claimed that Miss Lockey was a good sport, but that Cattie Harker was a hidebound old maid bitch.

We were in our room that Sunday afternoon getting dressed for dinner when Chico, the little monkey-faced Philippino houseboy, showed up in his clean white jacket, a wide bucktooth grin on his swarthy face. Chico was something of a character, a five-foot, wiry, jockey-sized, ageless man. The rules were for all the students to make their own beds, army fashion, under Chico's tutelage, but it was Chico who swept out with broom, dust rag, damp chamois and his prized Brussells carpet sweeper. The little Philippino had a grammar school education and two years of high school, but he spoke English with a peculiar accent all his own and when he got excited his sentences were a wild mixture of English, Spanish and Japanese, the words thrown in a haphazard fashion. Gimpy said the prep school students told him dirty stories and when he repeated them to his chums in The City they were always a scrambled mixture, telling the point of the story first, then going back from start to finish.

A chum of Chico's was a Philippino houseboy at Miss Harker's, and any time you wanted to send a note to a girl you slipped the note to Chico who passed it on to Pedro. Pedro always had the lowdown on every girl in the school and that made for a secret grapevine between the boys and girls.

"I press your pants," Chico announced as he stood in the doorway with a buck-toothed grin. "For nothing free. Good excellent like a tailor." We handed over the pants of our dark suits.

"Any news from Harker's?" Gimpy asked. "Any girls show up yet?"

"Two," Chico held up two fingers. "Tweens!" He held his two fingers close together now. "Blonde. Look-alike-together. Sophomores." Chico winked an opaque black eye at us.

Gimpy flipped a half dollar in the air.

"Your pal Pedro give you the lowdown on the twins?" he asked.

"Sure thing." Chico's beady eyes fixed on the coin Gimpy kept tossing and catching. "Them tweens came yesterday afternoon in a fancy carriage, fancy black team. Very polite, yes ma'am, no ma'am, when Miss Harker speak to them. You ever see look-alike tweens?"

"Sure," Gimpy replied. "The Siamese twins in a side show at the circus. Skip the big buildup, Chico, and let's have the lowdown."

"Pedro says them tweens were smoking cigarettes last night when Miss Harker caught them. Wow! Fourth of July fireworks!"

Gimpy flipped the four-bit piece and the grinning Chico grabbed it in midair.

"You find out the names of the look-alike gals, Chico?" Gimpy asked.

Chico took a folded piece of paper from his pocket and handed it to Gimpy who read the printed words aloud: "Milo and Margo Abernathy, Burlingame, California." Gimpy let out a silent whistle.

"Wow!" he said in disbelief, then told Chico to drop around about nine that night and he would have a note ready for his pal Pedro to give to the twins, saying that there was a dollar in it to split with Pedro.

When Chico picked up the pants which had no need of pressing and left, Gimpy began prancing around on his gimpy legs like a Cheshire cat, talking excitedly.

"You ever hear of the bigshot millionaire, Abernathy, Bowse?"

"Nope. I'm a green cowhand from Montana, a stranger in a strange land," I answered.

Gimpy explained that the Abernathy family lived on a palatial estate in Burlingame, and were very social.

"Get your thinking cap on, Bowse. A lot depends on the notes we concoct to send the twins. We'll ask them to meet us at the Wishing Tree at the far end of Lover's Lane on the spacious grounds of Harker's school and out of bounds for the Manzanita Hall gash hounds, an added risk to sweeten the love juices in our carcasses. I'll flip a coin to see which one you choose." Gimpy flipped a silver dollar. He got Milo and I got Margo.

Having an hour before our dinner date at the Shedds, we wrote the notes on Manzanita Hall stationery along similar lines, saying we had heard about the forbidden cigarette smoking and could offer a solution if they would meet us tomorrow night under the Wishing Tree. We addressed separate envelopes to Milo and Margo and signed our names Gimpy and Bowse.

Gimpy was taking it in his habitual nonchalant manner as we mounted the front steps of Dr. Shedd's home and rang the doorbell. But I had a swarm of fluttering butterfiies in my empty belly, and was as nervous as the proverbial tomcat on a hot tin roof. My first formal dinner at the Shedds would be a trying ordeal for this old country boy, but Mrs. Shedd proved to be a most gracious hostess, and made me feel right at home.

Miss Lockey and one of her teachers, Miss Tracy, were already in the living room, talking to Dr. Shedd, now dressed in a blue flannel jacket and white flannel trousers. Miss Tracy was the art and music teacher at Castilleja, a tall, slender, good-looking woman in her early thirties. Miss Lockey was also tall and slender, a handsome woman with a sprinkling of gray in her jet-black hair. When I was introduced to her she gave me a quizzical look and a warm smile, and in her soft voice she told me she had been born and raised in Helena, Montana, and was well acquainted with the Coburn family. She had gone to the Vistacian Convent with my sisters, Agnes and Edna, and my brother, Wallace, had been her best beau for a while in Helena. She said I had a strong resemblance to Wallace, and I was keenly aware that I had just made a lifelong friend.

Dr. Shedd led us over to a large punch bowl filled with grenadine punch, saying that the recipe dated back a few centuries to the First Battalion of French Grenadiers. The ancient formula called for Jamaica Rum and Burgundy Wine, a highly potent mixture for the hard-drinking soldiers, but he was truly sorry that the rules at Manzanita Hall strictly forbade the use of intoxicants.

"Hard lines, Bowse," Gimpy, the bold one, spoke in a stage whisper in my ear which fell during a hushed lull in the conversation.

"Bowse!" Miss Lockey's soft voice sounded. "What an unusual name. I suppose it's a nickname?"

I felt my face redden, and gave Gimpy a dirty look. I dreaded her next question asking the meaning of the moniker, but Mrs. Shedd saved the day as she came into the living room to say that Miss Harker had just telephoned she would be unable to attend dinner because a group of girls had arrived unexpectedly. Out of the tail of my eye I saw Miss Lockey and Miss Tracy exchange quick, furtive glances, and caught Mrs. Shedd giving the two ladies a left handed smile, a smile of relief if I had my guess.

The cold, icy mixture of fruit juices had a pleasant spicy tang, by far the best soft drink I had ever tasted. I surely needed that ice cold drink to cool down my flushed embarrassment. When we complimented Dr. Shedd on the grenadine punch, Mrs. Shedd asked us not to ask him for the recipe, that it was a deep, dark secret, somehow connected with some fraternal order he belonged to when he took a summer course at the University of Paris.

"A sort of military order, The Grenadiers," Dr. Shedd explained. "A society honoring the First Regiment of French Grenadiers in the late Eighteenth Century. In my youth I considered it quite an honor for an American to be invited to join the select group of French students. Part of the initiation was to down a huge silver goblet of potent grenadine punch, spiked generously with rum and the wine of Burgundy, and then sing the 'Marseilles' from beginning to end, to the fife and drum beat. The new initiates had to learn the secret formula by memory and were sworn to never reveal the recipe. A part of belonging to the Order of French Grenadiers was to grow a fierce military mustache and in my prideful youth at the Sorbonne I wore it all that summer."

When we sat down to dinner Chico, freshly bathed and wearing a starched white monkey-jacket, waited on table. Dr. Shedd skillfully carved the roast leg of lamb, which was the first sheep meat I had ever tasted. When everyone was served I almost made my first big mistake. My sisters, fresh from boarding school, had painstakingly taught me formal dinner manners and that training came in handy now, at least part way.

When Dr. Shedd bowed his head and said, "Let us give thanks to God" I noticed that every head except mine was bowed, so I promptly ducked my crewcut noggin while grace was said.

It was a vast relief when Gimpy and I took our departure and went to our room where we shed stiff starched collars, and got into comfortable cords and flannel shirts.

"You got it made at Miss Lockey's Castilleja School," Gimpy assured me. I told him that Montanans always stuck together.

Walt Coburn, Prescott, Arizona, 1927

We filled our pipes, smoked and chewed the fat until Chico showed up to get the notes and the dollar tip. It was a little after nine when Gimpy suggested we go on a preliminary scouting trip into enemy territory. Both girls' schools were surrounded by large live oak trees, and while no fence or barrier of any kind divided the two schools, there were well beaten paths on each estate and the students were forbidden to stray off those paths separating the boys of Manzanita Hall from the girls' schools, each governed by the same honor system.

It was a bright moonlit evening, with a white lopsided moon riding the star-choked cloudless sky. The giant oaks cast huge, misshapen dark shadows on the grass, and a hushed silence prevailed. We walked leisurely along this warm early September night, straining our eyes for a glimpse of the Abernathy twins. We were about to give it up when we heard the sound of girls' voices as they strolled along Lover's Lane, and stood grouped in the shadow of the Wishing Tree. All of them were dressed alike in dark skirts and white blouses, the uniform worn by Miss Harker's pupils. One girl was strumming a ukulele and the girls were singing "On the Beach at Waikiki" in blended chorus.

"A lousy chorus," Gimpy remarked disgustedly as we walked back to our room at curfew time and went to bed.

"Wait until you hear Lucy Diamond play the uke and sing real Hawaiian songs," Gimpy said as he described Lucy Diamond as the best looking Queen at Castilleja. "Lucy was born and raised in Hawaii and once a year she gives a formal ball at Castilleja, brings over a Hawaiian orchestra and serves real Hawaiian pineapple punch that has the kick of a mule. Until you've seen Lucy Diamond in a grass skirt, bare-legged and bare-footed, dance the hula, you ain't seen nothing yet."

Sleep was hard to come by that night as I lay on my bed in the dark, the faint perfume of Mrs. Shedd's flower bed sifting through the open window. I smiled faintly to myself as I compared Dr. Shedd to Mr. Sam Largent, superintendent of the Great Falls High School.

Will Shedd and Old Brockey were as different as black and white. Mrs. Shedd and Miss Lockey bore the same day and night comparisons with the gray-haired old maid Miss Edgerton, principal of the Great Falls High School. The red-haired Miss Huliston, my high school teacher, was on the same level as Miss Tracy, both good looking, full of fun and with a sense of humor. It was a far cry from Great Falls High to Manzanita Hall, and there was a vast difference between the city of Great Falls and the university town of Palo Alto.

I was in a different world here, but no longer a total stranger. Court Moore and Dr. Shedd and my roommate had made me feel the warmth of welcome. Tomorrow the two professors, Mr. Rowell and Mr. Kellar, were due to arrive and occupy the two large front upstairs rooms of the dormitory. The following day was registration day when the students of Manzanita Hall would be coming in to occupy the vacant rooms, the day the students who lived in Palo Alto, whom Gimpy called "day dogs" would sign up. I was eagerly curious about their arrival and wondered how I would fit in and how I would enjoy living with the other students cooped up in the same dorm, using the same bathrooms and showers. That eager beaver expectancy seemed burdened with grave doubts but I made up my mind to make a hand, regardless, and I carried that one encouraging thought into dreamland.

We were making our beds next morning when Chico showed up with his Brussels carpet sweeper, wet chamois, dust rags and broom. He handed each of us a sealed envelope, slightly scented. I split open my envelope and a single sheet of paper bore the inscription: "Bowse sounds like the name of the Dog-faced Boy in the circus side show!" Enclosed was an engraved invitation to an informal tea at Miss Harker's school on Sunday afternoon from three to five. It was signed Margo Abernathy. I read the note with mixed feelings of anger and sardonic amusement.

"To hell with that stuck up Margo," I told Gimpy as I read the note aloud.

"And to hell with Milo," said Gimpy as he proceeded to read his note: "The name Gimpy reminds me of the lame old plug hitched to the ragman's cart that collects old clothes in Burlingame."

His invitation to the tea was signed Milo Abernathy. Gimpy's laugh had a brittle sound when he said, "These twins have a bitchy sense of humor." We discussed them at length and profanely.

Gimpy explained about the Sunday pink teas. Each girl was priviliged to invite a boy to sit in the large reception room under the vigilant teacher-chaperone. Miss Catherine (Cattie) Harker met each boy personally and sized him up for future reference. As each swain entered, one of the teachers stood at the door to collect the invitations, these to be kept in the office of Miss Prudence Carter, better known as Prune Face Carter's Little Liver Pills. Prune Face for short.

Furthermore Gimpy explained, it was considered an honor for any Manzanita Hall student to receive an invitation, as well as the chosen few attending Palo Alto High School, or any nearby prep school, but that the Stanford students were barred as being too old and sophisticated. This was a strict ruling which started a few years back when one of Miss Harker's girls eloped at night with a Stanford sophomore, and got married by a Justice of the Peace at San Jose. It had been written up in the Sunday Edition of the *San Francisco Examiner*, and caused a big stink.

I was all for burning the invitations in the ash tray, but Gimpy claimed the sarcastic notes were a challenge, and anyway, we had a week to think it over. If we decided not to accept we could mail them to other Manzanita Hall students, and for a while we got excited about jobbing the stuck-up Abernathy twins, giving them a dose of their own sarcasm.

The two professors had arrived. Mr. Rowell, the housemaster, was a big, husky, handsome man, a Yale graduate who had won his letter in football. Mr. Kellar was a graduate of Dartmouth, another husky, good looking man. He was also a football player and track man, younger than Mr. Rowell. Both sported Phi Beta Kappa keys on their watch chains, as did Dr. Shedd. In spite of their scholarly and athletic records, both of them were out-going and friendly.

CHAPTER 6

Cowboy in Prep School

THE TOWN WAS FILLING UP with Stanford students, and because they had priority of the pool tables at Larkin's, we drank coffee at the long counter until they finished playing. Court Moore showed up with a tall, good looking man who sported a red sophomore hat. I introduced Gimpy to Court and Court introduced the sophomore as Harry Sepulveda. I was told later the Sepulvedas were one of the old Spanish families who had pioneered California and owned large Spanish land grants. Harry was a graduate of Culver Military Academy, captain of their famous Black Horse Cavalry Troupe. Court Moore told us before he left to meet the train that as soon as rushing season was over he would take us both out to the Chi Psi Lodge for dinner.

Gimpy's motorcycle was broken down as usual and he suggested we go back and work on the motorbike so we could head for Charlie Myers' Tavern, but I said to hell with the bike, and if we went to Menlo we would go by train. But we then decided Menlo would be crowded with Stanford men and we would be underfoot. Anyway this was no day to get tanked up on beer with the two professors in the dorm, so we ate lunch at Larkin's and took the streetcar back to Manzanita Hall. By then it was about three in the afternoon.

Rowell and Kellar were in their rooms getting settled when we climbed the stairs to our room. There was a jumble of voices and laughter from a room down the hall and Gimpy said that would be Swede Ole Carlson, Charlie Arthur, Cookie Cookson, Pinky Pinkson and Bud Owens whooping it up in Carlson's room. He took me into the crowded room and one of the students let out a war whoop.

"It's Gimpy from the gamblin' joints in Reno!"

And that motley crowd in cords and blue flannel shirts ganged up on my roommate, throwing him down and piling on top. I stood there in the doorway until the pile-up was over and Gimpy scrambled to his fet.

"This is Bowse Coburn," Gimpy introduced me, "from Montana."

I shook hands with each one in turn and no longer felt like a stranger in their midst. Then all of us went out into the grove of live oaks, walking scattered out along the wide lane, talking and loading our pipes, all glances fixed upon Harker's school pupils who were walking in groups along Lover's Lane.

The Harker Queens gathered at the Wishing Tree and the Manzanita Hall students gathered around the Council Oak, a giant old tree where every student carved his initials in the bark. A ruling laid down by Miss Harker was that no pupil of hers be allowed to call out or contact any Manzanita Hall boy or Palo Alto High School student, nor any boy at all for that matter, for she said such rude conduct was unbecoming and unladylike. While Dr. Shedd did not approve of the straight-laced ruling, he went along with it as a matter of policy to maintain a friendly relationship between the two schools, and all Manzanita Hall boys were honor bound to maintain that disciplined silence.

Swede Carlson and Charlie Arthur had gone steady with a couple of Harker girls the year before, and the two couples had made up a whistling signal of their own invention. The big handsome Ole and the slim dark-haired Chuck had spotted their Queens among the group and did their whistling act to renew their former relationship. Pinky Pinkson announced that his kid sister had enrolled at Harker's, but that she was only a freshman, and did not count in the eyes of juniors and seniors.

Gimpy soon spotted the Abernathy twins and was all hot and bothered, but I lost interest as soon as I saw them, because both twins were a head taller than myself. I told Gimpy I would feel like a midget wrestling with that six-foot beanpole Margo and that he could have both twins.

"What do you think I am," Gimpy laughed, "a Mormon Bishop with two wives?"

"Take your pick, Gimpy, and give the other one to Pinky, but deal me out," I told him.

I spotted a red-headed girl about five-foot two, more suitable to my five-six height. Gimpy told me her name was Wynn Martin and that she had freckles. He said her father was a San Francisco doctor. The way Gimpy said it you would think Wynn had smallpox.

It was time for us to go back to our room. At dinner that evening at the Shedds I was not about to pull the same boner twice when grace was said. After dessert, Dr. Shedd announced that Miss Harker had extended an invitation to all pupils at Manzanita Hall to attend the Sunday afternoon tea.

Back in our room Gimpy told me that when Cattie Harker extended a blanket invitation to all students of Manzanita Hall it meant that no Polly High boys were invited. He said that last year a couple of stinkers on the Polly High football team, Dink Rader and his brother, Bump, were invited and that whenever he and his roommate latched onto some good looking Queen, the Rader boys tried to beat their time. Dink Rader and Gimpy had no use for each other, and Gimpy said the Rader boys would probably pick on me because I was his roommate.

"Let me have your invitation that Margo sent," he said. "I'll send it with mine to the Rader boys and I'll guarantee those smart-aleck kids will show up promptly at 3 P.M. and the P.M. will stand for *post mortem* when they try to crash the gate. They'll be on Harker's blacklist for the rest of the school year."

Gimpy looked up the Rader address in the telephone book and addressed one invitation to Dink and one to Bump, and said he would mail them downtown tommorow, that dropping them in the school mail-box would be too risky and might leave a clue.

By the end of the week every room in the dorm was filled. All the day dogs had registered, including Tom and Ab Couch. I took the Couch boys up to our room and brought them up to date on the Great Falls and Montana gossip. Tom was captain of the Manzanita rugby team and was scouting for players. He, Herb Strawn, a day dog, and I tagged for front rank in the scrum. Both of us were short and stocky enough to lock heads with the two scrum players on the opposite team, and to kick the ball to other players. Because I was a green hand at rugby Tom explained that fifteen men played on the team, and that we were not allowed to touch the ball with our hands. It was all kicking and dribbling the ball with your feet, kicking, dribbling and running. You had to be fast and have good wind, and you had to keep in training, cut down on smoking, but chewing tobacco was okay.

Once school opened, our trips to Charlie Myers' ended. I was taking a special course, boning up on the subjects I had low grades in, in high school. I had already put in my application at the registrar's office at Stanford to enter on January 1 for the second semester, majoring in economics because economics was said to be an easy course. Anything to get into Stanford. Once I got my foot in the door I could switch to mining engineering, the course my family had lined out for me.

For the rest of the week the thought of the Sunday afternoon pink tea was in a far dark pocket of my mind, like a yellow-jacket hornet sealed in his mud cell and due to come out with his stinger. It seemed that every student was an eager beaver raring to go, and I was the only one who dreaded the ordeal. When that fatal Sunday came I had a doomsday feeling, but I showered and shaved the fuzz off my face, and got dressed in my blue suit and polished black shoes, stiff-starched collar and necktie. With a frozen grin on my scrubbed face, my crewcut hair brushed with two ebony-backed military brushes, my teeth brushed, I tried to take it in my stride like the others who were prancing around making wisecracks.

We went downstairs and lined up for inspection and a few words from Dr. Shedd regarding proper deportment. The upper classmen led the way with the freshmen trailing behind. Just inside Harker's entrance hallway stood Mrs. Shedd and Miss Harker. Mrs. Shedd introduced each of us as we entered and the tall, slender Miss Harker greeted us with a gracious smile of welcome. Then the Harker Secretary, Miss Prudence Carter (Prune Face), and Mrs. Shedd cut the upper classmen into one group in the front room and the sophomores and freshmen in another room. Confused and embarrassed as I was, I was reminded of rounding up a herd of cattle, the riders cutting out the yearling steers into the holding corrals.

The Harker Queens were lined up around the sides of the rooms for introductions, and when I was introduced to the red-headed, freckle-faced Wynn Martin, my clock stopped. There was a grin on her face that touched her gray-green laughing eyes when she said: "The grapevine said you were a cowboy from a Montana ranch named Bowse Coburn. Correct me if I'm wrong."

Wynn Martin, with me in tow, slid her way through the group to a bay-window seat which commanded a view of the gravel driveway. She wore a sage green dress that matched the color of her eyes. When she asked the meaning of my name, Bowse, I had been waiting for that and had an answer ready. I told her that Bowse was short for Bowser, and that according to legend of the cow country, a bowser was a cross between a Texas sidehill gouger and a wall-eyed Wallaby, and I proceeded to rattle off the whole pedigree, leaving out the breeding procedure, thus cleaning it up. Then I told her to look Bowse up in the dictionary.

"I already have," she informed me. "It means boozer. Aren't you a little young to acquire the reputation of a booze hound?"

"I've been working at it at Charlie Myers' Tavern," I answered.

Wynn wrinkled her short nose and turned to look out the window, and I followed her glance. Two teenage boys in blue flannel jackets and white flannel trousers were coming down the driveway.

"What the heck are the Rover boys up to coming here?" Wynn wondered aloud.

"Rover boys?" I questioned.

"Dink and Bump Rader, kids from Palo Alto High, crashing a Manzanita Hall tea party."

"I'll tell you about it later," I said. "Let's watch the fireworks."

It was Pedro who answered the door bell. He looked at the invitations extended by the boys and shook his head. Closing the door, he handed the invitations to Miss Harker, who went to the door and stepped outside. We watched the Rader brothers walk away in rapid strides, red faced with embarrassment.

I made Wynn promise not to repeat what I was about to tell her, and she agreed. I told her about Gimpy sending our invitations from the Abernathy girls to Dink and Bump Rader; that Gimpy and I were to blame, and it was up to us to plead guilty, to tell Miss Harker how it happened.

"You and Gimpy keep out of it, Bowse," Wynn advised. "You'd only add fuel to the fireworks. It would end up putting the Manzanita Hall boys on the blacklist. You and Gimpy keep your traps shut. Cattie will have the Abernathy twins shedding tears, but she won't expel them, not with the Abernathy money and prestige involved."

When we got back to our room after the tea party, Gimpy and I had plenty to talk about. It seems that Wynn and I were the only ones with a ringside seat when Miss Harker gave the Rader boys the bum's rush. I told Gimpy our best bet was to keep our traps shut or we might get our bushy tails caught in the wringer.

Gimpy told me he had made time with Milo Abernathy, and I said he was a hound for punishment. So far as I was concerned this dog-faced boy was not about to forget her insult. If the Abernathy twins were roasting their fannies on the hot griddle, I was not about to shed any crocodile tears, and told Gimpy he was welcome to his towel. If the Abernathy twins told Harker they sent the invitations to us we would wind up mousetrapped and Manzanita Hall would be on the blacklist. As I told Gimpy, it all depended on what Milo and Margo told Miss Harker.

For the rest of the week we kept our fingers crossed, and our ears to the ground to pick up the grapevine news. When we took our after-dinner walk, and there was no sign of the twins, Gimpy was sure they had been expelled. When he tackled Chico about sending the note by Pedro to Milo, Chico refused, saying that they were watching Pedro, and he was scared half to death.

I was half asleep that night when I heard Gimpy get up and walk down the hall to the bathroom. When he came back he shook me awake.

"There's a hell of a commotion of some kind over at Harker's," he said excitedly.

I went back to the bathroom with Gimpy where we got a birds-eye view of the school through a window. Every light was on and we could see Pedro and the Chinese cook and the Japanese gardner running around like crazy, armed with rakes and hoes. Miss Harker and her secretary were outside shouting orders. Just then a Palo Alto taxi drove up and Smiley Jones, the local policeman, stepped out.

In 1909 Palo Alto was a sleepy, peaceful college town, friendly and law abiding. Everyone knew the village cop and hailed him with the familiar greeting, "Hi, Smiley!" Smiley Jones was a fixture and part of this college town. He seldom had occasion to arrest anyone and the small jail remained empty. His revolver and billy club, shined and polished as were the brass buttons on his uniform and badge, were mainly for show.

After inspecting the school and surrounding grounds and consulting Miss Harker, Smiley took his departure in the waiting taxi, and all was peaceful and quiet at the school, but the floodlights remained on until dawn.

Meanwhile, Swede Carlson, Chuck Arthur, Bud Owens and Pinky Pinkson, together with the professors, had joined us in watching from the bathroom window, and we did some speculating as to what might have happened, figuring it must have been serious to have phoned for the police. Some said it could have been burglars, others said kidnappers, and so on until it was time for us to go back to bed.

"It could be Milo and Margo the kidnappers snatched," said

Gimpy back in our room, "Old Man Abernathy is a millionaire and then some."

"You'll read about it in the *San Francisco Examiner* tomorrow morning," I volunteered. "Big headlines on the front page, with pictures of the Abernathy twins snatched and held for ransom. It was that pigtailed Chink cook who tipped the kidnappers. That slant-eyed Chink belongs to some tong, and Nick Carter, the famous detective, will have to come to rescue the gals from some underground opium dive in San Francisco's Chinatown."

Gimpy heaved a pillow across the room at me, and I tossed it back.

Next morning after breakfast Dr. Shedd told us that during the absence last night of Miss Harker and her secretary, and most of the teachers, and all the students who were attending the opera in The City, a group of young vandals wrecked the music room, the living and dining rooms of the school. Dr. Shedd said he had assured Miss Harker that no Manzanita Hall students were involved, and he asked us to keep what happened a secret.

It was not until Monday morning when Chico showed up that we got his pal Pedro's version of what happened, after Gimpy tossed him a four-bit coin. Pedro told us that some young high school vandals had swiped two Nubian billygoats from the Mexican village, led them on picket ropes, pried open the window of the music room and shoved them inside. Besides turning the goats loose they had been given a shot of high life. Also a rag saturated with turpentine was wiped on the tender part of their anatomy beneath the short tails, and when turned loose they wrecked everything in sight. When Miss Harker unlocked the front door the two high-lifed billygoats came charging out, knocking her and some of the girls down. The gardener later found the turpentined rag which had set the goats on the rampage.

After Chico had taken his departure Gimpy and I held a little medicine talk. Our foregone conclusion was that Dink and Bump Rader were the prime instigators of the billygoat vandalism, but there was no way to prove it.

The Manzanita rugby team was fair-to-middling for a small school, with barely enough players to make up the team, plus only two or three substitutes. The football field was smaller than the regulation size, and as there was no second team we played the Stanford scrub freshman team or the Palo Alto High School on the campus practice field.

Mr. Rowell was our coach, but while at Yale he had played standard American style football, and the English rugby was new to him. So Tom and Ab Couch had to do the actual coaching on the field, with Mr. Rowell coaching on the sidelines.

Sandy Strum and I played front rank in the scrum. When the referee placed the ball on the ground between the front rank scrum on both sides, backed off and blew the whistle, it was up to front rank scrum to kick the ball back. To do this we crouched low with one arm locked across each other's shoulders. When one of our men started kicking and dribbling the ball with short kicks toward the opposite goal, the wing players tried to kick it out of bounds. The referee would toss the ball between the wing players lined up on both sides and there was a wild scramble to kick it toward the opposite goal. It was a rough game of blocking and shoving, kicking and running, with bruised shin bones and skinned knees.

Front line scrum men on the opposite team, when the whistle blew, tried to rush the front rank scrum who kicked the ball off center to foul up the kick. Butting heads or kneeing was considered foul play, but it was often tried, risking the watchful eye of the referee. We wore no helmets or shinguards. The front rank scrum men who had need of that protection suffered the most, getting bruised shins as the cleated shoes raked. We bumped lowered heads like billygoats, and if you lifted your head you got a black eye or a bloody nose.

Sandy was a little shorter than I, husky-shouldered and thick-necked. He was about five pounds heavier, but I was a faster kicker-backwards, so we made a good team. Head butting and shin raking was part of the game. It was the kneeing in the groin we had to watch. The second I kicked the ball back Sandy and I, still locked, twisted sideways toward each other for mutual protection as we met the rush of the two front rank scrum, and went down in a pile-up. It was then up to the front wing men to dribble the ball.

Bump Rader, a short, blocky-built lad, played front rank scrum on the Palo Alto team. Sandy told me Bump was a dirty player and when he tried a third time to knee me in the crotch I lowered my head and butted him hard in the belly. Bump went down, doubled up, his wind knocked out. The referee fouled me for butting and we lost five yards on the play.

We played the Belmont Prep School team, the freshman Santa Clara team, the scrub freshman Stanford team, the San Mateo High School team and the Palo Alto High team. Bump never tried kneeing me again and between Tom and Ab Couch they gave his brother Dink a hard time every game we played Palo Alto.

A couple of weeks after the Harker tea, an informal dance was given at Miss Lockey's Castilleja School on a Saturady night for the Manzanita Hall students, including freshmen and day dogs. That Saturday afternoon I forgot to duck and got a beautiful shiner in the rugby game with Palo Alto. It was something to be proud of, according to Gimpy Quinn, and a mark of valor on the football battlefield, in spite of the fact that we had lost the game. But one look in the mirror was enough. My swollen shiner and bruised cheekbone gave me a lopsided appearance. I was in one hell of a shape to go to my first dance at Castilleja, but in spite of my looks I was anxious to meet Lucy Diamond after the big buildup Gimpy had given the girl from the Hawaiian Islands.

When we got to the dance I was introduced to all the girls, all wearing formal evening gowns and looking beautiful and sophisticated. In my self-conscious embarrassment I could not remember a single name, and if I could have sneaked out I would have headed back for the safety of the empty dorm.

"Don't look so lost and bewildered, Bowse," a voice sounded behind me.

There was hidden laughter rather than mockery in the girl's voice, but somehow it added to my misery. When I turned around I saw the deeply-tanned face and shock of curly jet-black hair, the large, warm, laughing eyes, and a red-lipped smile.

"I'm Lucy Diamond," the girl said. "Miss Lockey suggested I ride herd on the bashful cowboy from Montana. That's some shiner you brought to the party, but on you it looks cute."

I managed a lopsided grin. Lucy took my arm and guided me to the wide, banistered stairway, and we sat down on the second step. When she informed me that I was allowed to smoke I lit up, took a couple of drags and handed the cigarette to her. She took a deep drag and puffed out a distant smoke ring, and we watched it dissipate in wispy shreds. She sure blew a neat smoke ring, but when she handed me back the cigarette I was not about to let a girl best me at a gent's game. I took a deep drag and tounged out three smoke rings.

"Injun smoke signals," I said. "Direct from Fort Belknap Reservation in Montana."

Lucy took the cigarette and puffed out a big round smoke ring, and a smaller one a split second later, and we watched the smaller, faster ring go through the larger one before they both collapsed.

"A message from the Hawaiian Islands to the Indians on the Montana Reservation," she said and lowered her jet-black lashes as she winked both eyes for all the world like Winkie Goodwin.

When the orchestra began playing "Shine On Harvest Moon," Lucy grabbed my hand and pulled me to my feet. When the waltz ended we went back to sit on the stairway. A slim girl with dark, honey-colored hair came up, a smile on her tanned face, and a twinkle in her dark gray eyes.

"Move over chum," she told Lucy. "I'm dying for a smoke."

Lucy introduced her to me as Alice Bacon, better known as Honey. When she told me she was from Butte, Montana, I asked her if she knew Denny Driscoll, a quarterback on the Butte High School football team.

"Denny Driscoll, the pride of Dublin Gulch. I've known Denny since he wore knee pants. A hell raiser if there ever was one, my darling Denny."

"For Pete's sake, Honey," Lucy held up both hands. "Don't start talking Montana. I'm fed up to the ears with your tales about Butte. Honey's my roommate, Bowse," Lucy explained.

And there came my stablemate, Gimpy Quinn, to cram himself in on the other side of Honey Bacon. Then, as if on cue, a young freshman girl with braces on her teeth came over and handed a ukulele to Lucy Diamond.

"By special request of Miss Lockey," she said.

Lucy, in a soft, contralto voice, began singing the songs of the Islands in their native language. Ancient, plaintive folk songs through which ran a thread of sadness, both felt and understood — songs of mingled love and tragedy. The final song was Aloha, a fitting farewell song to end the best party this young cowboy from Montana had ever attended.

Thanksgiving Day marked the end of the football season. The game between Stanford versus California was held at the Berkeley Stadium. The Manzanita gang, including the day dogs, with Mr. Rowell and Mr. Keller riding close herd on us, sat in the Stanford rooting section.

Thanksgiving dinner was at seven-thirty that evening which gave us time after the game to take the ferry across the bay to San Francisco, catch the six o'clock train at Third and Townsend, and make it back by the skin of our teeth. Some of the students whose homes were in San Francisco, or nearby towns took advantage of the four day holiday. The rest of us who remained at school were allowed certain liberties, and our curfew was extended until twelve midnight.

The wicked city of San Francisco, with its Barbary Coast and Chinatown, was out of bounds for us. San Jose and Monterey were our limit, but as far as we got was Charlie Myers' Tavern in Menlo. Thus we arrived home each night tanked up on beer, the pockets of our cords stuffed with blue ribbons to tally the bottles of Pabst Blue Ribbon consumed.

The rest of the first semester at Manzanita Hall was mostly routine. After football season there was no more practice every afternoon, and that time was now free. I was taking an extra load of studies, but since it was the second go-round for all subjects it was easy, especially as we were regimented to regular study periods. I was taking Latin and German from Dr. Shedd. I had four years of Latin and German in high school, and that gave me a basic understanding of the languages, but I learned more from Dr. Shedd in that four month semester than I had learned in four years in high school. Dr. Shedd was somewhat of a genius when it came to teaching languages, having the knack of making it interesting. He had a large pull-down map on the wall, showing the complete wars of Caesar and his campaigns, lecturing in Latin and translating into English. I had used the forbidden pony translation in high school, and Dr. Shedd had given us ten pages of Caesar to be learned daily with the aid of the pony in class room.

In my German class, held in Dr. Shedd's office, we spoke nothing but German, the fluent German he had learned at Heidelberg, with the correct guttural pronunciation. Before the second month I was speaking, reading and writing my essays in German script. It was advanced German under Dr. Shedd's tutelage. The same held true of Professor Roswell's mathematics class and I had conquered what for me was a series of obstacles in math. By the end of the semester I was thoroughly enjoying vaulting the hurdles, and I now passed the weekly oral quiz and the monthly written tests without trouble.

CHAPTER 7

John Barleycorn's Revenge

I WAS THE ONLY STUDENT at Manzanita Hall slated to enter Stanford for the second semester. In October, I had already put in my application. I had graduated *cum laude* from Manzanita at the end of the first semester, but Dr. Shedd had suggested I wait until the end of the second semester to receive my diploma with the senior graduating class and I was more than agreeable. He advised me to make a second application to enter Stanford, enclosing a list of my grades and a recommendation from him, which I did before I left to spend the Christmas holidays with my parents in San Diego.

I was pledged to the Chi Psi Fraternity, but Court Moore told me all the freshman rooms were taken and I might have to wait a couple of weeks to share a room. Meanwhile, I would get a room at the dormitory until after my initiation into the Chi Psi. I was stepping on air when I boarded the train for San Diego, ready and willing to tackle the four year course in mining engineering at Stanford.

I cut my holidays short by a couple of days. I was raring to get back to Palo Alto. I got there about 10 A.M., checked my suitcase at the baggage room, grabbed a surrey and told the driver to take me to the Stanford campus. Stopping at Rader's Clothing Store, I bought myself a freshman beany. I was dressed in my herringbone Harris tweed suit with the pegtop pants, my red beany cocked at a jack-deuce angle on my crewcut head when I entered the registrar's office and gave my name.

When the registrar consulted his files, he said:

"I'm afraid I have bad news for you young man. At a December meeting the Board of Regents made a new ruling, vetoing freshmen entering Stanford in mid-year for the second semester. I'm afraid you will have to wait until September."

This was a serious blow for me. As I headed for the door, I remembered I had made my first application on my birthday, October 23, so I turned and explained this to the Registrar. He went through his file again, and located my first formal application for entry January 1. It was then I voiced my almost tearful plea, enough to arouse his sympathy. He told me he would take the matter up with the Board of Regents and the powers that be at a meeting scheduled for next week. He said he was truly sorry about the complication but he would do all he could for me, and on that highly doubtful promise I took my departure.

There was no surrey around the deserted campus so I hoofed it back to town. I called Manzanita Hall from Larkin's on the odd chance Dr. Shedd could use his influence to plead my case, but Miss Cook, the art teacher, answered the phone and told me the Shedds had gone East for the holidays. When I told her my predicament she said my old room was available and to come out, but I would have to eat my meals in town. She assured me Dr. Shedd could straighten things out for me when he returned.

I got my luggage and took it to my old room. I changed into cords and blue flannel shirt, put my red beany in my suitcase, and took the streetcar back to town. I caught the next train for Menlo Park and went to Charlie Myers' Tavern, now quite deserted. I was lower than a snake's belly, and started to drown my sorrow in beer, and when I got enough suds under my belt I told my troubles to Charlie. He was a good listener and offered me plenty of consolation, but no pity.

It was then that Charlie Brownell came in. The six-foot, crewcut Brownell wore a long linen duster, a fore-and-aft Sherlock Holmes tweed cap, with a pair of rubberband dark goggles perched above his beak. He was singing in a half-swacked, husky voice as he came in:

> Some folks say
> That she can't play,
> But she sat right down
> And played by ear
> ALAMEDA TRAINS THIS WAY!

The last line was shouted in the leather-lunged voice of a train caller. He swaggered down the bar, took his TNE beer mug from its peg and slid it down the polished mahogany bar to where Charlie Myers stood listening to my sad story. The mug skidded to a stop within easy reach of Charlie who told Brownell he was improving, but would have to put a little more English on it for a proper skid.

"Put a head on it, Charlie, and I'll be there in time to blow off the suds," Brownell said.

I had seen the tall, lean, swaggering Charlie Brownell a few times and was remembering what I had been told about the junior at Stanford who was living out his legend as a two-fisted drinker, ladies man, international playboy and good-natured clown.

Charlie Myers introduced us and we shook hands.

"Bowse? That a family name?" asked Brownell.

"Nope," I answered. "A sort of nickname. Short for booze hound."

"You're working at it," he said with a grin, then asked, "Freshman?"

"Yes and no," I replied. "It's on the lap of the gods."

I then told him briefly that the registrar kept stressing "the powers that be, whoever they are."

"Rich alumni," Brownell announced. "They kick in with a gob of money. Besides the prestige it's the dough re mi that talks louder than words at the meetings of the Regents. My old man is one of them, otherwise I'd have been kicked out for keeps in my freshman year." He looked across the bar at Charlie Myers and said, "This young Bowse feller has the stuff it takes to be a member of the TNE, eh Maestro?"

"He can hold his liquor," Charlie said with a grin.

"On the strength of your word, I'm putting a bumble bee in my old man's cap," Brownell thumped me hard between the shoulder blades. "The hell of it is the old man's in Paris, but I'll cable him today. I came here hoping to pick up a drinking partner, to help me count the roadhouses both sides of the peninsula, and I've found the right man. Drink up, Bowse, and we'll be on our way."

When I put money on the bar to pay for the beer, Brownell shoved it back to me.

"The drinks from now on are on the TNE. Take my word for it, Bowse, you'll commence your freshman year at Stanford in January, but right now you're coming along with me on an all-night tour of the roadhouses. First we'll stop at the Western Union in Burlingame to send a telegram to pop."

He grinned at Charlie Myers and asked if he had any freshman beanies around the place. When Charlie said there were some in the trash bin in the back room, Brownell pawed through the lot looking for one which had not been beer soaked and tromped on. I put it on at a proper give-a-damn angle and Brownell led the way out to the fireman-red two-seated Chalmers car. My gloomy brooding had evaporated, and thanks to Charlie Brownell I was filled with new hope. The thought of my being rushed by the secret TNE added to the excitement.

We pulled up at the Western Union and Charlie sent a fifty word cablegram to his father, collect.

"That'll do the trick, Bowse," he said. "Those gentlemen of the Board of Regents and Dean of Men will vote you in like Flynn. That old man of mine swings a big money stick."

Back in the car Charlie tapped my red beany.

"Wear it in good health, and hold your liquor like a man. I hereby pledge you a member of the TNE and this night marks the first step of your initiation."

Charlie pulled down his goggles, buttoned up his duster and we were off like a sky rocket with the throttle wide open. He waved a black-gauntleted hand at a stone-walled Burlingame mansion visible beyond a graveled driveway lined with rows of tall date palms.

"That's our shack. Looks like San Quentin prison. The stable and polo field is behind. Ever play polo, Bowse?"

"Nope. But I've punched cows since I was a kid at my father's Circle C Ranch in Montana."

I got in my two-bits worth of bragging by telling him my old man was a pioneer, coming to Montana Territory in 1863, made his stake panning gold and invested it in land and cattle. The international playboy seemed to be impressed by my Montana background.

That was a wild and hectic, tipsy night as we stopped for drinks at the Log Cabin roadhouse and every other roadhouse along the way. We drank nothing but beer except at the Cliff House and College Inn in San Francisco where we drank Bass' Ale and Guinness' Stout. Charlie said we would pick up a couple of chorines from the *Floradora* show, so we pulled up behind the theater building at the stage door entrance. Charlie went in and showed up with a chorus girl on each arm. The tall one was a drugstore blonde. The short one Charlie called a pony had dyed hair. In the dim light they looked like teenagers, but in the revealing light of the first roadhouse, in spite of the heavy makeup, they were no spring chickens. Not wrinkled, but hard, sophisticated, their slangy talk sprinkled with mild profanity. I thought to myself that they could not hold a candle both for looks and ladies' behavior to the parlorhouse girls at Sylvia Bryant's and Crickett Rockwell's in Great Falls.

Judging from their conversation I got the idea that Charlie had propositioned them both and paid in advance for sleeping partners. But I wanted no part of that slumber party. Not that I had any moral objections, but I was scared to death of catching some venereal disease. On the way back from San Francisco we dropped in at the Bungalow roadhouse for a few drinks and breakfast, and Charlie called me to one side to say he had run out of money, and could I loan him fifty bucks, reminding me that the party was on the TNE and that he would pay me back. I had about fifteen bucks in my pocket so I wrote him out a check for fifty bucks and he again promised to return it. I told him to forget it and he got a little indignant.

What the hell! He was a Chi Psi and a TNE and didn't I, for cripes sake, know when I was being rushed?

We re-counted the roadhouses between The City and San Jose. It was about noon when he pulled in at the San Jose Tavern which had rooms for rent on the second floor. I was sticking to beer, the chorines, Blondie and Red, were drinking cocktails, and Charlie ordered a Scotch highball. After we downed our drinks Charlie carelessly mentioned it was time for the girls to take a nap and he handed me a room key. The chorines had mentioned that they had to be back for the night performance of *Floradora*, and a special New Years' Eve party the manager of the theater had planned for the troupe.

When Charlie and Blondie mounted the stairs I knew I was mousetrapped, and it was up to me to get myself out of it somehow, but I need not have worried because Red said she had been under a doctor's care and would not want to give what she had to a college kid, and if it was all the same to me we would stay in the bar. Red took a ten dollar bill from her handbag and handed it to me.

"That's what your pal Charlie gave me," she explained.

"Keep it, Red," I told her. "You just now earned it."

We ordered drinks and stayed in the barroom until Charlie and Blondie appeared. We then headed back for The City, but not until Charlie had tapped me for another fifty bucks. We dropped the chorines at the theater, declining their invitation to join the backstage party after the show, and headed back for Palo Alto. We ended up at Myers' Tavern in Menlo where there were half a dozen Stanford TNE's celebrating New Year's Eve. They filled a quart stein with beer and I was told to take a deep breath and guzzle the contents without stopping. Luckily I just made it or I would have had to repeat the performance. Then I was permitted to whittle a notch on the TNE table in the back room to become a TNE pledge.

After that Charlie yawned, belched and declared it was time to go, saying he was taking me to the Chi Psi House to spend the night. He bought a quart of whisky to take along and asked Charlie Myers to put it in a paper bag.

"No booze on the Stanford campus," Myers warned. Brownell just grinned and said, "I'll be holding the thought."

Charlie slid in behind the wheel, pulling down the dark goggles and starting the motor, and we left Menlo Park with the throttle wide open. Lights blazed in every house along Faculty Row and would until midnight. That did not bother my TNE brother for he was drunk and reckless as he drove the red Chalmers like a racing car, singing at the top of his voice:

> I was drunk last night
> Drunk the night before;
> Going to get drunk tonight
> If I never get drunk any more.
>
> 'Cause when I'm drunk
> I'm happy as can be,
> For I am a member
> Of the souse familee.
>
> Glorious, glorious
> One more drink among the four of us
> Sing glory be to hob there's no more of us,
> For one of us could kill it all alone.
>
> For we're all members of the TNE.

The tires screamed in protest as the car skidded around a corner. Suddenly both tires on one side where the pressure was blew out. It was like the explosion of a twin-barreled shotgun. Charlie gripped the steering wheel, fighting desperately for control as the front end side-swiped a high metal lamp post, upending the car which landed on its side on a wide lawn. The tremendous impact tossed me high in the air, my head hit the trunk of a palm tree and I went out like a light.

When I regained consciousness in the white glare of the flood lights which had been turned on, I saw a group of men in tuxedos gathered around. I recognized Professor Hubert Lane, the man at the registrar's office, and he was saying:

"This young man's apparently uninjured, but obviously intoxicated."

"The other one is none other than Charlie Brownell, drunk and maudlin," said another professor. "Better get him over to the Chi Psi House, and telephone for a taxi to take this other young man to town. Despite the freshman beany he's wearing, he is definitely *not* a Stanford freshman."

I stood there dazed and bewildered, doing my damndest to keep from swaying on my wide-spread legs. When the taxi pulled up I walked the imaginary chalk line and somehow managed to climb in the back seat without falling on my face. I was in no condition to go to my room at Manzanita Hall so I told the driver to take me to a small hotel. I managed to hold back the nausea until in my room and reached the toilet bowl. When I heaved up all the soured beer and food I had eaten, I stripped to the hide and hit the shower until I was cold sober and shivering. I then toweled off and got into bed.

I had blown my chance of entering my freshman mid-semester year, blown it to hell and gone. I was brooding over my hard luck when I heard joyous voices of a barbershop quartet coming from Larkin's, singing "Auld Lang Syne." One hell of a Happy New Year for this newly pledged member of the TNE.

Even though I had not slept the night before, sleep was hard to come by. So I lay there wide awake and tried to think of some solution to this messed up affair. Going back to San Diego to face my parents was out. Going back to Circle C Ranch was also out of the question. My only bet was to talk it over with Dr. Shedd, to come clean and tell the whole truth, so help me God. I repeated the last words aloud and a bit of a prayer went with that solemn promise from the black sheep of the Coburn Cattle Company.

Came the cold gray dawn of the morning after, I did not want to spoil New Year's Day for Dr. Shedd. But on the other hand I did not want him calling Professor Hubert Lane, the registrar, in my behalf, singing my praises as a scholar and a gentleman, not after last night's drunken mess, with Brownell wrapping his Chalmers around the lamp post in front of Lane's house, and the learned professors in tuxedos gathered around to view the disgraceful, drunken wreck.

Sick, sorry and cold sober, with hazy recollections of the previous night now revealed, I sat on the edge of my bed with a splitting headache inside a skull which felt the size of a pumpkin with an egg-size discolored lump on my forehead where it had struck the palm tree.

The memory of the lanky Charlie Brownell returned. Charlie arguing with the sourball campus cop known to all Stanford students as Gloomy Gus, a vinegar-faced, sneaky, mean sonofabitch.

"Lay a hand on me, you bastard, and my old man will tie the can to your mongrel hound dog tail — you know who I am? I'm Charlie Brownell and I'm heading for the Chi Psi House, and I'm going under my own power. Get out of the way or I'll shove that tin star up your arse."

I could still see Charlie in soiled, torn, linen duster, the Sherlock Holmes cap at a fighting angle on his head, the smashed goggles dangling on the elastic band, his face bleeding from cuts, staggering toward the safety of the Chi Psi House where his fraternity brothers would look after him.

I remembered the chill, cold words of Professor Hubert Lane as he held my red freshman beany gingerly in his hand.

"This intoxicated young man doesn't belong on the Stanford campus — he has no right to wear this beany."

There was a certain finality to his tone of voice as he gave me a cold and forbidding look which warned me that as long as he was the registrar I would never enter Stanford University. As shaken and half drunk as I was, I got the message, and I got it now on the morning after.

There was a drizzling rain as I walked across the street to Larkin's Coffee Shop to drink strong black coffee and eat a bite of scrambled eggs to satisfy my hunger. It was nine o'clock when I boarded a streetcar and walked a few blocks to Manzanita Hall. I found Dr. Shedd alone in his office.

"I've got some bad news," I told him as I stood there like a dunce. "I hate to spoil your New Year's Day for you, Dr. Shedd, but there is something I've got to talk over with you. I've made a mess of everything. I got drunk. I've ruined my chances of ever entering Stanford in mid-semester and for all time."

Once I got started I blurted my troubles out as fast as I could talk, and once out of my system I felt better.

"The world hasn't come to an end yet, Bowse," Dr. Shedd said with a smile. "*Sitzen sie, mein* friend. You are carrying a heavy burden of grief and remorse on your young shoulders. Professor Lane just called me and gave me the gory details. Just between the two of us, Hubert Lane, despite the fact he is a learned, scholarly gentleman with numerous degrees to show for it, is wholly lacking in that God-given sense of humor.

"I've just talked to the Dean of Men, Padric Ryan, a four-letter man when he attended Stanford, with a Phi Beta Kappa key on his watch chain. Padric said he had stepped out on the lawn for a breath of fresh air at the watch party, and he was an eyewitness when Charlie Brownell tried to climb the lamp post with his red firewagon. His version of it had me in stitches with his natural Irish wit," Dr. Shedd chuckled, then added soberly, "I'm fully aware of your bitter disappointment, Bowse, but I think I've got the solution to your problems. Looking back in thoughtful retrospect, I think we both made a grave error entering you as a freshman for the first semester. The sensible solution is for you to remain here at Manzanita Hall and graduate next June with the rest of your senior class. How does that sound?"

"You've saved the day for me, Dr. Shedd, and I can't find the proper words to thank you."

"Don't try. The smile on your face is far better than the spoken word. I imagine you'll find your roommate, Gimpy Quinn, upstairs, and we are expecting you both for New Year's dinner at one-thirty."

I was too choked up to speak as we shook hands. I ran up the stairs, two steps at a time, blinking unshed tears from my eyes.

Gimpy and I rough-housed and wrestled around the room, by way of celebrating the return of the prodigal son, with a turkey in the oven in lieu of the fatted calf.

Never before had I met a man like Dr. Shedd. He was a scholarly man, a gentleman in every sense of the word, a man with his own sense of quiet humor and a deep understanding of the younger generation which gave him a tolerance for our faults and careless mistakes.

During my first weeks at Manzanita Hall, when I was the only pupil taking German language lessons, after classes, and when Dr. Shedd had time to spare, I had told him about my father's Circle C Ranch in Montana, about my life as a cowboy, and before I was aware of it I was running off at the head like a magpie with a split tongue. I told him how I had earned my forty-a-month wages during summer vacations, putting in long hours, up before daybreak to wrangle horses in the pasture and do odd jobs no cowpuncher deserving of the name would do. During haying season I worked in the hayfields with the hay crew, and when the bookkeeper was on vacation I kept the books. I helped the cook wash dishes and carry in the stove wood. On roundups I stood two hours night guard, riding around the big beef herd, and also day herded the grazing cattle. I helped cut out the cattle and did my share of the branding. I told about the cowhands I had worked with, how the Little Rockies was the stomping ground of the notorious Curry Gang of outlaws and the Wild Bunch. I spoke of the Indians on the nearby Fort Belknap Reservation, how I had been raised with the Indian kids my age, and how I had gone to the reservation with my older half brother Wallace to sit in the lodges of the Old Ones to listen to their legends. I told about my father being a pioneer of Montana, how he had been left an orphan at fourteen in Canada, how he had been apprenticed out, according to Canadian law, to learn the carpenter trade; how he had run away and somehow made his way to Montana in the year 1863. With no education he had staked out placer claims and saved the gold which he invested in a small ranch and cattle until he had eventually made the Circle C Ranch into one of the large outfits in Northeastern Montana. He still retained his mines in the Little Rockies and that is why he wanted me to become a mining engineer, so that I could take charge of his mining interests at the Ruby and Alder Gulch mines. I told Dr. Shedd it was a job I wanted no part of because since memory began I had wanted to be a good all-around cowhand and eventually own my own outfit, my own registered brand and cattle. Bit by bit I had told it all to Dr. Shedd during our friendly talks.

But now that I had come back to Manzanita Hall after a New Year's Eve drunken mess I had a change of mind about a lot of things. On the second of January I had received a letter from the registrar's office informing me that my application for entrance in the second semester at Stanford University had been rejected, due to a new ruling. I put the letter in the top tray of my trunk, and with it went all hopes of my ever entering Stanford, or any other university. My college education was ended before it ever started. It was like a stillborn calf, dropped on the prairie for a hungry pack of coyotes to fight over.

It was not without a feeling of sadness and bitter regret that the abandonment of a higher education was decided, but I blamed only myself. Booze had been the cause of it. The kid called Bowse had lost the battle to John Barleycorn.

That afternoon when Dr. Shedd called me in his office for a medicine talk to outline my study schedule, I told him frankly that when I had graduated in June from Manzanita Hall I was going back to the Circle C Ranch. As much as I regretted being unable to go to Stanford, it just was not in the cards, and I was content with my decision to become a cattleman. Dr. Shedd agreed and so he outlined my study schedule. English would be my major subject, with general business a modern day cattleman should know about in connection with financing and land management, with a basic knowledge of bookkeeping included. So I was all set and ready to go.

I had been pledged Chi Psi, so the first thing I had to do was mail in my purple and gold pledge button which I proudly wore in the lapel of my Harris tweed coat. I enclosed an explanation to Courtney Moore, president of the fraternity.

There were many conflicting rumors of Charlie Brownell's last bust, and for a time the identity of the freshman passenger in the red Chalmers was a mystery. In his latest escapade the notorious Charlie Brownell had done it again, and by the end of New Year's Day the scandal had spread like wildfire throughout the Stanford campus. Every fraternity and sorority house buzzed like a disturbed beehive, with many conflicting rumors. The last escapade of Brownell's which happened over a year ago was now recalled . . . how after a wild weekend party he had shown up in a somewhat soiled tux, the front of his starched shirt liquor-stained and the collar wilted, and late for his nine o'clock class. With a tipsy, disheveled chorine on each arm, a wide grin on his unshaven face, he made the tipsy announcement that he was giving the painted chorus girls, who stank of cheap perfume and booze, a higher education. He had been expelled from Stanford, but somehow his old man had managed to reduce it to a year's suspension. And now the rich playboy of Burlingame and Paris had torn it wide open.

While Stanford was well aware of the existence of the booze fraternity TNE they chose to ignore its existence. Now every Stanford student with a TNE fraternity pin, the golden skull with the ruby eyes, pinned to his undershirt was shivering in his boots. Rumor had it that the Board of Regents and all faculty members, including the benzine board, were making a secret investigation and those students found belonging to the secret drinking fraternity would be expelled. Meanwhile Charlie Brownell had mysteriously vanished from the campus and his Chi Psi Fraternity brothers were covering his trail, thus avoiding the inevitable showdown with the benzine board. All members of the Chi Psi Fraternity were worried sick for fear the Regents and faculty would close the Chi Psi Lodge which had been built and elaborately furnished by Charlie's father, and was considered the finest fraternity house on the Stanford campus.

Meanwhile, Charlie Myers had good and sufficient reason to be worried. The TNE New Year's Day beer bust at his tavern had fallen flat on its face. Not a single TNE had dared show up, and the genial Charlie Myers had not only lost money, but he lived in fear of his license being revoked. The name of Charlie Brownell was now a dirty word at Charlie Myers' Tavern because the main source of his income was dependent on the Stanford students, especially the TNE's.

Courtney Moore showed up at Manzanita Hall the following afternoon, and we took a walk. I owed it to Court and the Chi Psi Fraternity to relate everything that had happened, including the expensive cablegram Charlie had sent to his father in Paris, how he was rushing me in behalf of the TNE's, the chorines and all, except the money he had borrowed.

Court listened to the somewhat lengthy story without interrupting as we sat in the shade of a live oak tree. As I finished there was a long silence, after which Court said:

"Charlie Brownell," he spat the name out like a dirty taste in his mouth. "The same old song, sung to the same old tune. Brownell played you for a sucker, Bowse. The innocent green freshman and the city slicker. The phoney cablegram to his old man was never sent. It wound up in the wastebasket. The telegrapher at the Western Union in Burlingame is an old drinking pal of playboy Charlie. And at which roadhouse did Brownell get taken by the shorts?"

In my ignorance I thought Court meant the back-door trots.

"Hell, I didn't follow Charlie every time he went to the can."

Court got a big laugh out of that.

"When was it Charlie started borrowing money from you, Bowse?" he asked.

"Right after we picked up the chorines, either at the Bungalow or the Log Cabin," I answered.

"How much did he stick you for?"

"A hundred bucks. And he kept saying it was the TNE which was footing the bills, promising to pay me back in a few days."

"You can kiss that hundred bucks goodbye. His giving you the old TNE rush was as phoney as he is."

Court went on to explain that Charlie Brownell was the Burlingame version of the British remittance man, with a handsome monthly allowance which he squandered on wine, wild women and ribald song. That when he went broke he would pick up a likely, well-heeled freshman, and give the greenhorn the big TNE rush, with the freshman footing the bill. That was Brownell's idea of a big joke and he had been getting away with it for the past few years. But this time he was not getting away with it because he had been blackballed at a secret meeting of the TNE. His initials on the TNE table at Charlie Myers' Tavern would be burned out with a red hot poker and his beer mug smashed.

Although Court had not told me beforehand, he had gone to Professor Hubert Lane as a representative for the Chi Psi, to plead my cause the day before New Year's and Lane had assured Court he would present my case to the Regents, and he was almost positive I would be admitted as a freshman for the second semester.

"That's like rubbing salt into your raw wound, Bowse, but I wanted you to know that the Chi Psi Fraternity was behind you all the way."

And Court cussed Charlie Brownell for every foul name he could lay tongue to, even though he was a fraternity brother.

"Take a look at this character," I orated, "who was kicked out of Stanford without ever having entered his first freshman class. A unique and doubtful distinction. I had my foot in the door when the notorious international playboy gave me the hotfoot. But to hell with it," and I grinned as if I meant it.

CHAPTER 8

Farewell Palo Alto

A DAY OR TWO LATER I received a note from Wynn Bryant by the Philippino grapevine. It was an odd mixture of condolence and congratulations, spiced with Wynn's schoolgirl humor and a sarcastic crack about the chorines, stating that the welcome mat at Harker's had been yanked out from under my erring feet. She further stated that the Rover boys' ban had been lifted and that she had been dating both Dink and Bump, but that on an evening stroll down Lover's Lane she would keep an eye peeled for the outcast, meaning me.

There was yet another note delivered by the Philippino grapevine. It was from Lucy Diamond, telling me I seemed to have lived up to my nickname, Bowse, the boozer. The grapevine had it I was under temporary ban at Castilleja, but she was hopefully praying the ban would be lifted in time for her Hawaiian party to be held at the Palo Alto Playhouse. She closed by saying she would learn the musical score of *Floradora*, "Tell Me Pretty Maiden . . ." and promised to sing it to me as soon as the blacklist ban was lifted. It was a sarcastic reference to the chorus girls Charlie and I had in tow, and was more of a threat than a promise. Right then I was too sick of the whole thing to ever listen to any song from the *Floradora* show and Lucy Diamond was probably aware of it, rubbing salt into my raw wounds. So to hell with the Queen of the Islands and the Stanford swimming champion Gimpy told me she was dating. To hell, too, with Wynn and the Rover boys.

I had already put myself on the "Injun List" at Charlie Myers'

Tavern. I was riding high on the seat of the water wagon. Kid Barleycorn had knocked me out when Ben Hur Brownell had wrapped his red chariot around the lamp post on Faculty Row. It took a month or so for the scandal to die a slow death, and it was rumored that Charlie Brownell had left for Paris.

At this time I received an invitation to attend a dance at Castilleja, signed by Alice (Honey) Bacon, of Butte, Montana. She said all was forgiven, and to quote Miss Lockey's exact words, "Us Montana folks have to stick together, regardless."

When I showed the invitation to my bunkmate, he gave me a wide grin.

"Not that I want to poach on your hunting ground, Gimpy," I said.

"Poach, hell," Gimpy chuckled. "Honey and I have been swapping notes by the Philippino grapevine for the past month, matchmaking on the sly. I got my gal Milo at Harker's, and I'm playing the field at Castilleja." Gimpy went on to say that Lucy Diamond wore her heart on her sleeve, and that she changed beaus like she changed underpants. Fickle was the Queen of the Islands.

So I accepted Honey Bacon's invitation to the dance at Castilleja, and enjoyed the evening. A few weeks later I got a bid to attend a Sunday afternoon pink tea at Miss Harker's, signed by Susan Brown.

"Who the hell is Susan Brown?" I asked Gimpy.

"Susan Brown," he answered, "is from Denver, Colorado, and related to the Brown Palace Browns. She's a new girl at Harker's. I met her last summer at Lake Tahoe."

"Is this another one of your matchmaking deals?" I asked as I eyed Gimpy suspiciously.

"You might call it that," Gimpy admitted. "Sue is lonesome, and besides, your friend, Wynn Bryant, is playing Queen to Bump Rover. You still carrying the torch for Wynn?" he asked.

"Hell, no, Bump can have her."

"That's the spirit. You and Sue will get along fine, but don't make any passes. I speak with the voice of experience."

Thus Prof. Gimpy Quinn, M.M. (Master Matchmaker), from Reno, Nevada, Divorce Capital of the U.S.A., Ambassador at Large, with or without portfolio of the Heart and Hand Society, chartered the love life of his friend and stablemate.

The halls of Harker's and Castilleja were sacred. The honor and and purity of their virgin pupils had to be kept inviolate by the lads of Manzanita Hall. Such was the understanding between the boys and girls with the bulk of the burden as gentlemen of honor heaped on the laddie-bucks at Manzanita. For the most part gentlemanly behavior was no problem, there always being a chaperone hovering about. The Spanish had a name for her, Duenna. At Harker's and Castilleja it was chaperone. But the girls themselves had their own irreverent names, such as she-warden, female Simon Legree, bitch-spy, and other choice titles.

As for the older Stanford students, if the juices of flaming youth got out of control there was the Creole Palace at San Jose, reputed to be the best parlorhouse south of San Francisco. Those French and Spanish Creole girls, imported from New Orleans, were said to be the most beautiful young ladies in existence, with not one drop of Negro blood. The Creoles of old New Orleans were of a proud heritage which dated back to the days when the pirate sailing ships cruised the Spanish Main. In order to enter the Creole Palace, you needed a card of introduction and you had to be dressed properly. There was a strict ruling that no minors were allowed, and that left the students at Manzanita Hall ruled out.

There was the select Beau Brummel Club at San Jose for the younger generation. To obtain an admittance card all you needed was a friendly bartender or Charlie Myers at Menlo Park.

In both parlorhouses the soiled doves had to undergo weekly medical inspection by a professional doctor. No rough stuff was allowed, gentlemanly conduct being the order of the evening. The Beau Brummel Club was the hangout for students of Stanford University, and the prep schools in the vicinity. Any violation of the house rules, and your membership card was confiscated. The offender was escorted to the door by a burly plug-ugly bouncer, and once you were blackballed you were banished for all time.

Only a handpicked chosen few of the Manzanita Hall gang had cards to the Beau Brummel Club stashed away. Gimpy Quinn, Swede Carlson, Charlie Arthur, Bud Owens and myself were among the chosen few, by courtesy of Charlie Myers, and we kept the secret carefully hidden from all others in the dormitory. Our visits were few and far between on Saturday nights when the group of the chosen few, dressed in dark suits, boarded the train after dark for San Jose, always traveling in a group. If Dr. Shedd or Professors Rowell and Kellar suspected anything they failed to make mention of it, and we were doubly sure when we checked in before midnight curfew to be sober.

As I mentioned before, I had put myself on the "Injun List" at Charlie Myers' Tavern, and I was sitting high and dry on the wagon for more than two months, until one Saturday afternoon when I received a letter from Jake Myers, the foreman of the Circle C Ranch, telling me that my first cowpony, Snowflake, had died of old age. I received the sad news in the noon mail and I went on a high lonesome at Charlie Myers', a one man wake for Snowflake. I sat in an empty back room with a pitcher of Blue Ribbon draft beer, drowning my sorrow with tears in my eyes as I conjured up kid memories of my first cowpony. Then along about ten o'clock Gimpy Quinn and Charlie Arthur showed up and my lonesome wake came to an end.

"How come you fell off the sprinklin' cart?" Gimpy asked.

I told him my hat had blown off and landed in the back room of Myers' Tavern, and that was the only explanation I gave them. The sad news about Snowflake was a cruel blow, and I was not about to tell any outsiders about it, knowing they would never understand.

The second semester at Manzanita Hall was a strange mixture of many varied things. Underneath, somewhere in a secret pocket of my thoughts was an awareness that my graduation in June, less than six months away, would definitely mark the end of my education, like a milestone on my life's trail. There was a feeling of sadness that

*Walt dressed for rugby at Manzanita Hall Prep School,
Palo Alto, California, 1910*

the bright bonfire of youth would die then, leaving the ashes of a campfire along the devious trail of the life of a mortal. A man has but one life to live, and the days of his youth are numbered. I would go back to Montana to work out my destiny as a cattleman on the Circle C Ranch. So I decided to live each day as it came like a bumblebee draining the honey sweetness from the blossoms. Live each day as if there was no tomorrow.

The business course studies which Dr. Shedd had so carefully outlined soon lost their zest and became routine, boring drudgery, but I owed it to him to get good grades and the study hours took care of that. The rest of the time I was free to glean what pleasure each day held. Most weekends I spent at Charlie Myers' Tavern at Menlo Park, checking in at midnight curfew. Stanley Ketchell was in training for his fight with Jack Johnson, the heavyweight champ of the world. On Saturday mornings I would board the train to San Francisco, go out to the Cliff House where Ketchell had his training camp and watch him work out with his sparring partners. On my first visit Stanley Ketchell remembered me from Great Falls when I rode my bike to his training camp at Box Elder Park, and he made me welcome.

An Eastern car manufacturing company had presented Ketchell with a Stanley Steamer with his name in bold black letters on the battleship-grey enamel, and there was a trained mechanic who acted as chauffeur. On my last visit to the training camp Ketchell invited me to go riding with him and Battling Nelson, one of his sparring partners. Bat Nelson was a good friend of my brother Wallace, who was no slouch himself as a welterweight fighter.

We headed straight for the Barbary Coast and Spider Kelly's Black Cat Cabaret, where we found Jack Johnson and one of his sparring partners, Kid McCoy, sitting at one of the tables with a couple of cabaret girls. Jack invited us and Spider Kelly to join the party. Boy, Howdy! Was I ever awed and impressed and a little excited, sitting there with five champs and drinking champagne. Shortly who should come in to join the party but Bob Edgren, the famous cartoonist and sports writer who worked for the *San Francisco Examiner*. Edgren was another close friend of my brother Wallace. I was surely in distinguished company, a two-bit young clown in the company of kings. I felt a little ill at ease, but after the second glass of champagne the tension eased.

The cabaret girls left the party to join the can-can chorus on the stage and I sat back and listened to the fight talk which dated back to the early-day, bare-knuckle champs when prize fights went on and on for fifty or more rounds to the knock-down decision. Bob Edgren, whose knowledge of those early-day pugilists went back to the beginnings, talked at length, naming dates and places, the number of rounds fought and even the names of the referees. He spoke of the old-time Irish and British champs who fought on large barges anchored in bays off the Irish and British coasts. He was a knowledgeable talker and the stories were spell-binders.

When Edgren consulted his watch and had to leave, Stanley Ketchell announced he and Bat Nelson were headed for Chinatown, to hit the pipe. Jack Johnson had a date to pick up a couple of girls for Kid McCoy and himself, and I was due to catch the train back to Palo Alto. Ketchell offered me a ride to the depot, but I declined. I could hop a streetcar which would take me to Third and Townsend depot and the ride on the open streetcar would sober me up.

Thus ended one of the most enjoyable Saturday afternoons I had ever spent, and never forgot. It was indeed a memorable day when I sat in the company of kings in Spider Kelly's Black Cat Cabaret in the heart of the famous Barbary Coast.

I was one of the few Manzanita Hall students to get an invitation to Lucy Diamond's Hawaiian show at the Palo Alto Playhouse. Gimpy Quinn and Charlie Arthur were the other lucky ones, and what I mean, LUCKY, in capital letters. For an old country boy from Montana who knew nothing about the Islands or Honolulu, to say nothing of Waikiki Beach, it was like some fantastic dream of another world.

Back in 1910 to the average person of moderate means, the Hawaiian Islands was a far remote place of volcanoes and dark-skinned natives, a fun-loving people who sang songs, wore flowers in their hair, and fought wars with the natives of other south sea islands, a semi-savage people of barbaric customs and strange religion. Only missionaries and the millionaires with yachts visited the Hawaiian Islands.

For me Lucy Diamond's Hawaiian performance at the Palo Alto Playhouse was then, and remains to this day, one of the most delightful and unique entertainments I ever attended. The stage setting was that of the Islands, a painted backdrop with snow-covered volcanoes, fronds of palm leaves and scarlet hibiscus blossoms. The Hawaiian string orchestra of steel guitars, ukuleles and native drums formed a circle. Beautiful brown-skinned native girls in grass skirts and flowers in their jet-black hair danced the hulu hulu with leis of orchids around their necks. But the outstanding hulu hulu dancer was Lucy Diamond herself, and her plaintive songs of the Islands touched the heartstrings of the audience with the feeling of sweet sadness.

After the performance the invited guests went to the patio of the Castilleja school where Lucy met each guest with a lei she draped around our necks, to partake of the buffet of specially prepared Hawaiian dishes and native pineapple punch.

Lucy's Hawaiian party came during the final two weeks of school, a fitting farewell to prep school life for me. I sat back in the shadows of the June night dressed in my tux, with a fragrant blossomed lei draped around my neck, holding hands with Honey Bacon. I had already told Honey I had given up my plans of going to Stanford or any other university, and that I was going back to the Circle C Ranch and would be wearing Levi's from now on.

"You'll have time to write me, Bowse?" she asked.

"Sure thing. A feller has time to write when snowed-in in some winter line camp."

"I'll drop you a picture postcard from Paris," Honey said.

She had told me she was going to Europe that summer with her mother and father, then would enter Wellesly in the fall. When she asked me about my love life on the ranch I told her I had a young Assiniboine squaw staked out on the Fort Belknap Reservation, while she would be parly-vooing with some frog in Paris, on the left bank, whatever that meant, the guy wearing a girl's beret.

"I have my sights raised to snare a Duke or a Russian Prince, and take him to Dublin Gulch on our honeymoon," said Honey.

"The shanty Irish will string him up to a telephone pole," I kidded.

"When I get back to Montana send your Injun girl back to the squaw camps, Bowse, and we'll elope without benefit of clergy, live in sin in South America. How about that?" asked Honey.

"It's a deal, Honey, providing I'm not making horsehair bridles in the Deer Lodge pen. I'll have to join the Wild Bunch and hold up a few trains to get a South America stake. Chances are we'll spend our illicit honeymoon at the Hole-in-the-Wall outlaw ranch."

"I'll be holding you to that promise, Bowse."

So we kept it on a lighter vein as we kissed and said goodbye. Honey and I had had some good times together when we went to home talent shows without a chaperone riding herd, but we had played the honor bound ruling of both schools, which at times was a hard game to play for this young cowboy and the attractive girl from Butte, Montana.

During those last two weeks of school there were dances and parties at Castilleja and Miss Harker's, but Honey and I had our farewell at Lucy Diamond's Hawaiian party. As for Sue Brown, she and I kept it on a feeling of comradeship and met only occasionally.

I graduated at the end of the second week from Manzanita Hall prep school, and on my farewell visit to Charlie Myers' Tavern we held our last Manzanita gang beer bust, and made it a good one. The genial Myers handed me a tissue-wrapped beer mug, and when I unwrapped it there was my TNE mug with the golden skull and the ruby eyes, and my name, Bowse Coburn.

The next morning I stood on the crowded depot platform with

Dr. Shedd, who had accompanied me in a surrey. I had already bade farewell to Mrs. Shedd, Professor Rowell and Professor Kellar, and the other Manzanita students who were still there. The platform was crowded with Stanford students homeward bound, including Court Moore, who shouldered his way through the mob to shake hands with me. When I shook hands with Dr. Shedd I was too choked up to trust my voice, but I promised to write him from time to time how I was getting along. As the train pulled out I got my last and final look at Palo Alto from the Pullman window, and I kept blinking the mist which filmed my eyes.

On the baggage rack above there was another suitcase beside mine, and the moving train had passed another station when the owner showed up. He was a good-looking, husky six-footer, with a block B on his sweater, his suit coat slung over his arm.

"I'm Nelson Barker from San Diego," he introduced himself as we shook hands. "I'm known as Nellie."

I had heard of Nellie Barker, captain of the Belmont prep school football team. I told him I was also going to San Diego where my folks had rented a house, then I was headed for Montana where my father had his cattle ranch.

"I know a guy from Montana whose folks have a home in Dago. Perhaps you know Harry Dunn?"

"Hell, yes. I've known Dunny since he was a kid in grammar school."

"I'm going back to the Club car," Barker said. "Want to join me in a beer?"

"You bet. I feel like a beer. Just graduated from Manzanita Hall prep school."

"I just finished at Belmont," Barker told me.

There were a few Stanford men in the Club car, but it was not crowded. There were also two middle-aged men playing cards at the far end. Nelson Barker said one of them was Baron Long, owner of the Tijuana race track, the other was Wirt Bowman, owner of the Bowman Hotel in Nogales, Arizona, a large cattle ranch below the border and also the Foreign Club at Tijuana, a large bar and gambling house. Both were high rolling gents, who between them, controlled the gambling at Tijuana.

When I asked Nellie if Baron was some sort of title, he said no, that it was his real name. They were both well-dressed, quiet-mannered and soft-spoken, the opposite to gamblers I had known in Montana.

The four Stanford students were harmonizing college songs, and judging from their blended voices, they probably belonged to some glee club. The four somewhat crocked students stood grouped together on wide-spread legs to keep their balance, heads lowered like a football huddle, arms across one another's shoulders as they sang in perfect harmony: "Down by the Old Mill Stream," " Shine On Harvest Moon," "Have You Got Another Girl at Home Like Mary," and a new popular song I had heard a few times, "When You're a Long, Long Way From Home."

It was apparent that Baron Long and Wirt Bowman were picking up the tab for the drinks the singers were consuming. When the train pulled into the Los Angeles station the Stanford boys got off, leaving Nellie Barker, Baron Long, Wirt Bowman and me, and before long we were all well acquainted and sitting together.

Wirt Bowman spoke of rumors of a revolution about to boil over in Mexico. He said a peon Indian named Pancho Villa in Chihuahua was stirring it up, buying guns from gun runners along the border from Juárez to Nogales. He said Villa was a power below the border, and every Yaqui Indian and peon Mexican was raring to throw in with his rebel army to overthrow Presidente Porfirio Díaz, and that Colonel Kòsterlitzky, chief of the Mexican Rurales, was getting worried.

I did not pay much attention to what Wirt Bowman was saying, knowing nothing about Mexican politics, and caring less. After all, Montana was a long way from the Mexican border. But in less than a year I had occasion to recall the words of Wirt Bowman in their true prophetic meaning.

CHAPTER 9

A Well-burned Bridge

I HAD LITTLE TROUBLE convincing my father that I had no need for a college education to make a successful cattleman, likening himself as an example. My half brother, Bob, about twenty years my senior, happened to be at our home in San Diego when I explained it would take four years to complete a course in mining engineering for me to take over the running of the Ruby and Alder Gulch mines in the Little Rockies. They both agreed that it would be a waste of time and seemed pleased that I was returning to the ranch.

My father was leaving in a few days to go back to Montana. I was to accompany him on the train as he never traveled alone. This gave me a few days in San Diego to bum around with Harry Dunn. I had no trouble talking Harry into the notion of entering Manzanita Hall in September. I also talked to a few other Montana boys whose parents had homes in San Diego: Elmore and Milton Roberts, whose father owned the Great Falls Lumber Company; Chester McNair, whose father owned a large real estate and insurance firm in Great Falls; Nelson Cooper, whose father owned a large sheep outfit near Cascade; and so I managed to get five Montana students for the September semester at the prep school. I wrote Dr. Shedd the good news, giving him the dope on each boy. I figured I owed Dr. Shedd something for all he had done for me, and a few weeks later I got a letter from him saying the five boys had entered and how much he appreciated what I had done.

A few days later I was headed for Montana with my father. We had our Pullman tickets and the train left San Diego at eight A.M. Father was awake at the crack of dawn, seeing to it that I, too, was up and dressed. We ate breakfast at six A.M., and he had me phone for a taxi, and at a quarter of seven we were sitting inside the depot with our baggage. Father kept telling me to go to the ticket window to see if the train was on time. This happened about every fifteen minutes in spite of the fact that I told him the train was made up in San Diego, and the departure time was already chalked on the bulletin board. Then he began worrying about the two trunks being checked properly, and now I had to go see if the trunks were ready to load. I was worn out by the time our train was ready and we were aboard. Even then I was sent back to make sure our trunks were loaded in the baggage car. At Salt Lake City, Utah, we had a two hour layover to catch another train bound for Butte, and there again I was put through the meat grinder, back and forth to the ticket window to check the bulletin.

That was my first experience traveling with my father. I had heard my older half brothers josh each other about it, and I knew what they had been through. Traveling with our father was a trying ordeal, the understatement of the year. I heaved a big sigh of relief when our train pulled into Malta, Montana, and we were on the stage for the Circle C forty miles away.

The following day I was once more in Levi's and boots, making a hand. When the outfit shipped another trainload of cattle late in September, my father was ready to return to San Diego. Since he would not travel alone, he again took me with him, and I had to go through the same procedure of checking the trains and baggage.

I was due to go back to the ranch the following week. During that week in San Diego I fell off the water wagon with a dull thud. I had run into some friends of Harry Dunn's and gone to Tijuana and started drinking tequila, Mexican style. A shot of tequila in a two ounce shot glass, a pinch of salt and half a green lime. You licked the salt from the back of your hand, downed the tequila and sucked on the green lime.

It was sunrise after an all-night drinking bout when I showed up at our home. My father had been walking the floor since daylight and was fit to be tied, for I was due to return to Montana that day. As soon as I opened the front door he lit into me, cussing me for a no-account worthless drunk. I was still drunk enough to talk back, the first and only time I had ever done this to my father, and when I blew up it was Kitty-bar-the-door. My father told me to get the hell out of his house. He never wanted to lay eyes on me again. And I went, taking my already packed suitcase and saying goodbye to my tearful mother.

I caught a streetcar to the depot, cashed in my return ticket to Malta, and bought a ticket to Los Angeles. I had my summer wages in my pocket and the money I had gotten for my Montana ticket. In Los Angeles I got a room at the Broadway Hotel and bedded down to sleep off my drunk. In my hangover I was sick and sorry, but it was too late to do anything about it. Once again I had matched a battle with Kid Barleycorn and got knocked out the first round.

When I awoke I had slept about eight hours. I left the hotel and went to Jim Jeffries Poolroom and Bar, the favorite hangout for race driver Barney Oldfield and prizefighters of all kinds, champs and meal-ticket pugs. There I ate the free lunch with a big schooner of beer, and took time out to get a tailhold on myself. I had better count my money and start looking around for a job, and get a room, I thought. The Broadway Hotel was too high-priced for a homeless guy without a job. The only thing I knew was punching cows, but right now I was not welcome at the Circle C Ranch, and too proud to go back home like a whipped hound with his tail between his legs. I bought a copy of the *Los Angeles Times* to look over the want ads for a job and a cheaper room.

The only time I had been to Los Angeles was with Harry Dunn and a couple of his high school chums on a sort of picnic. We had taken the streetcar to West Lake Park and rented rowboats. So I looked for an ad for a rooming house in that vicinity, and I spotted one which looked promising. I cut it out and put it in my wallet. I then went over to the YMCA and rented a front room for a week for five dollars to give me time to look around and get my bearings.

I spent the week job hunting, pounding the pavements of the City of the Angels, until I was leg weary and disgusted. I ate my lunches at Jim Jeffries free lunch counter and bought a schooner of beer. The rates of the better rooming houses in West Lake Park were too expensive, others were small back rooms, and others cluttered up with noisy kids. I spotted a vacancy sign in the front window of a three-story house with gingerbread trimmings, and large bay windows. It had a well-kept lawn and flower beds and an old stable at the rear which had been converted into a garage. Two men were playing croquet on the lawn, paying no attention to me when I stepped up on the wide veranda and thumbed the doorbell.

A tall, slender, handsome woman with streaks of white in her black hair answered the door. A pair of dark, amber-colored eyes looked me over for about three seconds, missing no detail, and I was glad I had shaved, had on clean clothes, and had my shoes shined. I told her I had seen the vacancy sign in the window and would like to rent a room if one was available. She told me she had a little attic room on the third floor if I did not mind climbing the stairs. She asked me in to show it to me.

I followed her into the hallway which had an old-fashioned hall-rack with a boxed-in seat and a long mirror. The carpet had a worn look, but everything seemed to be spic and span. On the second floor she showed me the bathroom I would be using. It had ancient plumbing fixtures, but was clean and in good shape. The attic room, except for the dormer windows, was an exact duplicate of my third floor room in our Great Falls home, and I could not help but mention it.

When I told her I was from Montana, she said her deceased husband had been a mining engineer with the Anaconda Mining Company at Butte, where they had lived for ten years. I told her I liked the room and asked its price. She said twenty dollars a month and I forked over a ten and two fives. Downstairs she made out a receipt, and said she would like me to meet the other roomers. They were her brother, Frank Brooks, and Rusty Riley, who worked for the Lowellyn Iron Works.

"It's time we broke up that croquet game before those Shanty Irish pals get to knocking each other over the head with their mallets. With them their Sunday morning game of croquet is a Donnybrook Fair. Lucky we have no close neighbors, or they'd be calling the cops."

As we stepped out on the vine-covered veranda the sounds of a heated argument could be heard.

". . . it's gettin' to where a man can't turn his back till you're cheatin' . . ."

"Cheatin' hell! Turnin' your back you call it, and nudgin' the ball a foot with your foot. I got a mind to break this mallet over your thick skull. This is supposed to be a gentleman's game."

"Break it up," the woman called out. "We've got company."

I liked both men as we shook hands and I was glad to stay when I was asked to have lunch with them. I now knew the woman's name was Ramona Tully and the men called her Mona. They got a big kick out of my nickname, Bowse. During lunch they talked about the impending strike of the Iron Workers Union, scheduled for sometime in October. Rusty Riley declared that when the strike hit he was heading for Bisbee, Arizona, where he had worked two years for the Copper Queen, saying that the Brophys and Douglases were fine people to work for.

"I heard that labor union flannel-mouthed Irish leader making a rabble rouser speech," said Rusty Riley. "He lit into Otis of the *Los Angeles Times*, calling him every dirty name he could lay tongue to. Before it's all over all hell will tear loose and when it comes I want to be long gone."

"That labor union organizer from Chicago," Frank Brooks, nicknamed Pancho, said, "talked about the famous lawyer, Clarence Darrow, who could get them off the hook if any of his goons got into trouble or were hauled up for murder. But we all know that Darrow wouldn't waste his talents on common laborers. They could hang or rot in prison for all he gave a damn."

It was my first contact in any way with labor unions, and it was all Greek to me. I grinned to myself as I conjured up a cowboy's union going on strike for higher wages in the broad middle of a roundup. A forty-a-month cowhand worked from daybreak until supper time, then stood a two hour night guard around a bedded beef herd, hoping to God they would not stampede on a stormy night. He had a certain brand of loyalty to the outfit for whom he worked, and come hell or high water he got the job done as best he could. But I kept my mouth shut and sat back to listen.

When I mentioned I had to get to the YMCA to pick up my suitcase, Pancho Brooks took me to town in the new black Ford in the garage. During the following weeks I pounded the pavements job hunting, a fruitless task thus far, and I was running short of money. I hit bottom when I tackled selling encyclopedias from house to house, getting doors slammed in my face. I gave it up the second day. Then I tackled the job of selling household brushes which lasted two days without a single sale. I still ate my free lunches at Jim Jeffries with a nickel schooner of beer. Then I would go upstairs to play a few games of pool, and one day I got the job of racking the balls and putting new tips on the cues and brushing the green cloth on the pool tables, as well as other odd jobs. I was making on an average of three dollars a day and I managed to pickup an extra buck here and there.

It was sometime in October when the iron workers strike went into effect, and Pancho Brooks and Rusty Riley were fixing to go to Arizona. My brother-in-law, Carl Evans, who married my sister, Agnes, had a good job as mining engineer at the Copper Queen at Bisbee, and I talked them into the notion of letting me go along with them. I had managed to save about twenty-five bucks for my train fare and traveling expenses. I wrote my mother I was hoping for some word from my father that all was forgiven, but it was wishful thinking.

Frank (Pancho) Brooks had received a telegram from the manager of the Copper Queen store at Douglas, Arizona, to report at once for the job of assistant manager. He was taking the first train out the next morning. Rusty Riley and I were packed and ready to go, but we were not planning on riding the cushions. We would ride in a boxcar. Pancho would take our suitcases on his ticket and check them to Bisbee. Rusty had ridden freights before. After he had graduated from the Butte College of Mines, he had lived the life of a hobo for a year, visiting every state in the Union. Just for the hell of it, and about six months of that year he had traveled with Ringling Brothers' Circus as a roustabout. He had no trouble talking me into riding the freight, and it would save the price of a ticket.

I had been wearing cords and a flannel shirt for my pool room job in order to save my good suits now packed in my suitcase. Rusty wore a pullover gray sweater and dark gray flannel pants, packing his good clothes. I kept about ten bucks in my wallet and put the rest of my money in a sock in my suitcase. Pancho said he would mail the claim checks for our suitcases in separate envelopes in case we became split up for some unforeseen reason. He would address the envelopes General Delivery, Bisbee, and drop them in the depot mail box, then go on to Douglas.

The prospect of hooking a ride on a freight train like a hobo had me a little excited, and I said so. But according to Rusty there was nothing to get in a lather about. The wise hobos rode in style in an empty boxcar. You slipped the brakeman a dollar to ride five hundred miles, or to the next division point, where there would be a new brakeman and you then paid another buck. All you had to watch for were the railroad plainclothes dicks who patrolled the railroad yards, and were mean bastards with a blackjack.

The three of us were standing at the front end of the long bar at Jeffries Pool Hall discussing tomorrow's plans when all hell broke loose outside. There was a terrific explosion, the loud blast of the fire station whistle, then the loud clang of the hook-and-ladder wagon, and the loud Klaxon horn on the fire chief's Ford.

At the first sound of the explosion we ran outside, and in less time than it takes to tell about it, the sidewalks were crowded with the curious. We could see the angry red glow of a fire a few blocks away, flames and sparks shooting skyward in the night. The three of us kept close together as the jam-packed crowd began moving as more fire engines, ambulances and paddy police wagons and police cars raced toward the fire.

"The Times Building! It's been dynamited!"

The milling crowd shouted as they tromped on each other's feet in their frantic efforts to get to the scene of the burning building. When we got there a cordon of police were swinging clubs and shouting warnings to stay back. They had roped off a section a block away from the fire. Firemen in black slickers and red helmets swarmed like red ants in the fireglow with long lengths of fire hoses resembling swollen, white boa constrictors, pouring water into the blazing inferno. Firemen on high ladders carried men out of the building, and on the ground were huge fire nets for those who had to jump. Ambulances carried away the maimed and the dead with sirens wide open.

Uniformed cops by the score were nabbing any men caught beyond the rope barrier, shoving them back with billy-clubs. Rusty, Pancho, and myself were sandwiched in by the crowd against the rope barrier, tight against our bellies. It felt like we were being sawed in two by the shoving mob, but we knew we would be clubbed down if we were foolhardy enough to go under the rope barrier.

A policeman with a megaphone was yelling: "Break it up!" and a mass hysteria now gripped the mob. Some were scared, some stubborn, and there must have been a lot of cop haters by the sound of their shouted curses as police clubbed their way through. Beyond the rope barrier was a line of cops with billy-clubs, enough to chill a brave man. As the milling crowd behind us suddenly gave way, a big red-faced cop shouted orders to grab those hanging onto the rope and haul them off to the nearest paddy wagon.

Before we could do anything about it we were crowded into the paddy wagon, and the wire mesh gate at the rear clanged shut. Pancho told Rusty that if he had his union card on him to get rid of it, pronto, before we reached the police station. Rusty said he had torn it up, and had thrown it away before he got into the wagon, as had Pancho. At the time it meant nothing to me, and it was only at a later date I found out that the Times Building had been dynamited by the labor unions because the owner of the *Los Angeles Times*, Harrison Gray Otis, was a leading open shop advocate. So now any member of the Iron Workers Union who carried a union card of the local branch would automatically be a suspect.

This was my first ride in a paddy wagon, and I was getting a big kick out of it. I had done nothing wrong, no burden of guilt bothered me. I had been picked up by the police only because I happened to be underfoot. I asked Rusty what we were being charged with, and he answered in a lowered voice:

"Listen, kid. Somebody dynamited the Times Building. God knows how many died in that fire. The police are looking for the men who set off the dynamite blast, and we got picked up in the dragnet. You got nothing to worry about, Bowse, unless you have a criminal record."

Two uniformed police, one with a sergeant's stripes on his sleeve, sat behind a large, flat desk in the police station. Three plainclothes detectives stood grouped, looking us over as the police lined us up facing the wall with our lifted hands pressed against the wall to be frisked. There were twelve of us lined up, and Pancho was the only well-dressed man. He wore a pin-striped blue suit, a white shirt and tie, and his black shoes were polished. A large elktooth with a gold band engraved with purple letters B.P.O.E. adorned his wide black silk watchfob.

When the detective stopped in front of him to look him over, Pancho stood at ease, comfortable, aloof, his dark eyes unflinching, a faint sardonic smile twisting one corner of his mouth. His whole attitude was that of a solid citizen who had been picked up by mistake. The detective wore an expensive looking Elk's pin in his coat lapel, and he looked Pancho steadily in the eye for a long moment, then with a jerk of his thumb motioned for him to follow him to the desk sergeant where the two officers talked briefly. Pancho removed his Elk's identification card from his wallet and handed it to the detective, then to the desk sergeant, who said:

"We have our orders from the Mayor to pick up all suspicious characters and you just happened to get caught in the dragnet, Mr. Brooks. It's been one hell of a night. My advice to you is to get off the streets, go home and stay there."

As Pancho headed for the door he and Rusty exchanged split-second meaningful glances.

The desk sergeant looked at the clock on the wall and yawned.

"You finished with these fish, Mac?" he asked the detective.

When the detective nodded the sergeant told the two police standing by to lock the rest of us up for the night, and that we would come up before the judge in the morning court.

We were ordered to line up single file and to keep one step behind the man in front. The jailer swung open the jail door and led the way down a long corridor with cells on either side. It was the first time I had ever been inside a jail and I was curious, though nervous. Every cell held two occupants, and they were at the barred doors making wisecracks, with cat-calls and derisive whistles, lip-farting at the police and jailor.

"Don't trip over your billy-club, Copper! Come close and we'll spit on your tin badge! One-two-three-four," they shouted in unison.

We were locked in the bull pen, a foul-smelling atmosphere of stale urine and sour vomit which battled with the pungent fumes of carbolic disinfectant. Rusty and I wove our way through the sleeping drunks and found a place to sit.

"We should have joined the Elks," Rusty laughed. "That's what saved Pancho Brooks, that and his glad rags. By now he's telling his sister that we're locked up in the clink."

"Maybe Pancho and his sister, Mona, will bail us out," I suggested.

"Not a chance. Pancho will be riding the cushions on the seven o'clock train tonight, and if his sister has the sense she was born with, she'll stay home where she belongs. They both had jobs at the iron works and by now every policeman and detective will have it figured out that the Times Building was dynamited by the labor union."

Rusty coached me on what to say when we appeared before the judge next morning. All I had to do was tell the truth, that I was a drifting cowboy from Montana, gone broke in Los Angeles. No job, no address. That I had a job waiting for me in Bisbee, Arizona. And Rusty would say he was a drifting hobo, no trade, no job, no address. He said we would be charged with vagrancy with the usual punishment of Ten or Ten (Ten days or Ten dollars), and when the judge put the fear of the law into us he would cancel the Ten or Ten and hand us a floater to leave Los Angeles before sundown, or else, and we would hop the first freight out as we had planned, headed for Arizona.

And that is about what happened, with one minor addition. Rusty and I, along with some other floaters, were given a free ride to the freight yards in a paddy wagon, and were allowed to purchase coffee, canned pork and beans, some bologna, cheese, crackers, and tobacco at a small grocery store near the railroad yards.

We heard that every jungle along the dry bed of the Los Angeles River had been raided by the police, and all vagrants and suspicious characters picked up, frisked, cross-questioned, and given a floater out of town. Thus the dynamiting and resultant fire at the Times Building had its repercussions of the hysteria which swept the entire United States that October in 1910 when the Times Building was destroyed by explosion and fire and twenty-one persons were killed.

Rusty spotted an empty boxcar belonging to the Great Northern Railway, and that Great Northern boxcar was as far from home as I was. A few minutes before the freight was due to depart, a brakeman walked down the long line of cars, carrying a pick handle he used to tighten the brake wheels on top of the cars.

"It'll cost you two guys a dollar apiece from Los Angeles to El Paso," the brakeman informed us.

Rusty had warned me beforehand, and we forked over our silver cartwheels without argument.

"Another buck apiece," Rusty told him with a grin, "if you don't pile any more guys in. Just me and the kid in this boxcar."

"It's a deal, feller. But you better close the door on this Pullman," the brakeman advised.

"Don't lock us in, mister."

"Hell no. You treat me right. I'll treat you right. Anyhow, the lock's busted. You can see for yourself."

Rusty took a look at the broken lock with a repair order posted beside it, and forked over another two bucks. When the long freight got underway we closed the door. We had bought a secondhand Army canteen at the store and filled it with tap water, also a can of tinned heat, and had managed to find a clean empty five pound lard pail. Our breakfast in jail at six a.m. consisted of a bowl of pasty oatmeal and weak coffee, and now with the coffee coming to a boil on the canned heat, pork and beans, crackers and a piece of bologna, it looked like a sure enough banquet.

I had always enjoyed riding on trains, but riding in a boxcar was something else, and I was getting a big kick out of it. We had rolled open the wide door and I was enjoying the passing scenery. Our boxcar was at the rear end of the train, and on the long curves we could see the other cars filled with the rest of the floaters. It was getting dark when we crossed the long bridge across the Colorado River into Yuma, Arizona, which marked the boundary line. We could see the old Yuma prison in the distance, a hell hole during the hot summer months according to Rusty, where the convicts died like flies, especially the white prisoners. After we had had a good look we closed the door before the railroad dick came along.

When the train got underway again, we opened the door to look at the star-filled sky and the lopsided moon for awhile before we lay down to sleep. It was sunrise when we came alive. It was two in the afternoon when the freight pulled into Benson, Arizona, the end of the line. It was only some fifty-odd miles to Bisbee, our destination, and Rusty said we would ride the cushions from here.

We piled out and hightailed it for the nearest saloon, before the railroad dick spotted us. We drank a cold beer and washed up in the john. We had half an hour before the Bisbee train was due to leave so we went into a restaurant and ate the first real meal since before we went to jail. We got into Bisbee about five-fifteen P.M. and hightailed it for the post office to get our claim checks and suitcases. We then got a room at the Miner's Rooming House down the main drag from the depot. The first thing we did was to hit the shower to scrub off the jail stink, and get into clean duds from the hide out.

Rusty Riley said it might be a good idea for him to attend the meeting of the Mine Workers Union at the Labor Hall at seven-thirty P.M., and when it was over he said he would meet me at the rooming house and show me Bisbee's famous Brewery Gulch. Meanwhile, I tried to find my brother-in-law's telephone number, but Carl Evans was not listed in the book, so I spent my time inquiring around town to see if anyone knew where Carl and Agnes lived. The only clue I got was from the bartender at the Butte Saloon. He was well acquainted with Carl, but he had not seen him during the past few weeks. He mentioned something about Carl being transferred to Lowell, a few miles from Bisbee, but as far as he knew Carl still lived in one of the company houses on the steep side hill up Tombstone Canyon, where there were no house numbers, no streets, only burro trails, and the houses all painted alike.

Rusty was waiting for me when I got back to the rooming house. He said he would go on to Douglas first thing the next morning, but tonight he would show me Brewery Gulch. There were rows of scattered saloons on both sides of the dirt street, with deep, ten foot concrete culverts on either side, and iron guardrails to keep the drunks from falling in. At hundred foot intervals iron ladders led down into the drainage culverts which ran full during the flash floods. At the far end beyond the saloons was a large lumber yard, and beyond

Will James illustration which was used in "Riders of the Purple" in the first issue of Lariat Story *magazine, 1925.*

that the red light district consisting of small frame crib houses scattered hit and miss up the sides of the gulch.

Rusty warned me not to venture near the lumber yard after dark alone, or I would get stabbed in the back or knocked in the head by a gang of hoodlums who would empty my pockets. We bought a bottle of colorless corn liquor before we hoofed it back to our room. The potent corn liquor, called White Mule, sold for ten cents a two-ounce glass, or three for two-bits across the bar. A lot of the miners preferred White Mule to bar whisky, with a small beer chaser to cool the pipes.

We sat on our beds, drank and smoked, and shot the breeze for an hour or two before we bedded down. Next morning I saw Rusty off with a handshake and a careless so-long, and said we would meet again soon. But it was not in the cards that we were destined ever to meet again. Never again was I to see Rusty Riley, Pancho Brooks, or his sister.

The quest for Carl Evans and my sister, Agnes, was like hunting for the proverbial needle in a haystack. At the end of a week's futile search, I had about given up, but Jerry Duffy, the bartender and part owner of the Butte Saloon, was certain that Carl was still living in one of the company houses up Tombstone Canyon. When I paid another five bucks for another week's room rent, I found I was running short of money. I was becoming a little desperate, and was rationing myself to two meals a day. In daytime I hung around Slim Livingston's Club Bar and Poolroom, suckering in some would-be pool shark for a game of two-bit kelly pool, and winning more games than I lost. Besides the ten dollar bill in my wallet, I had six-bits in change in my pocket for pool money, and by the end of the day I ran it up to two bucks on an average. It was enough to eat on. The cockney cousin-jack miners were easy pickings, but I was careful not to win more than a buck from any one of them, and thus kept all of them on a friendly status.

One night about ten o'clock I drifted into the Butte Saloon for a drink, because I was lower than a whale's belly, and worried about many things. Jerry Duffy, the bartender, informed me that he had heard Carl Evans and his friend, Emmett Fitzgerald, had been seen in the Shamrock Saloon, and they had both been working for the past month at the Lowell mine. He advised me to take a walk up Brewery Gulch and drop in at the Shamrock.

I had not been back to Brewery Gulch since Rusty Riley gave me my first look, and I was filled with renewed hopes of finding Carl. It was an uphill climb, and I was blowing like a wind-broken horse as I leaned against the waist-high iron guardrail of the ten foot concrete draining ditch to get my wind.

"How's chances to borrow the price of a pint, pal?"

The whisky-harsh voice sounded close behind me. It had a veiled threat which made me turn around with a sudden twist.

"Don't give us no trouble, pal," said one of the four toughs that had me boxed in. "Just hand over your dough and you won't get hurt. Holler for the cops and we'll beat the crap outa you and throw you arse-over-tincup over the rail."

I stood there with both hands gripping the iron rail, and when I tried to open my mouth to speak, my voice stuck in my throat with the fear of a trapped animal. As they moved in like a wolf pack, I kicked out hard at the groin of the nearest man, and he let out a wild scream of pain. In the next split second the other three piled on me, and tore my hand grip away, and then the inside of my skull exploded in a blinding flash. When I came to I could hear confused voices of men, and a feeling of panic swept over me with the flash of memory of those men closing in on me. I tried to open my eyes, but there was a wet towel over my face. When I tried to get up the wet cloth was removed, and I saw a group of men with strange faces. Then I realized I was stretched out on a poker table in a saloon. They sat me up with my legs hanging down, and my aching head felt like I had been hit with a double-bitted ax.

The big, red-haired saloon man gave me a drink of whisky, and explained what had happened. He said that a bunch of hoodlums had thrown me over the rail into the drainage ditch. A couple of miners had happened along in time to see the gang scatter, and they had gone down the ladder and brought me to the saloon.

When I got off the poker table and walked over to the bar, I knew I had no broken bones, but one side of my face was skinned up, and looked like a raw beefsteak. One eye was swelling shut, and turning a greenish-purple, and there was a black and blue knot on my forehead. When I reached in my pocket to pay for a round of drinks, the pocket was empty. That gang of bums had rolled me before they dumped me in the drainage canal. I was glad I had left my wallet locked in my suitcase in my hotel room.

A couple of men had just come into the saloon, and lined up at the front end of the bar. My one good eye gave them a casual glance and slid away, and then came back for a second look. There was no doubt that the tall, lean man with the pince-nez eyeglasses was my brother-in-law. Even in his khaki shirt and pants, his working clothes, Carl Evans had the unmistakable look of the gentleman he was. My long and well-nigh hopeless quest had ended. I shoved away from the bar, then had a change of mind about going over to greet him. I was afraid I looked too beat up, but I knew if I did not go now while I had the chance I might lose track of him. At first Carl did not recognize me, thinking I was just another drunk caging drinks. But when he looked me over the old friendly brother-in-law grin showed, and he placed an arm across my shoulders and asked me what I was doing in Bisbee, and asked what the hell had happened to me. When I had told it briefly, Carl introduced me to his friend Emmett Fitzgerald, saying I was Agnes' kid brother.

He told me Agnes had gotten a letter from my mother about the row I had with my father, and that I had quit home and they did not know where I was. He said Agnes surely would be glad to see me, but I told him I did not want my sister to see me in my present shape, and that I would rather wait a few days until I looked fairly respectable. My room rent was paid and I was anxious to find a job.

Carl was sure he could find me a job on the survey gang with his friend Shanty Ryan.

CHAPTER 10

Pancho Villa's Army

IN THE LIFE SPAN of the average man there are bound to be days, weeks, months and even years which in later years he has buried in the graveyard of his mind and thoughts in dark hidden pockets. Those are the secret things he tries to never talk or think about. With the passing of time he tends to obliterate and dim the memory of whatever it is the man has buried, be it grief, shame, or guilt. It remains buried for all time in the sands of time, until the cold winds of memory blow away the drifting sand and the buried memory is starkly revealed in skeleton bones which are bleached by time, like evil spirits dredged up to haunt pleasant dreams.

It is now more than a half century since the winter of 1910, and my brief sojorun in Bisbee, Arizona, as I write these words with reluctant pen which may falter at times, and then go on with this chronicle.

I recall the happy reunion of our small family gathering. The company house where Carl and Agnes lived had two bedrooms, with a combination living and dining room, a kitchen and a front porch. It was perched high on a steep hill which had a panoramic view of rough, barren mountains, honeycombed for the most part with tunneled mines rich in copper ore.

Carl had made good his promise of getting me a surveyor's job. The inimitable Shanty Ryan was about six feet seven, of lean, wiry build, somewhere in his forties, with an unruly shock of graying, carroty, close-cropped hair, a weathered face with squinting sky-blue eyes. His nose had been broken and set a few times, and the lobe of one large ear had been cut off with a knife by a drunken Mexican. By nature Shanty Ryan was a wild, fun-loving man with a true Irish wit, but he had a hot temper when he had a few drinks. He was a graduate of the Butte College of Mines, a confirmed bachelor, but like all true Irishmen, he had an eye for a good-looking girl, and a taste for whisky. He batched in one of the company houses up Tombstone Canyon. He called it the Crow's Nest. During the month I worked on Shanty's survey chain gang we traveled far and wide on every mountainside surrounding the mining town of Bisbee. With a transit slung over his shoulder that wiry, long-legged Irishman could climb like a mountain goat, while my partner, Chino Russell, and I dragged chain and surveyor pole and pounded iron stakes into the hard rocky terrain.

Shanty Ryan was the Copper Queen Mining Company's Chief of Party Surveyor, a hard taskmaster, and if Chino or I made even a slight mistake with our lead plumb bob we got chewed out to a fare-thee-well. Once I had a job my credit was good at the company store because Ryan paid top wages. The only fly in the ointment was that we would work steady six days of the week, with Sundays off, for two or three weeks, then from a week to ten days' layoff without pay while Ryan worked in his drafting room mapping blueprints of the land we had just surveyed.

Carl and Agnes insisted on my staying with them. I had the spare bedroom where their trunks were stored, piled one on top of the other. At the end of my second week I was aware that they were hard up. Back home in Great Falls Carl and Agnes had friends galore, their social life gay and happy, but here in Bisbee they seemed to have no friends and no social life. I knew Agnes missed the Great Falls social life where her sister, Jessie, married to Attorney Fletcher Maddox, was playing the social game to the hilt, with their son, Coburn, attending Shattuck Military Academy and daughter, Marion, enrolled in an expensive boarding school. She also missed another sister, Edna, married to Dr. Leonard Ellis, now in charge of the

Government Hospital at Hot Springs, Arkansas, raising a family in a luxurious home with Negro servants. Here Agnes was living in a damn shack up Tombstone Canyon at Bisbee, with a couple of unopened trunks full of unused wedding presents, living a gypsy life while waiting until Carl would be transferred to the Copper Queen Mines at Cananea, Mexico, where his brother, Tom, was Assistant Superintendent.

Of great comfort to Agnes, and the pride and joy of the father, was their six months old son, Carl, Junior.

Then came the Christmas holidays with a week's layoff, and no pay for Carl at the Copper Queen until January, so together we ate round steak for Christmas dinner instead of the traditional turkey. That evening we sat on the front porch and listened to the Cousin Jacks far below singing old English carols as they moved from house to house carrying kerosene torches on long poles. The harmony of voices reached us far above as we listened in silence to these carols sung by men far from their homes and the London docks. It was a clear, cloudless night with a full moon which shed a pale glow over the mountains, a typical southern Arizona night, with a slight chill in the December air. The stars seemed close, almost within reach like the Star of Bethlehem in the Holy Land, something to remember always.

The day before I had received a Christmas letter from my mother, with a curt message from father enclosed, telling me that when I decided to quit drinking and came to my right senses I could go back to the Circle C Ranch where I belonged. I did not show the letter to Agnes and Carl before I burned it. This curt message from my father was a blow, but I held no grudge nor hatred for him. He was a stern man, and a stubborn one, and I had inherited his stubbornness. But that cold message stuck like gravel in my craw, and I would sooner go to hell and back before I would return to the Montana ranch.

After I left Bisbee, I was destined never to see my sister, Agnes, again. She died in Miami, Arizona, in 1915, where her husband held a fine position with the mines there. They had a lovely home in Miami, and were able to use their wedding presents, and the beautiful hand-painted china Agnes had learned to paint while at the Vistacion Convent in St. Paul. Agnes was buried in the Masonic Plot of the old Miami Cemetery for Carl was a 32nd Degree Mason.

During the Christmas week in Bisbee when I was flat broke, I managed to earn twenty-five dollars working at Slim Livingston's Club Poolroom. Then during the month of January I had steady work on Shanty Ryan's survey gang. But by the middle of February that job ended because Ryan had been transferred to Miami, and Russell and I were without work. Chino's real name was Eludo, but was called Chino because of his curly hair. His mother had been Mexican. When she died in Chino's sophomore year at Bisbee High School, and his father remarried, Chino went to live with his mother's bachelor brother in Tin Town, the Mexican colony.

Chino Russell intended to go to Cananea, Mexico, where his uncle, Mateo Gonzales, worked as section boss for the Southern Pacific of Mexico. As I was out of a job and with no future prospects in sight, I decided to go with him because Carl Evans was sure I could get a job with his brother, Tom, at the Greene-Cananea Copper Company. Carl advised me to leave my good clothes in my suitcase with them, pack my working clothes in a denim barracks bag, and wear a pair of corduroy pants and a flannel shirt on the trip.

When Chino and I boarded the train for Cananea we were as excited as a pair of school kids. We rode the worn cushions in the smoking car, mostly filled with Mexican laborers, and a few Cousin Jack miners. It was a fifty mile ride from Bisbee, and was getting dark when we pulled into the depot at Cananea. I was a gringo stranger, had no knowledge of the Mexican language, and was strange to the customs of the country. But Chino spoke Spanish as fluently as the language of his Anglo father and was no stranger in Cananea.

It was too late to look up Tom Evans so I decided to see him at his office next day, not wanting to wish myself on his family. I was on my own, and aimed to keep it that way. We stayed that night with Mateo Gonzales in an old boxcar he had fixed up and made livable. Mateo lived in the railroad town which was set apart from the main town. It was called Ronquillo, and had its own store and cantina where I partook of a real Mexican supper of enchiladas, tortillas, chili con carne and cold bottled cervesa, the Mexican beer which was stronger than the United States brew.

Next morning we exchanged our U.S. currency for Mexican pesos. When I inquired about Tom Evans, I was told he and his wife had left a few weeks earlier for Butte, Montana, where Tom had a good position with the Anaconda Mining Company. I was told Tom's wife, Lucile, had become frightened by the wild rumors of a big revolution in the near future.

The rumors were that the Indian Pancho Villa from Chihuahua was backing Madero to replace Presidente Porfirio Díaz, and also that there was a lot of American money behind the revolution. Pancho Villa's headquarters were at his ranch in Chihuahua, but he was spending a lot of time in El Paso, Texas, buying guns and ammunition which were being smuggled across the border.

For the past ten or more years, this revolution had been slowly cooking to a boil. In every state throughout the vast country of Mexico a feeling of unrest had been brewing, in a gigantic widespread plot to shake off the dictatorship of Díaz who ruled Mexico with an iron hand. Even now, in almost every state the mayors and politicos were being 'dobe walled and the revolutionists had taken over. Almost to a man the Federalistas, the standing army of Mexico, had joined the ranks of Pancho Villa's rebel forces. Only the Rurales, the mounted police under the able command of Colonel Emilio Kosterlitzky, the Mexican Cossack, remained faithful to Díaz. Right now General Pasqual Orozco, Pancho Villa's right hand bower, was somewhere in the vicinity recruiting men to join the Villistas.

The mines in Cananea were laying off miners by the score. The dire threat of the coming revolution had its death grip on the big mining and smelting interests in the United States, and they were about to close the mines. It was only a matter of weeks until the small Cananea bank would close its doors and take its money across the border to Bisbee. In a very short time the mining town of Cananea would become a ghost town, and there went my job down the drain before I was even on the payroll of the Greene-Cananea Copper Company.

Back at the boxcar Chino Russell and I had a long talk, and Chino was enthusiastic about joining Pancho Villa's rebel army, and his firey talk built a fire under me and I decided to become a soldier of fortune.

Talking it over with Mateo Gonzales, it was plain to be seen that he was a hundred per cent strong for the revolution, and that if he were our age and single, he would join the rebel army. Mateo said he had been born in Sonora, Mexico, and that his grandfather had been a full blood Yaqui. He said when Presidente Díaz had ordered his soldiers and the Guardia Rurales under the command of Kosterlitzky to round up all the Yaquis in the Sierra Madre Mountains of Sonora and deport them as slaves to work in the tropical plantations of Yucatan, his grandfather and father had been among the vast number exiled into slavery, to die in the tropical heat of Yucatan. Díaz was the cabron responsible for the death of thousands of Yaquis thus driven from their homes and their lands confiscated. So when Francisco (Pancho) Villa, whose real name was Doroteo Arango, started recruiting soldiers for his rebel army, every Indian and peon in Mexico was eager to join up.

Once Mateo started talking, he told some wild tales. He had been section boss of the Mexican work crew in 1906 when the miners at Cananea, working for peon wages, had gone on strike for higher pay. William Greene, owner of the mines, took the train to Bisbee where he gathered his gringo forces, cowboys, miners and the Arizona Rangers, and returned with a force of three hundred armed men who were put under the command of Rafael Yzabal, Governor of Sonora, Mexico. In the prolonged battle they were unable to end the strike and had to wait until reinforcements arrived in charge of Colonel Kosterlitzky's Guardia Rurales who were heavily armed. Kosterlitzky, who took orders direct from Presidente Díaz overruling the powerful Sonora Governor, charged the Americans with illegal entry and ordered them out of Mexico. More than sixty men had been killed and the striking miners were given the choice of going back to work, being drafted in the Federal Army, or being shot by the Rurale firing squad.

Kosterlitzky ordered Cananea under strict curfew. All saloons, dance halls, gambling houses and stores were closed. Two hundred mounted Rurales patrolled the streets at night with orders to shoot any prowler on sight. A few days later when Kosterlitzky's Rurales marched a hundred striking Mexican miners to Hermosillo, the capital of Sonora, to be drafted into the Federal Army, the siege of Cananea ended.

Mateo Gonzales said the approaching revolution was a different story. General Orozco had recruited a vast army of a thousand or more men. American gun runners were smuggling guns and ammunition to Villa's rebel forces. Orozco had scattered large groups of armed soldiers throughout Sonora, outnumbering the Guardia Rurales fifty to one, and Colonel Kosterlitzky was in hiding somewhere in the Sierra Madres, and the Federal troops had deserted to join the rebels, now occupying most of the large towns and villages in Sonora.

General Orozco was marking time, awaiting orders from Pancho Villa to join his forces and move on the city of Ciudad Juárez across the Rio Grande from El Paso, now occupied by the Federalistas. Every night around midnight, Mateo said, one of Orozco's recruiting officers showed up at a certain cantina in Ronquillo, and Chino and I should go there to listen to what he had to say if we wanted to join the rebel army of Mexico.

Mateo warned us that we were both American citizens and subject to the hatred of the Mexicans and for good reason. He advised Chino to say he was born in Nogales, Sonora, and for me to say I was born in Canada. In this way we would not be called American gringo cabrones, despised and spit on. This is what we did when the recruiting officer signed us up for the cavalry, with the promise of five pesos a day to be paid when Villa's army took Ciudad Juárez.

I do not know exactly why I chose the alias of Tom Burke instead of giving my correct name. Perhaps it was because, back in my school days, I had read and still remembered a story about the adventures of Captain Tom Burke, a soldier of fortune, who had fought in some South American revolution.

> Viva Orozco!
> And me, tambien!
> We'll take Juárez,
> But we don't know when!

Thus sang the gringo battalion as we camped that month at Fronteras on the banks of the Nacozari River.

Cavalry hell! Those of us who had signed up for Pancho Villa's army hoofed it with the infantry from Cananea to Fronteras. It was two weeks or more before we were issued guns and ammunition, no doubt because it took that long before the busy gun runners got around to us with their strings of pack mules under armed guard. Meanwhile, using sticks for guns, we lined up for infantry drill, under the shouted commands of Mexican drill sergeants (all Federalista army deserters) who spoke no English. We soon learned what each toot of the shrill nickle-plated whistles meant. Line up; squad left; shoulder arms; present arms.

The guns issued us were German Mauser infantry rifles calibrated to shoot 7 mm cartridges. But the ammo we were given was 30-30 cartridges which should have been issued to the cavalry, armed with 30-30 carbines.

We were never issued uniforms. The majority of the Mexican peons were dressed in cotton pants and shirts, and native sandals on dirty bare feet. The miners wore Levi's and shirts and heavy work shoes they had bought at the company store.

We called ourselves the Gringo Rag-Tag Battalion, and before we reached the fifty-odd mile march from Cananea to the Mexican town of Fronteras, the majority of the outfit came down with the Aztec Curse, known as diarrhea. You name it and the Gringo Battalion had it. A few men died and were buried along the torturous trail to Fronteras. Chow for the most part was fairly good at the large army camps, if you liked a steady diet of jerky, chili beans, tortillas and chicory coffee, black as ink. Most of the Mexicans and a goodly portion of the Gringo Batallion smoked marijuana which was easy to secure.

So far there had not been the excitement of a single battle for the Gringo Battalion. If there was any fighting in store for us, Orozco's Mexican cavalry must have handled it days in advance of the slow, plodding infantry. For us it was a waiting game until word came from Villa's headquarters to advance to Ciudad Juárez, and rumor had it that this would be sometime in early April. Every week a fresh bunch of recruits arrived. None of the Gringo Battalion had been paid a single peso, and it was said it would be only after the Villistas had taken Juárez that we would be paid in full.

For the most part we were flat broke, and had been camped at Fronteras almost two months. Secret meetings were being held at night regarding desertion, despite the fact that it was nearly fifty miles to the border over rough terrain of mountains, high plateaus, and barren desert, and the penalty for desertion was death by a firing squad, without benefit of trial.

Day and night there was a cordon of armed sentries posted around the entire camp, with orders to shoot deserters on sight. There was a strict rule enforced by gun law that no soldier be permitted to leave camp after sundown. Despite all these warnings, a small group of six men from the Gringo Battalion slipped away after midnight from the sleeping camp. Half an hour later the rattle of gunfire shattered the night's stillness. At sunrise six bullet-riddled dead bodies were brought into camp to be buried in one large hole. We were told the gringo deserters had been shot down by Ley del Fuga (the law of escape) as a dire warning to all those contemplating desertion.

That night Cotton Top Jones, the long-eared, tow-headed renegade tinhorn gambler from Nevada, and big Josh Jefferson, the only Negro in the Gringo Battalion, and who had thrown in with Chino and me, sat around our campfire holding a pow wow. Cotton Top said the thick skulled bohunk miners were asking for it, that they did not have a snowball's chance in hell to make a fifty mile trip to the border, even if they had slipped past the sentries, and it took a desert rat prospector to survive in that kind of country.

"Come payday after the Villistas take Juárez," Cotton Top went on, "we'll get a Mexican standoff. Payday hell! I got no notion getting my guts shot off in a big battle in Juárez, so when we reach there I'm going to steal me a horse and ride across the bridge to El Paso, and if you fellers have got a lick of sense you'll throw in with old Cotton Top."

"Deal me in," the Negro said.

"Me tambien," said Chino Russell.

"That goes for me, too," I said.

We talked it over, making our plans to desert. This was in the first week of April. Many rumors were in the air. General Orozco had taken a hand-picked troop of cavalry with him as bodyguards to meet Pancho Villa at a secret rendezvous. Rumor also had it that Madero had declared some sort of armistice with Federalista General Juan Navarro, whose army occupied and held Ciudad Juárez, and the impatient Villa was getting fed up with Madero's efforts to make some sort of peace with Presidente Porfirio Díaz' representatives. Madero was the man whom Villa and Orozco were going to put in power to replace Díaz. Rumor now had it that Villa and Orozco were going to take Ciudad Juárez in spite of hell and high water, and the wavering Madero, and the officers in command of the rebel army on the Nacozari River, were anxiously awaiting news from General Orozco to move toward Juárez to join forces with Villa.

A few days later, after we had it made up to desert when we reached Juárez, Chino Russell became ill with chills, fever and diarrhea. There was no doctor available, the nearest one being in Cananea, and he was perhaps gone. Chino Russell died at sunset a couple of days later as I held him in my arms. We buried him in the hallowed ground of the Fronteras cemetery in the long shadow of the old fire-gutted mission.

I had lost a good friend. Sleep was difficult that night so I lay there watching the stars, waiting for one to fall from the dark heavens above, and when it fell I said a prayer for the repose of the soul of Chino Russell who had been raised in the Catholic faith, to which I belonged.

The following day we got our marching orders, and we were on our way. It was a forced march to the city of Ciudad Juárez about two hundred miles as the crow flies, and the Gringo Battalion sang its marching song:

> Viva Orozco!
> And me, tambien,
> We'll take Juárez,
> But we don't know when!

During the next couple of months no one had kept track of the exact dates, but once again dame rumor declared Pancho Villa had plans to take Ciudad Juárez on May fifth, the Mexican holiday of Cinco de Mayo, when Mexico had won its freedom. So it must have been about the first of May when our Gringo Battalion, and the tail end of Orozco's scattered forces joined Villa's army to surround Juárez, now held by the Federal troops under the command of General Juan Navarro.

Now for the first time those of us who had signed up for cavalry duty were issued horses, saddles and Winchester 30-30 carbine saddle guns to replace the German Mauser infantry rifles which we had never used. Villa's forces had raided the larger ranches, such as the vast Terrazas grant, and had rounded up the horses during March and April, and the huge remuda had been on pasture at Pancho Villa's rancho. The saddles were Mexican or second-hand U.S. Army McClellan saddles. I glommed onto a Mexican saddle, as did Cotton Top Jones and Josh Jefferson, and you could tell by the way those two acted that they knew horses. All the horses wore the Terrazas brand and were broken cowhorses. It was our job to tend our own horses which were tied to long picket lines. We fed them from huge piles of baled hay and stacked sacks of barley. There were leather halters and Mexican made hackamores to choose from. Along with the Winchester 30-30 carbines in saddle scabbards, each of us was issued a single action Colt .45 six-shooter, cartridge belts and holsters.

By the time our outfit reached Juárez, Cotton Top had recruited about a dozen Cousin Jacks and Bohunk miners who had had a bellyful and were anxious to desert. On the third day of May, at midnight, we were to slip away, take our horses from the picket line, saddle up and ride off into the night, one man at a time to not attract attention. The Villista sentries were posted about two hundred yards apart, on the alert for a Federalista attack rather than to shoot deserters.

We had no sooner made camp and settled down when the whisky peddlers from Juárez commenced to infiltrate the entire camp. Tequila, pulque, mezcal in two gallon wine sacks sold for one peso per quart. Dope peddlers were selling marijuana. Cotton Top, who had a knowledge of the Mexican lingo, had talked to a number of the whisky peddlers to get the lay of the land at Juárez, and also information about the guards stationed at the bridge across the Rio Grande which separated Juárez and El Paso, Texas.

According to the whisky peddlers, Juárez was full of drunken Federal soldiers and civilians, including gringos as well as Mexicans. The cantinas, dance halls and gambling and whorehouses had been taken over by rich Mexican Federal politicos. Madero was talking armistice with Díaz, while Villa and Orozco talked war.

There was a Federalista soldier sentry on the Mexican side of the bridge, and an American soldier guarding the Texas side, but neither sentry paid much attention or challenged the men on foot and on horseback, nor for that matter those in wagons and buggies, which traveled back and forth. Thus it looked like easy pickings for us deserters. Cotton Top and Josh had lived in El Paso, and both knew Juárez like a book. Our plan was for Cotton Top to ride in the lead; I would follow at a safe distance, and Josh would bring up the rear. And far behind, but close enough for them to spot Josh, would come the single file of strung-out miners. In this way we could ride slowly through the crowded streets of Juárez safely. Then every man was on his own. If stopped by soldiers each man would say he was alone, and was a citizen of the United States or Canada. Cotton Top warned everyone not to implicate any of the others, and to have his story down pat.

Cotton Top had somehow arranged it so that he, Josh and I were on sentry duty at the picket lines at twelve o'clock midnight on May third, and all we had to do was saddle up and ride off to meet a few hundred yards away, wait for the others to show up, then head for the bright lights of Juárez. And this is what we did.

I had goose bumps all over my hide when I saw the foot soldiers patroling the dimly lighted streets. I had no trouble keeping Cotton Top in sight. That lanky tinhorn renegade sat tall in the saddle as he rode at a walk through the tipsy crowd, but I sure was on edge as I sat in my saddle. When we reached the bridge Cotton Top had his hat pulled down and a brown paper marijuana cigarette hanging in the corner of his grin. When Josh caught up we rode three abreast toward the Federalista soldier on guard.

Cotton Top had a half-filled bottle of tequila which he raised in a drunken salute, and invited the soldier to have a drink.

"Borrachon gringo cabron!" the guard shouted. "Andale! Move on! Muy pronto!"

I held my breath as we rode past the little soldier with his threatening Mauser rifle and fixed bayonet. We were still riding three abreast as we neared the American soldier on sentry duty on the Texas side of the bridge.

"Have a snort of rotgut booze, soldier!" Cotton Top raised the bottle of tequila.

"Not on duty, cowboy. Where the hell you fellers come from anyhow?" the soldier questioned.

"Deserters from Villa's two-bit rebel army," Cotton Top admitted. "We've come this far soldier, and we don't aim to be stopped. There's a few more following, so don't give no trouble. Look us up at the Lone Star Saloon and we'll buy you a flock of drinks, sergeant." Cotton Top grinned down at the sergeant's stripes, and asked what outfit he was in.

"Utah National Guard," the soldier answered.

A few minutes later we were headed for the stockyards.

"Yonder come the rest of the deserters sitting in their saddles like so many big sacks of wool. Let's get the hell gone before they sight us. I don't aim to have them underfoot when I make a dicker for our horses with Pecos Simms, the gent in charge of the stockyards."

The stockyards were at the edge of town. When we reined up at a one-room shack near the loading chutes, Cotton Top called out in a guarded tone of voice, "Open up, Pecos! It's me. Cotton Top Jones!"

A light came on and a voice like a rusty gate hinge called out, "Hold your water, Cotton."

A short, heavy-set man stood framed in the door he had flung open. He was hitching up one side of his galluses as a pair of faded blue eyes peered out from under heavy black brows decorating a leathery, wrinkled face. A Colt six-shooter was shoved into the waistband of his saddle-warped Levi's.

"Last I heard you was doin' time in the Nevada pen, Cotton Top." He grinned as they shook hands. "Why you wakin' me up at four in the morning? You fellers on the dodge?"

"Hell no!" said Cotton Top. "We've been with Villa's rebel army. Got fed up and come across the bridge. Got three damn good cow horses for sale. How much will you give us for them, Pecos?"

"I see them geldings come from the Terrazas ranch. Not that I give a damn," Pecos said.

He motioned Cotton Top inside and shut the door. Cotton Top had handed me his bottle, and Josh and I had a couple of fast ones before Cotton Top came out. He had his fist full of money and said he had gotten fifteen dollars a round for the horses, and five bucks each for the saddle guns. We kept our six-shooters. He said he had thrown in the Mexican saddles because it was cash on the barrelhead. He divided the money evenly between us and we hoofed it for the Lone Star Saloon where we had a few drinks. I then headed for the Western Union telegraph office, and sent a night letter to Carl Evans to express my suitcase to El Paso, telling him I was heading back to the ranch in Montana, and I would write Agnes later. I then sent another night letter to Jake Myers, foreman of the Circle C Ranch at Malta, asking him to wire me a hundred bucks to get me back to Montana.

On my way back to the Lone Star Saloon to catch up with my drinking compadres, I stopped at the Paso del Norte Hotel to get a room. The white-collared dude behind the desk looked me over from head to foot with a fishy eye, like I had leprosy, and declared there were no rooms available. So I got the hell out of there before he called the house detective. Hell's bells! I had forgotten my unkempt, unbathed, unshorn ragged locks, or I would never have set foot in the plush lobby of the Paso del Norte.

When I lined up at the mahogany with Cotton Top and Josh, I took a good look at myself in the bar mirror. It was the first look I had had since I had shaved in Carl's bathroom in Bisbee. That seemed a long, long time ago, in the middle of February. I would not have blamed that desk clerk if he had called the cops, or the garbage collector. I had a moth-eaten growth of beard on a wind- and sun-weathered face which needed scrubbing with hot soapy water. My Stetson, simliar to a U.S. Army hat, was grimy with old sweat, my denim brush jacket faded and out at both elbows, my corduroy pants shabby enough for the ragbag.

Cotton Top called my attention to a printed notice tacked to the wall of the saloon: NOTICE! A REWARD OF TWENTY-FIVE DOLLARS FOR ANY AMERICAN DESERTER FROM PANCHO VILLA'S REBEL ARMY.

And below a duplicate notice was printed in Spanish. We figured it was time to get out of there before some bounty hunter tried to collect that reward. Cotton Top said he would not put it past the Texican bar dog to slip us a Mickey Finn.

Josh said his folks lived in Nigger Town, and he reckoned he would go home, so we said goodbye to him and headed for the nearest restaurant. It seemed strange to be sitting at a lunch counter with a menu to choose from. It was the first honest-to-god square meal we had eaten in months. After we got the wrinkles out of our bellies we located a clothing store, bought new underwear and sox, Levi's and flannel shirts. We did not have enough money to buy a Stetson hat or boots so we cleaned the ones we owned as best we could. We got the works at the barbershop, and took a hot bath in the cheap room I had rented for the night. Cotton Top had been promised a job by Pecos Simms at the stockyards, and so we said goodbye. Next morning there was a hundred dollars waiting for me at the Western Union. I had to lay over a day until my suitcase arrived.

I bought a new Stetson, and a pair of boots, and when my suitcase arrived I changed to better clothes. Just for the hell of it I went back to the Paso del Norte Hotel in a cab. The desk clerk failed to recognize me and gave me a room for the night. When I ambled into the hotel bar for a drink there were half a dozen or more newspaper reporters lined up shaking poker dice for the drinks. They were gathered in El Paso to cover the battle of Ciudad Juárez, and while I stayed apart, I bent both ears listening to their conversation concerning Pancho Villa and General Orozco. They were betting the scheduled battle would begin on the fifth of May, the Mexican national holiday, *Cinco de Mayo*. Sure enough at sunrise the morning of the fifth all hell broke loose across the Rio Grande. The long bridge had been closed, the Utah National Guard was there in full force, and a few cannonballs had been lobbed to the Texas side of the river.

I boarded the train out of El Paso at ten-thirty next morning. I sat on the rear platform of the observation car, scrubbed clean of my pasear into Mexico, with a twenty-five dollar reward on my hide. My brief sojourn as a cavalry soldier in Villa's rebel army had ended without a bullet scar to show for it.

CHAPTER 11

From Saddle to Cockpit

NEVER WAS THERE A NATIVE of Montana happier to get home when the train arrived at Malta at four-thirty A.M. I then had time to eat breakfast before boarding the stage for the Circle C Ranch in the long shadow of the Little Rockies forty miles away. Soldier of fortune, hell! I was a soldier of misfortune. I had not been within the sound of gunfire and when I took a good look at myself in the glaring light of reality, I had nothing to be proud about, but a hell of a lot to be ashamed of, from the time I quarreled with my gray-bearded father. He was in the right when he bawled me out. And now I was showing up at his ranch with my beragged bushy tail between my hind legs, eight months later. I decided to keep my mouth shut about where I had been for those eight months. If my father had discovered I had been a ragged foot soldier with Villa's rebel army he would have chewed me out. I found out later that Carl and Agnes had covered for me during the time I was in Mexico, and were worried sick until I had wired Carl from El Paso.

The first thing I did was write letters to my mother and father, to Carl and Agnes, and to Mateo Gonzales telling him of the death of Chino Russell, and that we had buried him in the cemetery at Fronteras, Mexico. By the grace of the Señor Dios, I was safe and sound at the Circle C Ranch where I belonged. Back home to pick up the pieces of my cowpuncher life, which was my destiny. With a red-inked debt of a hundred dollars on the company books which I would have to work out, I was content with my lot. When my father showed up at the ranch neither of us made mention of the quarrel we had had. It was now a closed book, water under the bridge. I never quarreled again with my father, but he laid down a strict ruling for me to follow. If I stayed sober and kept out of trouble of any kind and tended strictly to business for three months, my wages would be raised to fifty dollars a month. Another three months of good behavior and I would drag down sixty dollars, and another six months I would get straw-boss wages of seventy-five dollars. The only drawback involved was that as straw-boss I would have to give orders to a crew of older, seasoned cowhands with gray in their hair, old cowhands who had forgotten more about handling cattle than I would ever know until I reached their cow-savvy age. The very thought of giving orders to older cowhands seemed ridiculous and went against the grain.

The first three months while my father stayed at the ranch, I tip-toed the chalkline and earned my ten dollar raise. After he left for California in early October, for some unknown mule-headed reason, I broke the rules by riding to the mining-cowtowns of Zortman and Landusky in the nearby Little Rockies, and painting them as red as a war-painted sunset, because mainly I did not want that straw-boss job.

So it was that from 1911 until the Circle C outfit was sold, lock, stock and barrel, to the famous Matador Land and Cattle Company in 1916, that I sowed a goodly crop of wild oats in the Little Rockies country, the stomping ground of the outlaw Kid Curry Gang and the Wild Bunch, drinking and raising hell in general. This was probably because some years before the deal with the Matadors was signed, I was keenly, bitterly aware that some day before too many years the Circle C was to be sold, and with it my boyhood dreams of ever inheriting my share of the Coburn Cattle Comany's vast holdings as one of the largest pioneer cattle spreads. My rightful heritage would be gone with the wind. So from then on I did not give a tinker's damn, and I traveled high, wide and handsome, squandering my hard-earned wages across the bars, buying drinks for the house, bucking my horse down the main streets of the cowtowns, riding into the saloons for my first drink before stabling my horse to go on a hell-raising spree until the sheriff cut me down, paying my ten dollar fine for disturbing the peace, then riding back to the ranch flat broke, with a pint of whisky in the pocket of my chaps to sober up on. Then I would stand hitched while Jake Myers, the ranch foreman, would chew me out to a fare-thee-well, his cussing going in one ear and out the other like water on a duck's back, because I did not give a damn one way or the other.

When the Circle C outfit was finally sold in 1916, my boyhood dream of getting my share failed to materialize. My rightful share went in for boot and no one but me noticed it. My only bet now was to sack my saddle, roll up my roundup bed and head for Globe, Arizona, to work for my older half brothers, Will and Bob Coburn, who had acquired large cattle holdings on the San Carlos Apache Reservation.

There was a hell of a lot of difference between making a cowhand on the open prairie country of Montana and the rough mountain terrain in Arizona, with its brushy scrub-timbered steep slopes, canyons and deep arroyos, where the cattle were wild and hard to gather. Here the roundups consisted of pack mules instead of mess wagons and bed wagons; where the brush-popper cowhands rode double-rigged saddles with breast-strap rigging and their ketch ropes tied hard and fast to the saddle horn.

After about six months as an Arizona brush-popper cowhand I learned the hard way, I had gotten familiar with the range and was making a fair-to-middling hand when I received a telegram from my father from his home in San Diego, California, which contained bad news for me. He had bought a damned cotton farm in Imperial Valley, part cotton and part alfalfa and grain to feed a stinking mess of hogs. I was asked to come right away and run the outfit with my younger brother, Harold, and I had to swallow my pride and go. For me it was bitter medicine to take; three strikes and out! And I was out like Nellie's eye.

But just then came the First World War, and I made up my mind I would enlist when I got to San Diego, in spite of hell and high water and a bad ankle I had picked up in 1914 in a car wreck. I went to the cotton and hog farm near Seely in the hot Imperial Valley in the hell-hot month of July. But every time I got to San Diego I haunted the enlisting offices. First I tackled the U.S. Cavalry, but could not pass the physical on account of my stiff ankle. The Marines turned me down for the same reason, and the Navy would not have me, and it was a lead-pipe cinch I would be turned down by the draft for the same reason. A few of my San Diego friends were enlisting as cadets in the Air Branch of the Signal Corps at Rockwell Field on North Island. (The Air Force of today had not yet come into existence.) These friends took me to Rockwell Field to meet Major Lyons, Commanding Officer, who gave me a regular enlisting form to fill out as a cadet in the Air Branch of the Signal Corps. I filled it out at the headquarters building and was duly sworn in by the enlisting sergeant who then sent me over to San Diego for my physical. I went to our family physician, Dr. Oatman, and he passed me. Meanwhile my brother Harold's draft number was called, and he was now a buck private in the Infantry of the Ninety-First Division. So my cousin, Cliff O'Marr, a good farmer, was put in charge of the cotton and hog farm in Imperial Valley.

As a flying cadet I had to buy my own uniform, and I had my father's tailor make it. We wore a wide silk hatband on the regulation Stetson. Whenever I was in San Diego I put on my cadet uniform and did my share of swaggering. It was more than a month later that I received orders to report to a two-story barn-like place in Los Angeles for another physical. We had orders to strip down to the hide, and were handed a list of doctors to see: the eye doctor, the ear, nose and throat doctor, and the heart and lung doctor. It was "stand on your right foot, stand on your left foot, run down the bare stairway, run back up." It took all day and somehow I managed to pass. If the Army doctors noticed my stiff ankle, they failed to mark it against me.

Walt Coburn, Air Cadet, 1917

When a month went by without my being called for active duty, Jack Beaudry, a friend of mine, and I took the bit in our teeth and went over to North Island. The desk sergeant at headquarters pointed to a mile-high stack of enlistment papers and told us to do our own bird-dogging, that he was a busy man. When Beaudry and I finally found our papers we handed them to the sergeant who quit typing and took them into the adjutant's office. In a few minutes we were called in and told we were now attached to the Thirty-Seventh Squadron, due to report to Berkeley, and that the barracks building was on the University of California campus where we were to report.

Three days later Jack Beaudry and I got our travel orders and tickets. Resplendent in our cadet uniforms, we were raring to leave for our nine weeks of ground school hard-crammed study and infantry drill on the parade grounds, with latrine duty thrown in for boot. We were given our choice of airfields at the end of our training, Kelly Field in Texas, or Rockwell Field at North Island. I put in for Kelly, but was sent to Rockwell.

A civilian pilot named Coyle was my flight instructor on the Curtis OX5 Jennies. One morning my extra pair of shined shoes were out of alignment, a black mark against me, and I had to report to the tent house of the squadron commander. That put me fifteen minutes late, and I was doing double time to reach the Spot on the flying field when Sergeant Conomy, riding a motorcycle with a hand car, picked me up. We had just reached the field when a Jennie out of control came in low and crashed nose down. We could see the cadet in the front seat with both hands frozen on the half-wheel dip control, and the helmeted instructor on the rear seat with his hands gripped on the dual control trying desperately to get control of the ship.

If I live to be as old as Methuselah, I will still remember the sight and sound of that fatal crash. Sergeant Conomy and I were the first to get there. We climbed over the wreckage to unfasten the seat belts and lift the broken bodies from the front and rear cockpits, and wait for the ambulance to arrive. As we stood there badly shaken, our coveralls bloodstained, Sergeant Conomy read the number on the fuselage and lower wing.

"Three Seventeen. That's Coyle's ship."

And if I had not been fifteen minutes late that morning I would have been the cadet who was killed instead of Cadet Cullen, next name on the cadet alphabetical list.

Instructor Coyle dead, I had First Lieutenant Splain for my instructor the following day. I had five hours dual instruction before I graduated to solo, mostly taking off and making three-point landings, both tires and tail skid. Then came the cross-country flights to complete the flying training, which included East Field in the back country from San Diego to Imperial Valley, then to Fallbrook on the coast. Our maps were taped to one coverall leg by elastic bands, and the highway and railway from San Diego to Los Angeles were our guide marks.

I was due to take my final cross-country on a Saturday afternoon, checking in at East Field, then Fallbrook, and set down at Rockwell Field. I set down at Fallbrook just ahead of a peasoup ocean fog. Three Jennies with solo cadets were socked in at Fallbrook until the fog lifted.

The sergeant at Fallbrook checked my OX5 motor to make sure the overhead valves were not sticking, then tanked me up from the gas wagon, and filled the radiator. Everything was OK on the field sergeant's log book and I awaited the signal to take off. When I sighted a large patch of blue sky I told the sarg to twist the tail, and he swung down on the propeller and the motor caught. I motioned the ground crew to yank the chock blocks out and was dead positive I saw the field officer lift his arm and signal for the take-off, and I gave her the gun.

By the time I hit the coast at Del Mar the sun was visible in the overcast sky, the highway and railroad tracks in sight. When I circled North Island to get the direction from the wind sock there was a thick fog bank coming over the old lighthouse at Point Loma, and windblown wisps of fog were sifting like white spindrift down across Loma Portal and North Island. The sergeant in the tower at Rockwell signalled for me to land and I came in on a perfect three-point landing, taxied over to the whitewashed circle and cut the motor. I was full of beans and a little proud. I was the first of the dozen cross-country cadets home safe and sound. When I set down I was no longer a flying cadet, but automatically a second lieutenant with silver wings in the air branch of the U.S. Signal Corps. I did my best to mask my inner gratification, self-satisfaction, and an urge to give three cheers with the grim-faced, give-a-damn look of an ace member of the Lafayette Esquidrille.

When the tall athletic Captain Splain walked over to where I sat in the front cockpit of the Jennie, I expected to see a grin on his face instead of a storm cloud.

"Wipe off that silly grin, Cadet," he said grimly. "East Field is socked in. Fallbrook's socked in. Rockwell Field's socked in. The Lieutenant in charge of Fallbrook Field telephoned that some smart-aleck cadet had taken off on his own, without permission. He gave me the number of your ship. Report to your squadron commander. Before you get your weekend pass I'd advise you to take a look at the bulletin board at Number One Hangar.

With that Captain Splain, a West Pointer, turned and walked away to rejoin the other instructors.

I left my helmet and goggles on the seat, unfastened my safety belt and climbed down over the wing. I headed to where Sergeant Conomy sat straddle of his motorcycle and climbed in the side car. Conomy gave me a lopsided grin, trod hard on the starter and left like a bat out of hell, making a short half-circle that tilted the side car at a precarious angle as was his habit to scare hell out of his cadet passengers, halting abruptly in front of the Commanding Officer's tenthouse at the far end of the squadron street. According to the rule-book I checked in and then walked to my tent down the line.

As a rule all cadets were entitled to a weekend pass, with the exception of those confined to the island on some demerit infraction of the many rules that governed the cadet camp, like sloppy bed-making, sloppy dress for morning inspection, a loose button on a uniform, unshined shoes, sloppily wrapped putties, shoes out of alignment, and I had come through the week clean as a whitefish.

The bulletin board at Number One Hangar had nothing to do with demerits. It was a daily log of cross-country flights. By the time I had checked in with my squadron commander the peasoup fog had rolled in. Rockwell Field and the Naval Aviation base at the far end of North Island were socked in, as was the sand-spit connecting Rockwell with Coronado, and you could not see the city of San Diego across the bay for the dense fog. There was not a plane airborne until the fog dissipated.

Captain Splain, who went by the book, had spoken a bitter mouthful when he chewed me out, but I could have sworn the commanding officer at the landing field at Fallbrook had given me the go signal, but it was a case of my word against that of the commanding officer, and in the army you do not dispute the word of a superior officer, even a non-com corporal or sergeant. That is why I dreaded to look at the bulletin board at Number One Hangar. Opposite my name would be the word "Grounded," and that meant I would be ordered to face the benzine board for infraction of rules, taking off without orders. I would be grounded, perhaps washed out.

Alone in my tent I lifted the lid of my foot locker. There was the small envelope containing my two gold bars of a second lieutenant and the silver wings to pin to my blouse, the gold and black officer's hat cord. Come twelve o'clock noon the bugler sounded mess call and I lined up with the others to march to the mess hall. After dinner I forced myself to hang around the canteen drinking coffee and eating Hershey bars until three-thirty P.M. Then I went over to Number One Hangar to get the bad news, and found my name at the top of the chalked list. "Cadet Coburn. Finished his last final cross-country at ten-thirty A.M." It was signed Captain Splain.

I felt like hollering and putting on an Injun war dance, but instead I headed double time to grab my weekend pass, then shower, shave and get dressed in my cadet uniform with the white silk hat band. And God bless Captain Splain. He had chewed me out and that ended it, and I knew he would be telling it for a joke.

This called for a celebration of some kind. I knew better than to pin on the gold bars and the black and gold hat band, but I put the silver wings in the pocket of my blouse to show my friends. I would borrow my father's new Apperson Eight Jackrabbit seven passenger car, get booze from the bootlegger at the U.S. Grant Hotel, and Wow!

That evening I was at the wheel of the big tan Apperson with Sergeant Starr, the mechanic who had the care of Captain Splain's Jennie, a First Lieutenant from the cavalry at Camp Kearney, a sailor I had picked up, and two taxi-dance girls we had picked up at the Dreamland Dance Hall. I had gotten two quarts of genuine Canadian Club from the bootlegger at the U.S. Grant Hotel. He was a former saloon keeper who had been closed up by the Volstead Prohibition Act. We were on one big joy ride, cruising up and down the coast, La Jolla, Del Mar, and as far as Oceanside, then back through Balboa Park, and into the back country as far as Ramona. We were feeling no pain by one A.M. as we headed back for San Diego.

During World War I on a Saturday night San Diego was something for the book. There was the large army camp at Camp Kearney, Rockwell Flying Field, and the Navy Aviation Base at North Island, as well as the naval station at the World's Exposition Grounds at Balboa Park, and the Marine base. Also the MP's from the 21st Infantry at Camp Kearney, a part of the standard army which had been stationed for several years in China, who looked down their noses at the volunteers and draftees of the civilian army and lost no chance to push us around. They were a tough, hard-boiled bunch of MP's who had done at least one four-year hitch, and the sergeants had hash-marks on their sleeves to show for fifteen to twenty-five years which took in the Boxer Rebellion of 1900. The Shore Patrol took care of the sailors, from the gobs in boot camps to the battleships and sub-chasers of the Pacific Fleet at anchor in San Diego Bay. The Marine MP's on shore patrol took care of the leathernecks.

On a Saturday night, with countless bootleggers peddling rotgut whisky, the MP's and Shore Patrol had their hands full. San Diego's red light district, called the Stingaree, did a land office business, with the Navy and Army prophylactic stations keeping busy.

It so happened that on this particular Saturday night General Strong, Commander-in-Chief at Camp Kearney, was giving a blowout and formal dance at the U.S. Grant Hotel. San Diego's Mayor Wadham, state senators, and the army brass from Camp Kearney were in full attendance. By one o'clock the traffic was thinning out so I slowed down to the speed limit with the cavalry captain and a taxi-dancer in the front seat, and Starr and the sailor and another taxi-dancer in the rear seat. I cruised down Broadway and just as I passed the front entrance to the Grant Hotel a seven passenger Packard army car, painted olive-drab green, pulled away from the curb. A star pennant signifying a General's car was on the left front fender, and the smart-aleck sergeant driver gave no signal nor waited for the line of traffic to clear. The traffic on my left prevented me from turning, and there was no way of avoiding the Packard as it swung away from the curb. The heavy bumper of the Apperson raked the under front fender of the Packard, lifting it up with a metallic crash, and I had to step on the gas to rip clear. Once clear I gave the Apperson the gun.

The MP station was on the corner next door to the Grant Hotel, and two Ford paddy wagons stood at the curb. The smart-aleck sergeant driving General Strong's car was bearing down on the siren with which the car was equipped and soon the MP paddy wagon sirens added to the raucous chorus.

I made a right turn which would take me into Mission Canyon, and by the time I had reached the canyon I had left the Ford paddy wagons far behind. The cavalry lieutenant wanted out of the mess and I did not blame him, then the dance hall girls wanted out for fear of being pinched as prostitutes. I told them to hold their water while I cruised around Mission Hills, and then back to Old Town, past Ramona's Marriage Place, then along the back streets to the Dreamland Dance Hall just off Broadway. There I let the girls and the lieutenant out.

Just as I was pulling out from the curb, I sighted a cruising MP paddy wagon coming out of an alleyway. I had wanted to dump Sergeant Starr and the sailor, but Starr said he would not quit a man in a tight, and the gob said he was having the time of his life. The driver of the cruising paddy wagon must have recognized the tan Apperson and bore down on the siren, so I got the hell out of there. There were two cut-outs on the Apperson, one for each four cylinders, and I opened them both and the roar was like a racing car. I hit the coast highway and traveled at a cruising speed along Sunset Cliffs where I pulled up and got out, taking the flashlight from the glove compartment, to see what damage had been done to my father's car. There was no damage to the front fender, just a long smear of O.D. paint on the scratched front bumper. Sergeant Starr said he had gotten a quick look at the crumpled left fender of General Strong's official car, and the star pennant which was hanging at half-mast.

I turned the flashlight on the gob in the back seat, and he had apparently passed out. Starr wanted to slap the sleeping sailor around, and set him afoot, but I talked him out of the notion, saying I would drop him at the docks at the foot of Broadway, which I did. Then I conceived the crazy notion of playing one more game of tag with the MP's before I drove the Apperson home, and Starr had enough booze under his belt to agree with me. So I cruised around the Grant Hotel, and slowed down in front of the Brewster Hotel across the street where I had spotted a couple of white-collar civilians.

"Let's recruit the slacker bastards, Sarg," I said and stopped the Apperson, opened the door and got out.

Starr followed me out, and when the two civilians sighted us they must have realized what we were up to because they ran for it, so we gave it up as a bad job. When we got back to the Apperson there were two MP paddy wagons drawn up on either side, and a big MP sergeant sat behind the wheel of the Apperson.

"No damned MP drives my father's car!" I was just drunk enough to put up an argument as I yanked open the door and made a grab for him.

Then a big red-faced MP grabbed me from behind and another MP had Sergeant Starr in tow. They hauled both of us into the back seat, and drove the car to the MP Station, where a trimly built first lieutenant sat behind the desk, a military blond mustache on his upper lip. A pair of pale blue eyes looked us over from head to foot as if we were some garbage the dogs had dragged in.

"Sergeant Carver reporting, sir!" The beefy MP sergeant had hashmarks from here to hell and gone, and the way he saluted betrayed the old adage that it was the sergeants who won the battles while the generals won the wars.

"Two prisoners. One buck sergeant, one boy scout. The boy scout was driving the car!" He prodded me in the back with the end of his polished billy club to move me forward.

"Salute! Stand at attention!" he barked the order like an old-time drill sergeant.

I straightened up fast. Somebody had handed me my hat which had fallen off and I had it on straight, the white silk hatband a little soiled. I was not certain in my booze-fogged mind whether to stand bare-headed or keep my hat on. Not that it made a hell of lot of difference. My goose was cooked, regardless. I snapped to attention, and threw the desk sergeant a snappy salute I had learned at ground school. He kept me standing at attention while he asked my name, rank and where I was stationed.

"General Strong," he said, "commanding officer at Camp Kearney, has preferred charges of a grave nature against you, Cadet Coburn. Your preliminary hearing will be held at ten o'clock Monday morning. Have you anything to say for yourself, Cadet?"

"Yes, sir. I alone am to blame. Sergeant Starr from Rockwell Field had nothing to do with it."

The first lieutenant motioned to the sailor we had dropped at the foot of Broadway, and who was now standing at the back of the room.

"Seaman First Class Raymond, Sir!" he said as he saluted smoothly.

"At ease, sailor," said the lieutenant as he handed the gob a card and told him to fill in his intelligence report in the back room. The damned gob had moved in on our party as a naval intelligence man, and he slid me a grin as he passed.

"You slimy bastard," I said, wanting to take a poke at him. The first lieutenant gave me a grin. He was human after all.

"Empty your pockets, Cadet." I was told.

When I emptied my pockets there was that damned corkscrew. The first lieutenant's grin widened. Then the MP sergeant put me in the paddy wagon and headed for the guardhouse.

"The first step to Alcatraz, boy scout. That's where the Old Man's sending you!" he said with a chuckle.

This time I was in real trouble, thanks again to old man John Barleycorn.

The guardhouse was next door to the MP barracks, both large shedlike structures in the warehouse district of San Diego. All the windows in the guardhouse were barred like any other jail, and an armed sentry stood guard at the front door. The Apperson was in the parking lot between the guardhouse and the MP barracks.

Besides the desk sergeant there were half a dozen MP's with webbed-belt holstered Colt .45 automatics and polished hardwood billy clubs playing poker in the back room. They were tough looking regular army soldiers from the 21st Infantry, veterans of the Boxer Rebellion.

The desk sergeant who booked me was talking on the telephone. There was a sort of grin on his weathered face which deepened the crow's feet at the corner of his gray eyes.

"Yeah, the Apperson car is in the parking lot," he said over the phone. "I got the keys here on my desk... Yeah, Sergeant Bronski just fetched him in.... Okay I'll ask him. Call you back."

"Front and center, boy scout," the big sergeant ordered.

I stepped up and saluted while the desk sergeant looked me over with a look of amusement in his eyes, then made some notes on his pad.

"At ease, soldier!" he said. "What about the cavalry captain who was with you on the big joy ride? What's his name?"

"I don't know his name," I answered. "I'd never seen him before. I just picked him up. He had nothing to do with anything."

"How about the sergeant from Rockwell Field?" he asked.

"Sergeant Starr? He had nothing to do with anything that happened. I borrowed my father's Apperson car and furnished the booze I got from some bootlegger. I don't even know the name of the damn stool pigeon sailor who just moved in on us. I'm willing to take all the blame. All I ask is to get my father's car back to him without letting him know the mess I'm in."

"You're in one hell of a mess, no fooling," the desk sergeant told me. "General Strong's got it made to send you to the federal pen at Alcatraz Island."

"I gotta get back on the job if you're finished with me," the MP sergeant interrupted, and Bronski was told he could leave. As he passed me he said, "Good luck, boy scout. No hard feelings."

After Bronski left, the desk sergeant offered me a Camel which I took and thanked him.

"I'm off duty at six," he said. "I reckon we can manage it for you to drive your old man's car back home. You are booked to show up at seven-thirty A.M. today (Sunday) at the MP Headquarters. Your friend Sergeant Starr has been dismissed without charges. That gob you picked up belongs to the Navy Intelligence, and has filed his damned report."

The desk sergeant's name was Jim Coffee. He was from Albuquerque, New Mexico, where he had punched cows for one of the large cattle outfits, and when he found out I was from Montana, and a cowpuncher, we became good friends. It was now four-thirty by the clock on the wall, and I was put in the drunk tank. Jim Coffee said he would get me out at six A.M. when he got off duty, and he did.

There were about a dozen drunken soldiers in the bull pen, and when one of them made a crack about me being a boy scout, I was not about to stand hitched for it like I had had to do from the MP. So we tangled. I had the drunken bastard whipped when the others in the tank grabbed and held me, letting the drunk get in a couple of Sunday punches. Just then Sergeant Coffee showed up and let me out. He showed me the washroom and can, and I got my bloody nose stopped, my face washed and my clothes tidied.

Once I got behind the wheel of the Apperson with Coffee alongside in the front seat, I was in fairly good shape, considering what I had been through. I did not intend for my father to find the nearly empty bottle in the glove compartment, so I took it out and handed it to Sergeant Coffee, who uncorked it and we both had a drink. I needed a few snorts for a brave-maker to face my father and stand the gaff at the MP Headquarters. That big belt chased away the butterflies, horseflies and yellow jackets which were having a field day in my empty belly.

I got a lucky break when I drove the Apperson into the open garage. My father was still asleep and my mother was preparing breakfast. I made up a lie about being temporarily transferred to March Field near Riverside where I expected to be stationed for a month or two. Then Sergeant Coffee and I walked the block to the MP paddy wagon waiting to take us back to town. I had shoved the empty bottle deep into the garbage can at the back door of our house where no one would find it.

Back at headquarters the same first lieutenant was there. He had me stand at attention while he read off seven charges on my arrest slip. I was charged with hit and run driving, colliding with General Strong's official automobile, evading arrest, drunkenness, resisting arrest, engaging in a fist fight with another prisoner in the guardhouse, and with disorderly conduct unbecoming to an officer of cadet status.

I was told to report to Colonel Harvey Burwell, Commanding Officer at Rockwell Field, then to Captain Dunnington, adjutant to Colonel Burwell. I was handed a sealed envelope containing my wallet, wrist watch, and the tell-tale corkscrew which had gotten me into this disgraceful situation.

"You are released from MP custody," the desk sergeant told me. "But when you leave here you are ordered to go straight to the dock and take the first shore boat to North Island. Dismissed!"

I saluted, about-faced, and went out the door and headed down Broadway to the docks to board the first Star and Crescent launch to North Island. I duly reported to my squadron commander, then to the adjutant's office in the Headquarters Building. Captain Dunnington was a typical West Pointer who went strictly according to the book. He kept me standing at attention, ramrod-backed and eyes front to what seemed eternity, while he read my seven count arrest slip and chewed me out.

First I was reduced in rank from a flying cadet to private first class, confined three months to quarters except in line of duty, and fined three months pay except for a five dollar monthly canteen ticket. By my drunk and disorderly conduct in public, I was unfit to become an officer and gentleman in the United States Army.

"For as long as I am stationed at Rockwell Field," Dunnington told me, "you will never be given the status of a commissioned officer in the United States Army. If you apply yourself and keep a good conduct record there is a possibility of your being promoted to sergeant. If you pass the written examinations of sergeant first class, you have a possible chance of again retaining your flying status as a non-commissioned officer. It will be left entirely up to you to get your wings. You are lucky General Strong dropped his first orders of a formal court martial in favor of company punishment by Colonel Burwell."

When at long last Captain Dunnington dismissed me, he gave

me my final orders .I was to get my foot locker and barracks bag from the Cadet Squadron Building and report to the commanding officer of B Squadron, to be assigned my tent and bunk in that unit. On Monday morning I was to report to the officer in charge of the Field and Hangar Division. Then I was dismissed. Dismissed! I was sure as hell dismissed in every sense of the word. Once again I had been knocked out of the ring by the champ, Kid Barleycorn.

There went my two gold bars of a second looey, the silver wings I had won and lost overnight, the brand new, never worn cordovan boots which had set me back fifty bucks, and the black and gold cord hatband. I removed the soiled white silk hatband and replaced it with the orange and purple cord of a private first class. But I had escaped the black disgrace of a dishonorable discharge for which I owed thanks to Colonel Harvey Burwell.

I was told that if I behaved myself for the three months I was confined to the Island and kept my nose clean, I would be made a sergeant first class and get back on flying status. And this is exactly what I accomplished during those long summer months of confinement. The written examinations for sergeant first class were tough, requiring knowledge of airplane motors, and tougher than the exams at ground school at Berkeley. But by then I had wised up on a lot of things, including slipping five bucks to the sergeant in charge of the printing department for a precious copy of the test. I needed to bone up on the correct answers, but was careful to get only a passing mark.

During that first week I wrote my mother that I was *back* at Rockwell Field, and would be unable to leave North Island for a month or so because of duty.

At ground school I had met the World's Olympic Champion Swimmer, Norman Ross, who was now a Second Lieutenant Cadet Instructor in command of the 36th Cadet Squadron. He was a six-footer, with jet-black hair, and for some infraction of Army Regulations he was confined to Rockwell Field like myself. On a Saturday or Sunday he would put on his bathing suit, put a few silver dollars in an empty Bull Durham sack tied to the string of his dog tag, and walk out to the sandspit connecting North Island to Coronado Island. He would swim out in the Pacific beyond range of the sentry guards and spend the day swimming with friends on the famous Coronado Beach.

I had learned to swim in the wide Missouri River in Montana as a kid, using the breast and side strokes. Norman Ross taught me the Australian Crawl, but when I tried to follow him I was unable to keep that black head in sight and slowed him down waiting for me to catch up. After a few times I did not want to embarrass the famous Olympic champ swimmer and gave it up. Besides he was an officer who had his select group of friends while I was only an enlisted non-com.

But there was Earl Kyle whose father owned the salt water swimming pool at San Diego, where his older son taught swimming. Earl had washed out at ground school and he and I were tent mates at B Squadron. He had been swimming since he was knee high to a hoptoad and while in high school had broken a few amateur swimming records. So on a couple of weekends we would put on our bathing suits and swim around the sentry on the sandspit to Coronado Beach and Tent City where a number of San Diego families rented tents. We would spend the day there, swimming back at sunset. But I decided it was not worth the risk of being caught, and gave it up after a couple of times.

My three months' confinement were June, July and August. By October I was back on flying status, sergeant first class in charge of the Field and Hangar Division under a second lieutenant commanding officer. With weekend passes I would go home and drive the Apperson, taking my parents for long drives in the country with their friends, since I was now walking the straight and narrow with no drinking.

Then came the deadly Spanish Influenza epidemic which took devastating toll of life throughout the entire country. Army, Marine and Navy boot camps were hard hit along with the civilian population. My father, Robert Coburn, then 83 years of age, died of pneumonia caused by the flu.

While I somehow managed to escape the Spanish Influenza, I had a close brush with death one day when I walked away from my second forced landing on a cross country flight to Imperial Valley. The trip over the mountains bucking a head wind had emptied the gas tank of the Jennie, and I had made a dead-stick landing in the desert at the foot of the mountains, with Sergeant First Class Starr in the back cockpit, and for a minute or two it was a little hairy.

So with my brother, Harold, an infantry soldier in the trenches somewhere in the Argonne Forest, and me flying by the seat of my government britches in a crate which had too many hours on its OX5 motor, both of us were living on borrowed time. At the suggestion of my half brother, Bob, my father, after providing for my mother in his will, left the rest of his estate to Bob with the provision he would take care of Harold and myself when the war ended and we were back in civilian life, which, of course, he never did.

Then came Armistice Day, and with it all my hope of ever going overseas washed down the drain. On March 30, 1919, all the squadrons at Rockwell Field were due to be discharged. As sergeant first class I had a pass to live at home at night, catching an early streetcar, and taking the shore boat to North Island each morning. The morning of March 30 I decided to travel in style so I took the Apperson in time to catch the Coronado ferry, and drive the sandspit to Rockwell Field to line up with the rest of B squadron to receive my discharge.

On the way I sighted Major Smith, adjutant to Colonel H. H. (Hap) Arnold, the commanding officer at Rockwell Field, as he waited for the early streetcar, so I stopped and picked him up. We caught the early ferry to Coronado, and Major Smith said he would like to stop at the Del Coronado Hotel for a few minutes. His few minutes lengthened into fifteen, then thirty minutes before he hurried out, saying he was sorry for the delay, and that if I was late for formation to tell my squadron commander that he had delayed me, and he would telephone him at the adjutant's office to verify it.

I dropped him at the headquarters building and drove down the main street past the squadron street, and before I had gone far I noticed that all the squadron streets were deserted, empty of any soldiers. Every tent was empty save the first tent house of the squadron commander. When I parked the car and went in, Sergeant Englebrect sat at his typewriter. He was the one guy in Rockwell whose guts I hated, and it was mutual. He gave me one of his nasty, nice smiles and said:

"You're in for a bad time, Sergeant Coburn. Lieutenant Coolidge is fit to skin you alive."

"To hell with you, you keewee bastard," I said as I walked past him.

The tent flap to Lieutenant Coolidge's tent was open. I marched in and saluted, standing at attention.

"Sergeant Coburn reporting, sir," I said.

Lieutenant Coolidge, enlisted for the duration, had been a tool dresser in a Douglas Aircraft factory in civilian life, a pompous bastard desk officer without wings. He had me stand at attention while he bawled me out for being the only soldier in B squadron half an hour late for his discharge. He would have gone forever and a day chewing me out had he not been interrupted by the phone ringing.

"Yes sir! . . . Sergeant Coburn is here in my tent . . . Reported half an hour late for . . . Yes sir . . . Yes sir . . . I understand sir . . . His joweled face was red as a beet when he hung up.

"Why in hell didn't you tell me you had Major Smith in your car and he made you late for your discharge?"

"You never gave me a chance to explain the cause of my delay, sir," I said.

"At ease, sergeant!" Lieutenant Coolidge spoke in a milder tone.

He picked up a typed letter from the pile on his desk and said with a thin smile:

"Captain Slattery, Commanding Flight Officer, has recommended you for a second lieutenancy and a transfer to Kelly Field, Texas, for a six months course at Garrison School to complete your studies in aviation, providing you wish to continue your army career."

He handed me the letter of recommendation and I glanced at it briefly. I was remembering the three times during the past year and a half that I had passed the examinations posted on the bulletin board and Captain Dunnington had refused to sign my papers. The last time was for a second lieutenancy in the Philippine Scouts. I had applied just for the hell of it. I recalled Captain Dunnington's words that as long as he was in the army I would never be a commissioned officer. Now standing at attention I spoke my piece.

"If you have my discharge papers on your desk, sir!"

Lieutenant Coolidge handed them, signed by Colonel H. H. Arnold, to me, together with a check for $173.80 which included a $60.00 bonus. I took it and saluted, about-faced smartly and left the tent, thumbing my nose at Sergeant Englebrect as I passed. I got behind the wheel of the Apperson, gunned the motor, opened both cutouts and drove the sandspit road to Coronado.

With my honorable discharge from the U.S. Army and the letter of recommendation from my good friend Captain Jack Slattery, West Pointer, in my pocket, my eyes felt a little itchy in the morning sunlight. I had been a day late and a dollar short on the day of my discharge, and that was part of the story of my misspent life.

I was free, white and twenty-nine years of age, flat broke and back in civilian life. On the first day of May I got off the train at Prescott, Arizona, to take a forty-a-month cowpunching job on a large cow outfit in Blooody Basin owned by my two half brothers, Will and Bob Coburn. I had sold my saddle when I went into the army so Will took me to Frank Olzer's Saddle Shop where I bought a second-hand saddle for twenty-five bucks, charged to my account. I still had my old high-heeled Hyer boots which had a lot of wear left, and my brush-scarred, batwing chaps and spurs, but that was all. I loaded my outfit into the old beatup Haynes car which Will was driving. Alpheus Favour, attorney for the Coburn Cattle Company, went along with us to spend a week on the spring calf roundup. We left Prescott at daybreak, headed for the Horseshoe Ranch in Bloody Basin, over a bumpy mountain road, and on the way we busted a rear spring.

When we got to the ranch Will gave me a green bronc to ride, and we started for the roundup camp about fifteen or twenty miles from the ranch headquarters in the heart of the rough country. We were about halfway there when Will sighted a big two-year-old maverick bull and took after him. He was one of the few cowhands in Arizona who still took his dally wraps instead of tying hard and fast to the saddle horn, and he was one of the best ropers I have ever known. He always rode top cow horses and he was riding a fast Steeldust quarter horse which overtook the big maverick in nothing flat. Will caught him on the first loop, but for some reason lost his dally winds and lost his rope. He shouted for me to head him off, and I took after the bull, and got into a pile-up. Tied hard and fast to the saddle horn the bull went over a brushy cutbank, dragging me and my horse after him. I wound up with a busted kneecap, fifteen miles from the ranch. At the time we thought my knee was just out of joint so I lay on the ground while Attorney Alf Favour held me under the arms and Will pulled on the leg to try and snap it back into place, but they soon gave it up as a bad job. Since it was my left leg that was stiff, I had to use the right, the Injun side, to crawl into the saddle. The bronc was gentle enough to ride, but he kept walling the white of an eye at my leg, which stuck out where it should not be as I sat half-assed in the saddle, leaning my weight in the right stirrup.

Will had ridden ahead to get the old Haynes in shape to take me to Prescott as there were slow leaks in both rear tires. Alf Favour rode beside me on the way in. When I felt a dizzy spell coming, I pulled my right foot out of the stirrup and keeled over sideways, and hit the ground with a jarring jolt, and Alf had to help me back in the saddle. It was nearly sundown when we got to the ranch house, and I was put in the back seat of the Haynes with my game leg propped up on the lumpy cushions and Favour drove the car to town. Talk about the rocky road to Dublin, it was a paved highway compared to that rocky, rutted mountain road.

Dr. Looney, considered the best cow country doctor in Arizona, took X-rays of my bum knee which revealed the kneecap broken straight across. It would be a week or ten days before the swelling reduced enough to operate. It was after the operation ten days later that I got the verdict from that wise cow country doctor.

"Your cowpunching days are over," he told me. "You can't make a brush-popper cowhand in Bloody Basin or anywhere else. Hard lines, son!"

Thus ended my career as a cowhand. Twenty-nine years old and set afoot. A stove-up cripple in the prime of life, cut into the culls. Everything shot to hell. A mess of pottage at the end of the rainbow . . . Those were the bitter thoughts which haunted my nights like a black nightmare as I lay in the hospital bed at St. Mary's Hospital in Prescott. Then I quit feeling sorry for myself and took stock of what I had left out of the wreck. I could always whittle out a tin bill and head for the manure pile with the roosters. Hell, I had not wanted to work for my two much older half brothers in the first place, getting the crappy end of the stick. I had had a bellyful of their treatment of me at the Circle C Rranch in Montana, and over on the San Carlos Reservation. If I had not been broke in San Diego I would never have tackled it in the first place. That busted kneecap had set me afoot, so what the hell! I would manage somehow.

Came the day when they sawed off the knee cast and I could hobble around on crutches. Will bought me a ticket to San Diego, and gave me fifty bucks for expense money, generous as hell for a million dollar cow outfit. It was then and there when I boarded the train that I made my decision to be on my own. To hell with my half brothers and their handouts of chicken feed. I vowed never to take another nickel from them, and I kept that promise.

I was glad to get back to San Diego and my mother's house. I limbered up my stiff kneejoint at the Los Banos Swimming Pool at

Walt, right, with Chinese cook at Parker, Arizona survey camp, 1920

the foot of Broadway, and in a few weeks I could walk without a cane. I got a job as a civilian at Rockwell Field, North Island, assembling a lot of crated Jennies shipped from the factory. The job paid a hundred and fifty a month. My boss was my friend, former Sergeant First Class Conomy, now a civilian. A two-man crew was assigned to each plane, and we started from scratch, taking the fuselage and wings from the crate. My crewmate was former Sergeant Starr, now a civilian.

For an added bonus the employed civilians had access to the commissary store, army surplus clothing and blankets, tobacco, cigarettes, Hershey bars, toothpaste, shaving cream and medical supplies, plus food, all below wholesale prices in San Diego. I kept my mother's kitchen well-stocked with canned foods of every sort.

During the year I saved enough money for a grubstake, and purchased an almost new second-hand Model T Ford. Then we were laid off from that job and I managed to get a job as civilian night watchman because there were no longer soldiers stationed at Rockwell Field. It paid a hundred and twenty-five a month and this cushy job lasted about six months until a squadron of soldiers moved in. I then landed a job managing a garage at Del Mar, California, for fifty bucks a month and board at the Stratford Inn which owned the garage. I had one assistant mechanic, and we bunked in a loft in the garage. During the summer months I filled in as an extra lifeguard on the hotel beach. Meanwhile I had applied for a civil service job as railway mail clerk. I had been working at the garage for more than a year when I was called for mail clerk duty. I only worked two weeks at the Los Angeles railway depot post office before being transferred to Albuquerque, New Mexico. My run was from Albuquerque to Needles, California, where I deadheaded back to Albuquerque. I was supposed to study "throwing" cards for the City of Los Angeles, but I failed to keep up with my studies. I received notice at the end of four months to report to Los Angeles for my examination, but knowing I would fail to pass, I used my railway pass to ride the cushions to San Diego. I managed to get my old job back at the Del Mar Garage. In the meantime, I sent in my resignation as railway mail clerk along with my books. Before I quit I loaned my two keys which unlocked the registered mail sacks to my roommate, Fred Ferdelli. He was also a railway mail clerk, and lived at the YMCA, in Los Angeles. He mailed them to me at Del Mar, and I promptly sent them to P. I. Moore, Postal Inspector, at the Los Angeles Post Office.

A few days later Moore showed up at the garage and began cross-questioning me about the delay in forwarding my two keys to him. I explained how I had loaned them to Ferdelli. Then Moore informed me that there had been a mail robbery during the period my keys had not been turned in, and the mail robber had used keys to unlock the registered mail pouches. He told me I was under suspicion of being in cahoots with the captured mail robber, but in cross-examining him he had not implicated me. I proved my alibi by the garage mechanic, Chic Evans, and the manager of the Stratford Inn, regarding the dates and hours I had been at the garage. So I was in the clear and Moore caught the train back to Los Angeles.

That evening when I went to supper, the hotel manager called me into his office. As usual he had been hitting the bottle, and when he started accusing me of mail robbery and being a suspicious character, I blew up and quit. I then went back to San Diego and began reading the want ads.

A reliable man was wanted for a survey outfit at Parker, Arizona, preferably one with experience as a rod and chain man. The ad stated for the applicant to report to Mr. Boudineau at the U.S. Grant Hotel, giving the room number. I lost no time in applying for the job, and got it. It paid one hundred and twenty-five a month. The survey was on the Mojave Indian Reservation near Parker. We lived in tent houses, and there was a large mess hall with a Chinese cook. The survey crew, the powerhouse crew and the construction crew building the ditch we were surveying, shared the grub bill, and Mr. Boudineau did the purchasing of the food supplies. It averaged each man about five dollars a month, and we lived high on the hog.

That Chink cook was one of the best camp cooks that ever came down the pike. The tent houses were free, as were the army cots and army blankets, with a Sibly army stove for heat which burned the plentiful mesquite wood.

The survey job lasted nine months, and then I got the ditch-rider's job on the irrigation canal which furnished water to the Mojave Indians and white farmers, including the Goodrich Tire Company's cotton land. Riding a beat-up Model T flivver along the wide canal banks, I would open the sluice gates, measuring the alloted water to each farmer and cotton field. This job lasted another six months.

It was during my stay at Parker, Arizona, on the Colorado River Mojave Indian Reservation that the Señor Dios laid His hand on my shoulder, to change the destiny of my entire future life.

My boyhood dreams of one day owning my own cow outfit had been shattered when I busted my kneecap at Bloody Basin, and the cow country doctor told me my cowpunching days were over. My life as a cowboy had ended.

Nothing other than a modern miracle by Almighty God could save my destiny, and out of a blue sky on a Sunday afternoon this miracle came to pass. Perhaps somewhere in my subconscious mind there had been that silent prayer. I had no way of knowing then or now. But the hand of God, who wrought such miracles, decided my destiny in a strange and devious manner.

CHAPTER 12

$25 for the First One

ON THIS SUNDAY AFTERNOON I was lazing around in my tent with a beat-up copy of *Adventure Magazine*, reading a western fiction story with a critical eye. There were enough mistakes to convince me the writer did not savvy anything about cowpunching. It was only after I had finished the yarn, which had enough plot and character delineation to make good reading in spite of my biased opinion, that I looked to find the name of the author. The story was written by Robert J. Horton, and this surely rang a bell.

The author was the same old friend and drinking companion I had known back in Great Falls, Montana. The same Bob Horton who was sports editor for the *Great Falls Tribune*, with a daily column under the by-line of "Sporticus." I had been completely out of touch with Bob for a number of years, and had no idea he had started writing western fiction.

Re-reading the story, I was vaguely reminded of one of the windies I had spilled to Bob when in our cups at the Mint Saloon. The nucleus of the plot was the same.

According to my boneheaded cowhand way of thinking, if an Eastern tenderfoot like my old friend Horton could bat out a fiction story about my own cow country, I certainly could do the same. I spent the rest of that afternoon writing a lengthy letter to Bob in care of *Adventure*, asking his advice regarding my tackling writing a western fiction yarn, informing him that my cowpunching days were over.

The following week I received a lengthy letter from Bob, now living in New York, encouraging me to start writing without delay. When Bob Horton was enthusiastic about anything he was like a prairie fire backed by a forty mile wind. He said the only way to start was to get at it; borrow or steal a typewriter, buy a ream of good bond paper, a ream of second sheets and a box of carbon paper. He enclosed the carbon copy of one of his stories he had just sold, to give me a working example.

I was instructed to send him a copy of my manuscript for his criticism and blue-penciling, informing me in no uncertain terms that I was his protégé from then on, that it was the interesting letters I wrote him from the Circle C Ranch which gave him the idea of writing western stories, and it was because of those letters and our talks in the Mint Saloon that he was now sitting on top of the world. He told me that I was a natural storyteller, and that I had a way with words, predicting in his outgoing exuberance that someday, if I could weather the storm of rejection slips, I would climb the rungs to the top of the ladder of success.

It was this first letter from Robert J. Horton which launched me on the rough and rocky road as a writer of western fiction for the pulp magazines. Something of his absolute confidence in my unproven ability as a writer, along with his buoyant enthusiasm, must have rubbed off on me because it has lasted throughout many long years.

The first letter from old Sporticus marked the beginning of a somewhat sporadic correspondence between us which was as unpredictable as the weather, until his untimely death some years later. In his letters there was invariably some sage advice, along with caustic criticism of a manuscript, but the barbed words were always blunted by his dry humor. I regret that those letters Bob Horton wrote me have been lost in my travels. But some of his advice, given in that first letter, has stuck in my memory like a sandburr to a saddle blanket.

For example, the few rules he laid down at the beginning, long before I sold my first story are: "Buy a copy of Roget's *Thesaurus* and study it as you would a text book. Quit reading western stories of any kind, because no present-day writer of western fiction knows as much about the cow country as you do and reading their stories would only confuse you. Read every story written by O. Henry, because he has mastered the art and craftsmanship of the short story. Read the books and stories of Jack London, because red meat is in everything he writes. Also read the books of Joseph Conrad. Study the style of these authors, then forget the stories, and soon you will develop your own style without being aware of it.

"Live each story as you write it. Live the part of your characters. Let your characters work for you to develop the story as you dream it out. Set your working schedule at four hours each day, the limit of creative writing. Any hour after four or five will be forced writing and apt to be wooden. Let your first copy tell the story. Do not attempt any rewrite or polishing, or you are apt to ruin the yarn.

"Once you get onto the ropes with your two-finger hunt-and-peck system on the typewriter, you should make a fairly clean first copy, and be able to knock out two thousand words a day. And remember that every time a manuscript is returned with a rejection slip, it will be a blow, but also a hard-earned lesson, because the story is lacking in some way, shape or form. So read it over carefully, find out what is wrong. Don't try to rewrite the rejected story. Start a new yarn. Let each rejection slip count as a lesson and profit by it. The school of rejection slips is one of hard knocks, and it will take all the guts you have to make the grade, but you do have the gift of a natural writer and all hell and high water will not stop you from reaching the top."

Those were some of the rules set down by Bob Horton, a newspaper man of the old school, and one of the best writers of western pulp fiction of his era. I took his advice in every rule he set down for me to follow, as mentor, guide, philosopher and friend in need. Thanks to him, I had the courage to continue on through the several years of my writing career before I sold my first story.

My job at Parker, Arizona, petered out, and I was now back in Del Mar working in the hotel garage while acting as part-time lifeguard on the beach. It was during those lean years that I got tossed around and almost gored on the sharp horns of a dilemma, and like the matador in the bullring, I faced the moment of truth. Now at the beginning of my writing career it seems I came face to face with one of the most crucial and monumental decisions of my life.

I was earning fifty dollars a month plus room and board at the employees' dining room at the hotel, and sleeping quarters in the cubbyhole loft of the garage. During the summer I earned ten dollars extra for lifeguard duty in the afternoons. This was all on the credit side of the ledger.

On the debit side, every month on the exact date I paid thirty-five bucks on a second-hand Model T one-seater runabout which I had bought from a used car dealer called Honest John. I had bought this when I was a civilian employee at Rockwell Field, North Island. An additional five bucks were paid on a beat-up Oliver typewriter I was renting from a local realtor. And there was the ream of bonded manuscript paper, a ream of second sheets, and a box of carbon paper, together with large mailing envelopes (with return postage to be enclosed) to drain the nickles and pennies. So, even during the summer with the added ten bucks for lifeguard duty, it was very slim pickings. I did my laundry in the garage, and used discarded bathing suits for underwear.

After two years of writing with nothing but rejection slips to show for it, being flat broke at the end of each month, a prayer and high hopes went out with each manuscript seemingly fore-ordained to return with a printed rejection slip. Each took a heavy toll. Licking my wounds for a day or two, I walked the long stretch of sandy beach, swimming out through the breakers and staying out until I was pooped, then riding in on a big comber. Summer and winter, every day regardless of weather, peasoup fog or rain, it was good medicine. Then after a time, when the dreams returned, I would bat out another beginner's masterpiece.

It was sometime in December with another sad and sorry dead-broke Christmas coming up, and two more rejection slips to add to my collection of failures, that my future prospects as a writer loomed bleak and barren. I had put on my bathing suit and worked out, chinning myself on the horizontal bar at the bath house, then shadow-boxing and trotting the deserted beach, before swimming out. I wrestled around with a mess of kelp to warm up for the swim through the breakers and around the long pier where Al Howarth, the engineer at the powerhouse, bundled up in mackinaw, cast his line to catch fish for his female cat and her litter of kittens. John Bludworth, the tall, grizzled deputy sheriff, was there to keep Al company, both sharing the secret opinion that I had lost a few marbles to swim on a cold rainy day in the ice cold ocean, with winter riptides cutting a wide channel.

Once that first chill was gone, it was much warmer in the ocean than on the cold end of the pier. Then too, I was swimming off the results of rejection slips, but the two men on the pier did not know that.

Oftentimes I would ride out in the back country with Les Zuerner, who had the rural mail route contract, leaving the garage in charge of the mechanic, Chick Evans. He did the repairs of the automobiles and had done several hitches in the U.S. Cavalry, and we got along first rate.

On this particular morning I rode out with Les in his old Packard, and I sensed that he had something on his mind besides his hat. He had some sort of proposition he wanted to lay on the line, but did not quite know how to approach it. Working as he did in the Del Mar post office, helping his father-in-law, the postmaster, he was aware of every returned manuscript which came back to me to roost. Finally he dropped the bombshell.

"How would you like to make a thousand dollars?" he asked, right out of the cold overcast sky.

It sure caught me off balance, and I figured Les must be ribbing me.

"Robbing the United States Mail," I answered, "is a federal rap. But if there's a Chinaman's chance, I'm your huckleberry, Les." And so help me Judas, I halfway meant what I said. "You're talking to one of Butch Cassidy's Wild Bunch," I added.

"Nothing like that," Les said hastily.

The idea of robbing his father-in-law's post office rather shocked him.

"No larceny involved, Walt. A thousand bucks clear. That's the solid truth. I'm not kidding you. Cash on the barrelhead. Money is of no concern to this millionaire."

"What's the deal, Les?" I asked.

I knew a man would not be handed a thousand smackers without earning it. I was looking for the skunk in the woodpile, for there was bound to be a badger game somewhere with this old country boy holding the dirty end of the stick. But a thousand bucks was a thousand bucks, and I was willing to take a few chances.

"Whether you take or leave it," Les lowered his voice to a confidential tone, "what I'm going to tell you goes no farther, understand?"

"You have my word on it. Want me to cross my heart and spit into the wind?"

"Might be a good idea at that," Les sounded serious as hell. "Maybe you've read in the newspapers about monkey glands being transplanted into humans?"

"Monkey glands, goat glands," I agreed, a little puzzled.

A recent Sunday section of the *Los Angeles Examiner* had devoted a full-page detailed account of the latest discovery in medical science. It was called a boon to aging manhood, a surgeon's answer to the fabled Fountain of Youth, still in the experimental stage, although some doctor had claimed success.

Les had pulled off the road after he had completed his rural mail route. He killed the motor on a high bluff overlooking the Pacific Ocean, rolled a Bull Durham cigarette, and I followed suit. I remember it was one of those bleak days with low fog blanketing the sea.

It was high tide, and the booming surf as the breakers broke against the sandstone cliffs and caves below had an ominous sound.

In that fog-bound solitude my good friend, Les Zuerner, laid it on the line. Stripped of its excess verbiage, this was the gist of the proposition he outlined as confidential spokesman for the "other half" of the experiment.

A well-known and highly reputable surgeon had been specializing in the transplanting of goat and monkey glands to humans over a period of a dozen years. In his own private clinic this M.D. had gone a step further in his scientific research. He had learned to transplant human glands with proof of benefit to the sterile recipient, and no harm whatever to the donor.

Les then revealed the fact that for the past week or more, I had been under critical observation, and had passed the test as to physical fitness. Les had been chosen to broach me on this delicate subject. He handed me a large manila envelope, saying it contained various medical articles, documented over the years regarding gland transplants. This envelope, the kind long familiar to my gaze as containing rejected manuscripts, was indeed an ironical touch.

"The doctor guarantees the operation will not deprive you of your manhood if you live to be a hundred," Les announced convincingly. "And you'll be paid a thousand bucks, with nobody but me and you and the doctor and the other family the wiser. You got till day after tomorrow to think it over. In case you turn them down, they'll have to find another man. You can best decide after you read the proof of this doctor's success in this field."

On the way back I was sweating from every pore under my heavy sweater in spite of the cold, bleak day, holding onto the envelope like it contained nitroglycerine, as well as my future destiny as a writer of western fiction. With a thousand-dollar grubstake I could hole up somewhere and devote all my time to writing. With a thousand bucks the deciding factor, I knew I could make the grade. It was a windfall, the answer to a writer's prayer and wishful dreams, my writing career assured. These and other confusing thoughts milled around inside my skull on that ride back to the hotel garage.

Day after tomorrow was the deadline, and during the long day and night hours I went through a period of anguished indecision. Sleep was hard to come by, and I walked the deserted beach night and day. I am not ashamed to admit that I prayed to God to help me make a decision during those black hours at night. The following day I received another rejected manuscript from Street and Smith which added to the gloom. Meanwhile I read and re-read the medical report.

I had given my word not to divulge the secret which now hung around my neck like the dead albatross of the Ancient Mariner, so there was no one I could confide in.

I went for a long swim around the pier that night when every star in the moonlit sky lent a faint glow to the white sands, I let the riptide carry me out in its path and it landed me about a mile north of the sandstone cliffs where Les had parked his car that morning a hundred years ago. An hour in the cold water and angling through the rip had winded me and left me chilled to the bone. Exhausted, I lay on my back on the cold damp sand and made a promise to the Creator of mankind from Whose mold I was made whole and unblemished. The following morning I found Les loading the rural mail into his pickup, and gave him my answer.

"Tell that millionaire to get another boy," I told him as I handed over the envelope, thus ridding myself of the dead albatross.

I learned later than an Australian fighter agreed to this proposition for the same price offered me plus a one-way steamship ticket to Sydney. The operation was a total failure and a lawsuit ensued. As I read the news account of the charges, the dread feeling came that I was reading the obituary of a fine athlete, and that there but for the grace of God, went I. It was an eerie feeling like someone had just walked across my grave.

Meanwhile, it was on my daily trips to the Del Mar post office that I met Lee Shippey, a newspaperman and war correspondent recently returned from France. It was an informal introduction of comparing rejection slips which marked the beginning of a lifetime friendship. Shortly after that meeting, Lee went to work for the *Los Angeles Times*, and for many years had his own column, "The Lee Side o' L.A."

He was at the Del Mar post office when, instead of a returned manuscript, I was handed a letter with "Munsey Publications" stamped on the envelope. It was from the editor, Bob Davis, acknowledging receipt of a short story I had sent *Argosy Magazine* entitled "The Peace Treaty of the Seven Up." The letter stated that *Argosy* had accepted the story and would pay me $25 for it, but being an unknown author they would require some identification.

CHAPTER 13

More Money—Good Advice

AFTER TWO LONG YEARS of negative reports, it was almost impossible to find words to express my emotions that day. I was sitting on top of the world. I had at long last made the grade. I was too choked up to trust my voice as I handed the letter to Lee Shippey to read, and this kindly newspaperman, with his deep understanding of human nature, read my thoughts and shared my unbounded happiness as he shook hands and thumped me between the shoulder blades. I felt like hollering the glad tiding out loud, and doing an Injun war dance, but instead I stood tracked, grinning like a first grader with a gold star on his report card.

Lee Shippey explained that *Argosy* needed this identification because occasionally frustrated writers were known to copy verbatim another author's published story. Suddenly I remembered Bob Horton who sold stories to Munsey and could identify me. I rushed back to the powerhouse and knocked out a letter to him on the old second-hand Oliver.

The following is quoted from the letter Bob Horton wrote to Robert H. Davis of Munsey's, dated Great Falls, Montana, March 25, 1922.

> My friend Walter J. Coburn, of Del Mar, California, writes me that he has sold you people a story and given me as reference. All I can say is that he's been trying for a year and a half, and I'm surprised he didn't break in before. He's OK. His father owned the largest cattle outfit in Montana in the

days when it was a cattle state. Walter rode the range when it was good, and he's still young. I've read some of his stuff and when his characters talk range talk they spill the genuine thing. If anybody is entitled to write western stories he is, and I hope he climbs to the top of the grade.

Selling my first story was all the encouragement I needed. In my cowboy ignorance, I firmly believed I had it made. The sun had risen on my success. But it was a false dawn, because it was about six months before I sold my next story to *Western Story Magazine*, a Street and Smith publication. I then received a letter from the editor, F. E. Blackwell, asking to see another story of mine, as if he had not read the dozen or more which had been returned by *Western Story* with a printed rejection slip, and perhaps he had not. He bought my next story, a novelette of twelve thousand words, for a cent and a half per word.

This put me in the chips. I quit my job at Del Mar and headed for Santa Barbara where I rented a small cottage near the old mission. I was soon selling enough stories to pay the rent and grub.

In a moment of desperation I had signed up with one of several correspondence schools of short story writing. I paid them five dollars a month, and sent them manuscripts for criticism. I then sent the corrected manuscripts to different pulp magazines. All came home to roost. I still owed the school fifty dollars when I went to Santa Barbara. These books on short story writing were on a bookshelf in the living room when I received a telegram from Bob Horton saying he was due to arrive in Santa Barbara on a certain day, and I met him at the train as he requested.

It was during the prohibition era, and I had bought a pint of prescription whisky at the drug store. Because it was about all I could afford in those lean years, I also bought a pound of round steak, a few potatoes and a can of corn.

During the time I had known Bob Horton as a sports editor for the *Tribune* in Great Falls, he was always a fancy dresser, in tailored suit and well-barbered. The last word I received from him was that he was batching in a log cabin at Logging Creek, Belts, Montana. He was there to "get atmosphere" when the first snow fell for a story he was writing entitled "Till the Wolves Come Home." He had enclosed a snapshot of himself dressed in long wool sox, high-laced boots and a flannel shirt, and these were the clothes he now wore when he stepped off the day coach in Santa Barbara, plus a mackinaw coat and woolen cap with the earflaps turned up. He needed a haircut and shave and looked for all the world like a lanky, dead-broke lumberjack with a hangover. And that is exactly how he was, down to the loose change in the pockets of a soiled pair of army issue riding breeches. There was a sprinkling of gray in his untrimmed hair. His only luggage was a large brown paper bag which held a Gillette razor, a shaving stick, a toothbrush, a tube of toothpaste, a new pair of long wool sox and a union suit. His long-legged stride was a cocky swagger, and he had a grin on his lantern-jawed face with its three-day's stubble of wiry whiskers. As always, there was an amused sardonic twinkle in his eyes.

About a month earlier, Bob Horton had sent me a wire announcing his arrival, with instructions to reserve a suite of front rooms at the expensive Samarkand Hotel, but he failed to appear. Now here he was a month later. It was a chilly day in November when I took him to my small one-bedroom cottage. I built a fire in the fireplace, and broke the seal on that pint of whisky. Horton had a habit of walking the floor when relating one of his colorful stories. I was in the kitchen peeling spuds for pan frying and occasionally I would go into the living room where we would have a drink.

As Bob paced the floor he tossed something into the fireplace and the blaze would flare up. I paid no attention until in passing the bookcase I saw his gesturing arm flick out and toss one of the correspondence school books into the fire.

"What the hell are you doing, Bob?" I demanded. "I still owe $50 on those books."

"Trash!" Bob spoke contemptuously as he consigned the rest of the unpaid-for pamphlets to the flames. "Trash!" he repeated. "You don't need any damnfool books to teach you how to write. That correspondence school outfit's got you on the sucker list."

"I still owe them fifty bucks. I signed some sort of agreement. I've already paid them fifty bucks."

"And how many of their corrected manuscripts have you sold?" Bob quirked a lifted eyebrow in my direction.

"They all came back to roost."

"You're out fifty bucks. As P. T. Barnum once remarked, 'There's a sucker born every minute.' " He tossed down a shot of liquor.

I got Bob a room at a good rooming house, went good for his meal ticket at a restaurant where I was known, rented him a typewriter in my name and in three weeks he had finished writing a thirty-five thousand word story. When he mailed it he instructed the editor to wire him the money.

During those three weeks he wore the same outlandish lumberjack mackinaw, high-laced boots, and wool cap with the flaps tied up. One afternoon when I went over to his rooming house, the landlady informed me Mr. Horton had paid his rent and moved out. A strange man of eccentric habits, the good woman confided as she told me how she had accompanied him to the Western Union office to identify him so he could obtain the money the editor had wired him. In return for this favor he had had two dozen American Beauty roses and a five pound box of candy delivered to the house by special messenger. She proudly showed me the card signed "Robert J. Horton, author of 'Outlaw Code.' " This was the title of the story he had written in three weeks.

He had paid his bill at the restaurant, returned the typewriter and squared his account for rental and stationery, and boarded the train. It was typical of old Sporticus to leave without bidding me goodbye.

A month or more passed without word from him. I figured he had gone back to Montana or New York. In spite of the fact that I was accustomed to his odd habits of negligence, I was a little hurt by his strange disappearance.

I had formed the habit of working mornings, and going to the beach every afternoon for a swim regardless of the weather, to keep in good physical condition. I had located a deserted stretch of beach in the sand dunes near the exclusive Montecito Estates, near a lake and bird refuge. This was a secluded spot where I could change into a bathing suit. Once while Bob was in Santa Barbara, I had picked him up and he had spent the afternoon at the lake, watching the waterfowl and other birds. He had brought along a thick illustrated volume on bird life and a notebook. That evening after supper he took an almost childish delight in quoting off-hand the scientific names for mallard and teal ducks, jack-snipes and sandhill cranes, and various other waterfowl, along with lectures on migration, mating habits, and so on.

One evening a month or two after Bob had left Santa Barbara, I had finished my swim about sundown and was headed for town in the flivver along the sparsely traveled Channel Drive when I heard the blaring of one of those fancy lah-de-dah French horns, the kind expensive automobiles were equipped with. It was a superior snooty summons to make room, and get the hell over. Even though I was on my own side of the road and the Ford was chugging along at the edge of the speed limit with no traffic ahead, that high-toned horn kept up its imperious summons.

In the beat-up rear view mirror I got a look at the long, brightly polished, black hood of a big Packard, with a large nickle-plated radiator cap in the replica of a winged Statue of Mercury. A liveried chauffeur, with cap and goggles, was driving. I assumed the car belonged to some Montecito millionaire, driven by a very arrogant chauffeur, and to hell with him and his fancy horn! I tooted back in answer to his road-hog challenge and kept going. A few minutes later the big Packard overtook me and instead of passing kept alongside, crowding me toward the sandy shoulder. I had my mouth open to yell an insult at the driver when I caught a brief glimpse of the man in the back seat.

A tall figure in tailored pin-stripe blue suit and derby, sat stiff-backed with both gloved hands on a polished cane. And so help me Hannah, he had a monocle screwed up in one eye. One quick look at that long cadaverous face was all I needed to know it was the one and only Robert J. Horton. I pulled off the pavement and stopped.

"Drive that rattletrap into the lake, old chap, and leave it in the mud," Horton instructed me in a haughty London House of Lords accent, poker-faced without a sideway glance. The silk cord of the monocle hung alongside the white carnation in the buttonhole of his tailored coat. His creased trousers were pulled up to show the pearl gray spats, and his chamois gloved hand waved the walking stick imperiously. I could not help thinking that Broadway lost a ham actor when Horton turned his talents to newspaper and fiction writing.

There was old Sporticus, dressed to the nines, riding in a custom-built Packard, with a uniformed chauffeur, and me in faded Levi's and a pair of old beat-up tennis shoes. The top was down on the old flivver I had named Calamity Jane, and a damp bathing suit hung from the radiator cap to dry. But what the hell! I was healthy and full of beans, and making a living putting words on paper. I had the world by the tail with a downhill pull.

"It's open season," I grinned, "for glass-eyed sandhill cranes." I pointed to the sign, BIRD REFUGE. "Tell your keeper in the monkey suit he'd better camp here at the frog pond. As long as you keep within the confines of the bird refuge you'll be fairly safe from the snipe hunters."

"I have a reservation at the King's Rest Court," Sporticus announced haughtily. "Cottage Number One. My man Giles will prepare dinner promptly at seven-thirty. Cocktails at six. I'd advise a hot bath to rid you of barnacles and surplus sand. I'll expect you promptly at the cocktail hour, old bean. Drive on, Giles, and don't spare the horses."

All this was spoken as he stared straight ahead, the sunlight reflected on the polished lens of the monocle. Sporticus was playing the role of Prince and myself the ignoble part of Pauper.

The newly constructed King's Rest Court was a plush, expensive tourist attraction in the mountain foothills near the old mission, within easy walking distance of my humble cottage. I showered, shaved and donned a new pair of gray flannels, a lightweight navy blue crew-necked pullover sweater, Argyle dark blue and white sox and buckskin oxfords, recently purchased at the Sport Shop. They had taken a sizeable bite out of the check I received from Street and Smith the previous week. I timed my arrival at six to humor my whimsical friend.

The front door of Cottage One was partly open when I arrived. In the living room, with its heavy oak furniture, was Sporticus in white flannels, open-necked white shirt, and two-toned shoes, pacing the carpeted floor, a highball glass in one hand, a manuscript in the other from which he was reading aloud. He waved me in with the highball glass, motioning toward a table which held a bowl of cracked ice, and a bottle of bootleg Scotch.

He resumed reading aloud, reciting the dialogue, gesturing as he mimicked the voices of the different characters as he paced back and forth, paying no attention to me. I had long ago become accustomed to the peculiar antics of old Sporticus, for as far back as his newspaper days he was always acting a part. A taste of the Scotch of some unknown brand proved to be palatable and I gulped it down, and helped myself to a refill.

Horton let out a loud snort of disgust and tossed the manuscript into the waste basket.

"Ruined!" he exclaimed. "A pox on that scriptwriter in Hollywood for spoiling an excellent story. Little did I think when my Hollywood agent sold the story that I was selling the murder rights!"

He gulped the rest of his highball and popped some ice into the glass and splashed in the Scotch. There was a grin on his face and a humorous sparkle came into his eyes as he quoted:

"The time has come the Walrus said, to speak of many things — of ships and shoes and sealing wax, of cabbages and kings."

He told me he had dismissed Giles for the night so that we could talk. That was a memorable evening, never to be forgotten, as we sat in deep armchairs and talked of old times and future dreams. I smoked my pipe and Bob smoked his Turkish cigarettes as we worked on the Scotch. The icebox was filled with cold cuts of ham, turkey and rare roast beef, salads of all kinds, and a large bowl of home-cured olives.

Bob brought me up to date as we drank and ate. He said he had spent the money he had gotten for the novelette on several suits of tailor-made clothes and bootleg whisky. Broke and in debt from his stay at the Los Angeles Ambassador, he had wound up in jail, in the company of Willie Giles, the bellhop and bootlegger at the hotel. He had served five of his ten days before his Hollywood agent finally located him, the bearer of good tidings that he had sold two of Bob's stories to the studios for a handsome figure. Bob had bailed out Willie Giles, bought the second-hand Packard, and fitted Giles out with a chauffeur's uniform. So Giles was now his valet. chauffeur and traveling companion.

Bob said he was going to San Luis Obispo to utilize the hot mineral baths, to boil out the nicotine, alchohol and jail stink. Then he would go back to Los Angeles, sell the car and board a train for New York. From there he was going on a trip to Europe, and propositioned me to go along. We could write our stories abroad and live the life of Riley. He was in the chips, and while it was whisky talk, he meant every word he said. It was a tempting offer, but while I had less than fifty bucks in my bank account, I was not about to live off any man.

With us both well into our cups and enjoying a celebration, I was not going to spoil it by any drunken argument. Nor did I make mention of the fact that I was moving to Carmel, California, right away.

Bob departed the following day. The day after that I climbed aboard Calamity Jane and headed for Carmel. On the way I stopped at San Luis Obispo and left a letter for Bob at the hotel, and drove on north.

That memorable evening at Santa Barbara when we talked of

cabbages and kings until daybreak was destined to be our last get-together. It was the parting of our trails for I never saw my old friend Sporticus again. The following is quoted from a letter I received from F. E. Blackwell, editor of *Western Story Magazine*, dated August 23, 1927:

> Dear Coburn: Your friend, Bob Horton, shook hands with me last Friday in a wild state of excitement. A child going to the circus is nothing to him. He was off on the Leviathan Saturday. I think his feelings were hurt because I was going to be out of town and wouldn't be there to wave him goodbye. Bob is a good scout and loyal to the core. He has just finished a very good serial for me, and has promised to do some work on the other side. It's a wonder to me that the liquor hasn't done him in long ago. For years I have been saying, "Well, this is the end, he will never be able to do another story." Now, however, after having seen him bob up serenely after frightful and terrifying experiences in frightful and terrifying places, I say that he is one man I don't understand.

I guess Bob had been dead for a year or more before I received the word from a mutual friend, Steve Doyle, of Great Falls. Steve, now gone to his own reward, was cashier at the Stanton Bank. He had once loaned Horton five hundred dollars on the strength of the synopsis of a story, and Bob had paid off the thirty-day note on the date due. Steve told me in his letter of the time when Horton, then sports editor of the *Tribune*, tubercular-looking to start with, had come down with a touch of pneumonia which had left him with a hacking cough. Bob quietly spread the word that he was dying of quick consumption, a deadly disease. From the result of this the newspaper took up a collection. Alex Warden, the owner and editor, donated a hundred dollars. Others chipped in. Sid Willis, owner of the Mint Saloon, Billy Rance of the Silver Dollar, Cut Bank Brown and Highnote of the Maverick, generously fed the kitty. Other saloon men and gamblers sweetened the pot. Abe Nathan of Nathan's Clothing Store and Mose Kaufman of the Red Front Clothing Store, vied with each other in their generosity.

When Alex Warden, with a fitting speech, presented the surprised (?) Horton with a ticket to California and a fat bank account sufficient to last the winter in the balmy south, Sporticus wept and sobbed aloud, coughing into his handkerchief which came away from his mouth with tell-tale crimson spots.

Later Horton confided to Steve Doyle that the crimson stains came from a small vial of red ink palmed in the white linen handkerchief. Thus Sporticus, wetting his cigarette cough with Tijuana liquor, lived it up in San Diego, supplementing his depleting TB grubstake with money earned as waterfront reporter for the *San Diego Sun*, a Scripps-Howard newspaper.

News of the costly hoax trickled back to the owner of the *Great Falls Tribune* in devious ways from time to time. Alex Warden was wont to relate it often in later years as a good joke on himself.

A touch of sadness dwelt in the pages of Steve Doyle's lengthy letter. I had lost not only an old friend and drinking companion, but the man who had given me the courage I so sorely needed to start and continue my writing career. Bob Horton had followed the ghostly rider on the pale horse into the darkness, without my knowing it. I heard later he had died at sea aboard a homeward bound steamship, and that relatives in New England had buried him, but a shroud of mystery seemed to cloak his untimely death.

In spite of his infectious gaiety, his dry humor and play-acting, there was an unfathomable aura of loneliness and sadness in his life. He had a keen, brilliant mind with a flair for genius. His zest for living had its moments of probing the black depths of despair, though few who knew him were aware of it. He had a gallant sort of courage which he carried like a banner throughout his life.

"The dedicated life of a writer," Bob once said, "is a life of loneliness."

No truer words were ever coined.

CHAPTER 14

Carmel and Calamity

DURING MY SOMEWHAT CHECKERED CAREER as a dedicated writer, I have lived in many places, confining most of my restless wanderings to California because of my love for the Pacific Ocean, and to Arizona and its cow country.

In California there was Del Mar, where I sold my first story, then a few months at Lake Elsinore, then on to Santa Barbara for a few years, where I became friends with such artists as Ed Borein, famous for his etchings of cowboy life. When I finished my morning's stint at the typewriter I would drift into Borein's studio in the old De la Guerra adobe in El Paseo, where we would smoke Bull Durham cigarettes and swap yarns of cow camps and roundups in Montana where he had once worked as a cowhand for my father's Circle C outfit.

When Charlie Russell, the great western artist, and his protégé, Joe De Yong, and Carl Oscar Borg, a western artist of repute, came to Borein's studio, it was indeed a red letter day. We would sit and listen spellbound to Charlie Russell's endless fund of original cow country and Indian anecdotes. With the exception of Joe De Yong, who did not smoke, we rolled our own cigarettes, tossing the short butts into the huge open fireplace.

At other times Charles F. Lummis would drop in at Borein's studio, another red letter day. Lummis was a famed historian of the Southwest who had spent many years living among the Pueblo Indians of Arizona and New Mexico. He was a white-maned, leathery man, dressed in tailor-made corduroy suits, the cloth imported from Spain. Ed Borein and his wife were old-time friends of Charles Lummis. In fact they had been married in Lummis' home in Los Angeles and called him Daddy Lummis.

Carl Oscar Borg, when a young man, had signed up as an able seaman, and sailed before the mast around The Horn in a clipper ship, and later had lived a year or two with Pueblo Indians in Canyon de Chelly, Arizona. His landscape paintings of the canyon and the Painted Desert, along with his portraits, were among the very finest.

There were several other well-known landscape artists who lived in Santa Barbara at that time, and perhaps the greatest of all was Moran. His paintings of the Grand Canyon, the deserts of Arizona, and the mountains of the West, are now collector's items and beyond price.

For many years I had read Jack London's books, and I now studied them along with O. Henry's short stories, which were masterpieces with a surprise ending. Jack London was my favorite writer. He was a hard drinking man, and I guess I patterned his way of life. For a long time I had planned to visit his fabulous ranch in the Valley of the Moon, and perhaps this is why I moved camp to Carmel. But I was too late, for a tragic death had already overtaken him.

When I reached Carmel in my Model T flivver, I rented a house on a hill overlooking the ocean, and in time I became personally acquainted with many of the well-known greats of that period. Among them was Jimmy Hopper, the great football player at the University of California, and one of London's closest friends. There was Harry Leon Wilson, a writer for the *Saturday Evening Post*, and author of numerous books, Sam Blythe, another writer for the *Post*, who did mostly political articles and spent much of his time in Washington, D.C.

There was Frederick Bechdolt, author of many books of factual stories about old West characters, famous law officers and outlaws.

Also there was Robert Wells Ritchie, writer of western fiction, and John Kenneth Turner, author of *Barbarious Mexico*, a highly controversial book banned in Mexico. His vivacious wife, Adreana Spadoni had written *The Swing of the Pendulum*, a bestseller in that era. All were former top newspaper men, veterans of their trade and craftsmanship.

Again there was Ira (Rem) Remsen, a skilled artist, playwight, and playboy. And Steve Glassell, owner of Cabbages and Kings Men's Shop which handled imports from England, a character if ever there was one. These were the days of prohibition and if you desired a case of Scotch, Steve was the man to see, that is, if you were his friend.

Carmel at that time was at its peak as a famous artist colony. There was the great poet Robert Sterling, who had just ended his life by suicide, and Ambrose Bierce, who had mysteriously disappeared in Mexico during the Pancho Villa revolution. Both had lived in the shadow of Edgar Allan Poe and the black wings of brooding death which lingered in the wind-whipped cypress of Point Lobos and the roaring surf below. In the high cliffs above cults supposedly communicated with the spirits of the dead.

The legend of Jack London and his book *John Barleycorn*, and his tragic death at forty-one was still fresh in the mind of this young man launching his career as a dedicated writer together with the legends of Sterling and Bierce, and the other greats who had dwelt in Carmel. It was only in later years that I came to realize the full impact of my brief year in Carmel-By-The-Sea. I seemed destined to see some of its brooding tragedy of death hanging like a black fog over the mysterious Point Lobos where the spirits of men and beautiful women haunted the place. One of those tragic deaths was destined to brush its black-winged flight close to this man and along with it the memory of laughter and the gay and happy carefree days of my youth. The youthful gaiety and sunshine, sparkling like Burgundy, of which I drank freely, drowned past regrets and future tears.

There were the Sunday afternoon ball games of Carmel's Abalone League, with the cars lined up at the ball grounds, where the umpire's close decisions were hotly argued with horn tooting, pro and con. We watched the San Pipers versus the Sand Dabs, the Sea Gulls against the Pelicans, the Sharks playing the Swordfish, the Killer Whales against the Barracudas, and Jimmy Hopper, the All-American football player, was the only real pro.

Each team of the Abalone League had its portion of female players, dressed in faded Levi's and baseball caps, and the females were more deadly than the males in the hotly disputed arguments over the umpire's every decision. There were the picnics at the end of the ball game, sandwiches, salads, cold cuts, washed down with dago red, the fisherman's wine, bought from a Portuguese bootlegger at Monterey. There were impromptu dances, gay parties, both formal and informal, and the Saturday night poker sessions at the home of Harry Leon Wilson, well-known Carmel author.

H. L. Wilson, Bob Ritchie, Sam Blythe, Fred Bechdolt, John Turner and his wife, Adreana Spadoni (the only woman allowed), were the poker players and it was during the long intervals between jackpots that the comical anecdotes were told. Adreana's story about her uncle who had been an officer in Garibaldi's Army, fresh from Italy and speaking only a few words of English, always topped these hilarious tales.

There was a large bulletin blackboard at the post office where every writer gathered each day waiting for the mail to be sorted — letters which held checks or rejection slips — and I held the booby prize for rejection slips for the first six months, then finally I began hitting the jackpot.

Every day there was at least one humorous bulletin thumbtacked to the board, especially during city elections which were hotly contested, and the incumbent office holder was the target of humorous and sarcastic wit-barbed typewritten bulletins. The following day the incumbent posted rebuttals in barbed answers. Humor begot humor, sarcasm a sarcastic reply, the lost and found bulletins were in a class by themselves, and the want ads were classics.

Carmel's Little Theater Group staged their shows at the Golden Bough Theater. Ira Remsen was at the head of the group. He wrote the sketches for the vaudeville, minstrel and burlesque performances. He was at his best writing the three-act corny melodramas, a mixture of the popular ones at the turn of the century. *Ten Nights In a Barroom, The Drunkard, The Mortgage on the Widow's Farm, The Farmer's Daughter*, and so on, all mixed and blended into heady "mellerdrammer," complete with the dashing young hero, the beautiful gal with the drunken father, the tinhorn gambler, the widow with her mortgage, the whole works.

The plays were staged with live puppets. In the loft above were the comely, shapely, young girls in black leotards who worked the strings as the live actors performed. Rem, the choreographer, standing in the wings on one side, and his petite wife opposite with her promptbook, were both visible and part of the show.

At that period the Golden Bough Theater in Carmel matched the most modern up-to-date trick lighting of any much larger theater on the Pacific Coast, in addition to an expensive pipe organ.

Rem's "mellerdrammer" with the puppet dialogue, the jerky movements of the living puppets, was the work of a genius, both in the clever writing and the direction. It required talent on the part of the actors, and the "accidently on purpose" mistakes in dialogue added a touch of humor, and the prompting from the wings was hilarious. An occasional accident which fouled up the white silken-cord puppet strings added to the fun, the young girls in the loft pantomiming panic in trained ballet form. The spotlight of soft rainbow-hue colors would be turned on the loft to show the chalky white faces of the girls in black leotards, scarlet lips and jet-black eyebrows. The live puppet actors on the stage below were lighted by the floodlights, each actor responding with jerky movements, making wrong gestures, with Rem fit to be tied going through his pantomime motions, and his wife prompting the mixed-up dialogue.

John Kenneth Turner, a tall, lean, black-haired man, was the villain with his flowing black false mustache. Fred Bechdolt's good-looking wife, who rolled her own Bull Durham cigarettes, was the black-gowned widow. Kit Cook, the best-looking girl in Carmel, played the farmer's daughter. Steve Glassell, a handsome man, was the tinhorn gambler. Ernie Sweigart, the star football player, a Stanford graduate, played the clean-cut hero, and Jimmy Hopper the town drunk.

To the best of my knowledge it was the first time that live human puppets were ever staged. There was always a full-house audience and from the opening curtain they were more than enthusiastic, demanding curtain calls from the actors, Rem and Jodie, and the leotard girls. A midnight supper for all the cast was held backstage after the performance.

Carmel, like most art colonies, had its share of minor scandals, as well as its share of genuine writers, artists and sculptors. Then, too, it had its share of would-be artists and writers who basked in the reflected glory of the greats. It also had its share of wealthy citizens who dwelt in palatial mansions at Pebble Beach, along Seventeen Mile Drive from Carmel to Monterery, and ranches in Carmel Valley with its country gentlemen, and country club golf players and tennis enthusiasts.

One outstanding scandal which left its black mark on Carmel concerned a young teenage girl who had been expelled from one of the exclusive and expensive prep schools near Pasadena because she was pregnant. When her wealthy father, a prominent stockbroker on Wall Street, now living at Pebble Beach, demanded to know who the father of the unborn child was, his beautiful, spoiled daughter named a list of prominent men in Carmel and Pebble Beach, some gay young blades, some young married men, and a few men in their forties, millionaires, writers, artists, poets and other local gentry. Apparently she had played the field, including a couple of queers who lived together in a luxurious cottage on the Seventeen Mile Drive.

While some claimed they had never met the girl, every man in Carmel was walking a tightrope with no net below, guilty or innocent as the driven snow, they shared the blame of guilt until the wealthy parents took their pregnant daughter on a year's cruise. After they had gone sailing the Seven Seas the men accused, both innocent and guilty, formed the Adulterer's Club and threw a champagne party at the Pebble Beach Hotel, inviting one and all, and the bootleggers reaped a big harvest.

For a time the accused men were in the dog house, until the rumor spread that the spoiled rich girl had faked her pregnancy and just for the hell of it had made her adulterers list at random. There was no way of knowing if this rumor was true or false, but the palatial home at Pebble Beach was listed for sale at the realty company in Carmel, furnished, including a well-stocked wine cellar.

The tell-tale list of adulterers resulted in at least two divorces and a couple of separations, but soon the rancid stench of the scandal died and was forgotten.

Robinson Jeffers was the poet laureate of Carmel. The rock castle he was building with his own hands was well under construction by the time I got to Carmel, and he was working on the tower. Jeffers and his wife and two children were living in the unfinished castle. His wife was a noted musician, and rumor had it that her former husband was a wealthy man who had financed the construction of the Golden Bough Theater and had installed the expensive pipe orgon for his wife before she left him for the renowned poet Jeffers.

The Jeffers refused to let their children attend public school, and it was rumored that the youngsters had an artificial language of their own. This was during the time Esperanto was in vogue among the art colonies throughout the United States. For some unknown reason, the Jeffers family chose the life of a recluse, perhaps because the building of the rock castle occupied all their spare time. It was Adreana Spadoni who coined the phrase "the two white worms" for the Jeffers children as they sat silent and aloof on the rear seat of the family's beat-up Model T Ford. Rumor had it that Jeffers' beautiful wife no longer played the organ due to the breath of scandal which had touched their lives.

The Carmel Volunteer Fire Department was both utilitarian and social and was worth mentioning. The hose cart with red buckets was man-powered, each member owning his own black slicker and red fire helmet. The firehouse was painted red, the large brass firebell on a raised platform was kept highly polished, and the loud clang of the fire alarm could be heard for a great distance. At its sound, any hour, day or night, every volunteer fireman within earshot dropped what he was doing to respond promptly.

On certain occasions the Cabbages and Kings Clothing Store closed for the day with signs posted on the door: BASTILLE DAY, BOXING DAY, SAN JUAN DAY, CHINESE NEW YEAR, or whatever. If you happened to meet Steve Glassell, the store owner, on Bastille Day, he spoke French or English with a French accent, a red carnation in the buttonhole of his jacket. On Boxing Day Steve spoke with a British accent, a Sherlock Holmes cap on his head and a monocle hung by a black ribbon around his neck, sporting a Harris tweed suit, spats and a London walking stick. Chinese New Year called for a Mandarin costume with false pigtail and Steve speaking sing-song pidgin English, and the store window displaying a Chinese dragon. On San Juan Day he spoke English with a Spanish accent, and wore a Spanish costume. On Jewish holidays he spoke Yiddish and wore a black silk skullcap.

Steve let it be known to his friends when a new shipment from England was due, and they would show up to help uncrate the imported stock. In this way they had first choice of purchasing any article. When the Cabbages and Kings stock ran low, with a new shipment on the way, Steve and his cronies, after imbibing freely of bootleg Scotch, hit upon the brilliant idea of a fire sale to dispose of what stock was still on hand, a fire which would easily be extinguished by the volunteer fire department of which Steve was a member.

At the back of the store was a lean-to shed full of empty wooden boxes, just enough to kindle a small fire to cause a lot of smoke, but very little blaze to set the main frame building afire. A bundle of oakum was suggested, loose fibers shredded from old rope, dipped in tar, used for caulking boats, and easily obtainable at one of the ship chandlers at Monterey.

The faked fire was perfectly timed for the night of the annual formal ball of the Volunteer Fire Department, given at the Town Hall. The fire alarm would be sounded at midnight and by the time the fire laddies manned the hose cart and grabbed fire axes and water buckets, the Cabbages and Kings would be shrouded in dense black smoke, with a rear window open to let in enough smoke.

The planned fire went off like clockwork. The fire laddies had imbibed freely of the potent punch and when the fire alarm sounded they rushed out to don their slickers and fire helmets. Reaching the fire, they found the shop filled with black smoke and outside great billows of smoke rolled skyward attracting a throng of citizens mixing freely with evening-gowned girls who had come from the ballroom to see the excitement.

"Save the drygoods!" some inebriated fireman shouted. An eager-beaver fireman wielded an ax and smashed the lock on the front door, and the other firemen swarmed in. Soon they were out again carrying armsful of jackets, plus-four knickerbockers, imported Argyle sox, neckties, shirts, boots, golf shoes, and anything they could grab, while the firemen on the cart formed a bucket chain to pour water on the smouldering oakum in the back shed. Within half an hour every shelf and counter was bare. Every imported item in the store, including a case of Scotch, had miraculously disappeared, carried off in waiting automobiles and taken home.

Unbeknownst to Steve Glassell, the rest of the Carmel Volunteer Fire Laddies had planned in advance the rape of his Cabbages and Kings exclusive men's shop.

It was a rollicking and merry bunch of brave fire laddies, with soiled shirt fronts, wilted collars, and their tuxedos smelling strongly of oakum smoke, who went back to the Town Hall to partake of the buffet supper being served. Steve Glassell was left behind in the midst of the smoke-filled empty shelves and display counters, a look of sad betrayal in his dark brown eyes, his ruddy-jowled face smoke-grimed and his carefully barbered black hair in disarray. A lone, sad figure, deserted by his erstwhile friends who had made off with his case of bootleg Johnnie Walker Black Label he could have sold at a profit. Steve was rescued later by the inebriated hose-cart brigade, to which he belonged, and was presented with a crying towel and carried back to the Town Hall to rally 'round the punch bowl, going along with the practical joke when they sang "For he's a jolly good fellow!"

The carefully plotted fire sale had really gone up in oakum smoke, and the following day there was a sign in the front window saying the store was CLOSED FOR REPAIRS.

But the Carmel Volunteer Firemen were honest men. Each compiled an itemized list of what he had salvaged, and to each list was written "Reduced to half price — Fire Sale. Check enclosed."

The only law which prevailed in Carmel was a big stalwart Swede named Gus, the constable. Astride his gentle coal-black gelding, and resplendent in his brass-buttoned blue uniform and polished black leather boots, he was a ruddy-faced man in his forties. There was a sprinkling of gray in his cropped straw-colored hair, and he was a good-natured man who took his job seriously, and on occasion was the butt of good-humored practical jokes.

His pride and joy was the sleek black horse, Midnight, which he kept carefully groomed and grain-fed. On cold and foggy mornings Midnight would crowhop a few jumps with a hump in his back. Gus was no bronc rider and on these cold mornings he would lead Midnight around to get the hump out of his back. His regulation .45 automatic in its leather holster which hung from a Sam Browne belt was kept polished, as was his nickle-plated law badge. But as far as anyone could ascertain, the Colt had never been fired.

Gus's favorite hangout was Bashum's Ice Cream Parlor, and the strongest drink he ever imbibed was ice cream sodas. When a strange automobile belonging to some tourist parked along the main street, by word-of-mouth the rumor spread that it was a stolen car. Gus would jot down the number in his official notebook, and astride his black charger would keep an eagle eye on the parked car, awaiting the innocent tourist who was shopping at the Cabbages and Kings, or the Seven Arts, a book and stationery store, to return to his car to be sternly questioned by Gus and required to show his identification. For some reason the gullible Gus seldom failed to grab the bait of the practical jokers.

There was the rumor of a vicious dog which turned out to be a coddled Pekinese lap dog belonging to some society matron and the rumor of a grizzly bear or mountain lion roaming the pine forests of Carmel was another hoax which sent Gus on his black horse through the pines in futile search. And there were the weasel and skunk, the infamous chicken yard robbers, still another hoax which kept him on the run.

Everyone in Carmel, including the kids and dogs, knew and liked the amiable Gus. The kids vied to hold his horse when he went into Bashum's to guzzle ice cream sodas and banana splits. So far as anyone ever knew the small Carmel jail with its one barred window remained empty of prisoners. Bachelor Gus was in demand during the evening hours as a baby sitter, and as a caretaker of houses when the owners were traveling.

The strange disappearance of Evangelist Aimee Semple McPherson created great excitement for a time when rumor had it that she had shacked up in a secluded house in the pines of Carmel with a man believed to be her organist at her Foursquare Gospel Temple in Los Angeles. Shortly after the long-lost leader of the Foursquare Gospel was mysteriously found alive on the Arizona desert south of Tucson, a real estate woman showed me the house in Carmel where Aimee was said to have hidden out, and I had a strong hunch the talkative real estate woman was tacking on a higher rental because of the scandal involved. So I told her I wanted a cottage near the ocean as I liked to swim, and thus got a better cottage, better location and half the rental price.

For the past year I had been engaged to a young married lady who had separated, but was not divorced from her second husband then living back East. She had a fifteen-year-old son by her first marriage and when she was free we planned to be married. She was one of the finest and most loyal friends I ever had, a tall, slender girl my age with long jet-black hair and warm brown eyes, and who shall be known here as Barbara Hill. Barbara and her son moved to Carmel from Santa Barbara where we had first met, and stayed in Carmel during my stay.

During the time I had been engaged to her I had done very little drinking. I had been working my four hour stint at the typewriter batting out two thousand words a day and selling every story I wrote. It was during prohibition and the bootleg Scotch was mostly cut or doctored with grain alcohol and selling for seven and eight bucks a fifth, and which I could not afford. So most of my drinking was confined to the red wine I got from Pedro, a Portuguese bootlegger at Monterey, to whom Jimmy Hopper had introduced me. Pedro owned a ship chandler's store and a couple of fishing boats, was a good amigo of Hopper, and one of John Steinbeck's cronies. I paid two bucks a gallon for the pure rich sour red wine which had been aged in the wood.

By this time I had saved enough money to trade the old beat-up Model T Ford in on a good second-hand Cadillac at the Cadillac Agency at Salinas.

It was the middle of December when Barbara and her son left for the East to visit her parents for the Christmas holidays and to obtain a divorce.

I will never know what motivation or combination of motivations triggered the drunk I went on when Barbara took the train East to Chicago. I had met Willie Tripp, a California cowboy and another of Steinbeck's cronies, who lived on the outskirts of Monterey. He owned a few head of good saddle horses he rented, and often when I had finished work in the afternoon I would head for his stable, and Willie and I would ride the trails of Carmel Valley until sundown. While I could no longer make a brush-popper cowhand in the rough country of Arizona, I was more at home riding around with Willie Tripp than I was on foot.

The day I put Barbara on the train at Salinas I drove the Cadillac to Tripp's place, stopping in Monterey to buy a bottle of bootleg Scotch from Pedro. I had just gotten a check for five hundred dollars from *Adventure* and felt flush. Now with a good horse between my legs and a bottle of Scotch in the pocket of my old batwing chaps, I was sitting on top of the world. Willie had to stay at the stable to dude-wrangle some guests at the Del Monte Hotel, so I was on my own. I had been nibbling at the bottle along the trail and when I rode the black Morgan gelding down the main street of Carmel I dimly remember challenging Gus, the constable, on his big black horse, to a race which Gus refused. Then the rollicky grain-fed horse I was riding spooked at something, bogged his head and crow-hopped a few jumps. He was easy to ride and I gigged him in both shoulders and bucked him down the street, fanning him with my hat every jump, until I yanked his head up and called it a day.

Fred Bechdolt owned a big bald-faced sorrel gelding, and I tried to talk him into saddling up to ride with me to where there were some cattle grazing in Carmel Valley and to team tie a few gentle white-faced steers with me, but Beck said he had a deadline to meet on a story. Though the author of some good western factual books, Bechdolt was a dude newspaperman, and made no pretense of being a cowhand. But I was drunk enough to kid him about it which did not set very well with him. After all, he had gleaned his knowledge of the frontier West secondhand, from old newspaper files and articles written by historians, and I found some of his stories as full of holes as a hunk of Swiss cheese.[1]

---

1. See: Bechdolt, Frederick, *Burs Under the Saddle*, by Ramon F. Adams, pp. 27–33; *Six-Guns and Saddle Leather* (revised ed.), by Ramon F. Adams, nos. 179, 180.

When Beck showed me what he had written about the Wild Bunch, taken from newspaper morgues and the Pinkerton files, one evening at my house, I had pointed out the errors he had made. B. M. Bower, the schoolmarm author, had made the same mistakes. The B. M. Bower article had appeared in *Adventure Magazine* and I had written a letter to Arthur Sullivant Hoffman, then editor of *Adventure*, correcting her, and Hoffman had printed my letter in the magazine. I showed it to Beck and to Bob Ritche, who was there at the house that evening.

I had had enough dago red under my belt to loosen my tongue that night. So I told the two writers about my father's Circle C Ranch being located in the Little Rockies outlaw country of Montana, that Kid Curry and his brothers, Lonny and Johnny, had worked for the outfit when I was a kid, and that I was there when the Curry Gang held up the Great Northern train near Wagner in 1901. I told them I had met the outlaws and had been to the Kid Curry Hideaway near the Thornhill Ranch, not far from the Circle C Ranch, and that Jim Thornhill, former ranch partner of Kid Curry, was a close friend of mine. I told them that when the sign was right, perhaps fifty years from then, I would write the facts of the Curry Gang and the Wild Bunch, but that right then I was content to write fiction stories.

Bob Ritchie and Fred Bechdolt sat bug-eyed and all ears while I ran off at the head telling them just enough to whet their newspaper reporter appetites. From that evening I gained a certain stature because I had been there, and all my fiction yarns were based upon facts.

But the day I started ribbing Beck I was vaguely aware that I had somehow violated the unwritten laws of Carmel by bucking my horse down the street, challenging Gus for a race and playing drunken cowboy in town, and somehow Willie Tripp had learned that I had bucked his Black Prince horse down the main street of Carmel. When I offered him a drink from my bottle he refused and I was damned sure I had broken my pick with him, and that he would never again rent me Black Prince or any other gelding in his stable.

So I loaded my saddle and chaps in the back seat of the Cadillac, picked up another bottle of Scotch from the Monterey bootlegger, and headed for home. Those were the days when the men in Carmel wore plus-four knickerbockers, golf sox and sport coats, so when I got home I shed my Levi's, showered, shaved, and got dressed in my rompers and Harris Tweed sport coat. All I craved now was a drinking companion and I thought of my good friend, Earl Radikan. Rad had been a sophomore at Dartmouth when he joined the American Ambulance Corps, serving with the French Army before the U.S. became involved in the First World War. He was a tall, mild-mannered gent who had won the Croix de Guerre and was wounded in action when a German shell blew up his ambulance. So I headed for Rad's place where he was living with his common-law wife, who had separated from her husband. Rad and Edie had been high school sweethearts in Boston, but while Rad was overseas she had married a rich playboy, and the marriage had gone on the rocks. So Rad and Edie had somehow drifted to Carmel about the time Barbara and I arrived.

It was a natural gravitation for Rad and me, both living with women without benefit of clergy, to become friends. At Rad's house after a few drinks we three decided to head for Pop Ernst's Café on Fisherman's Wharf at Monterey which specialized in seafood. Later we drove back to Carmel to join an open-house party at Ira Remsen's place. Rem had concocted a strong rum punch and Steve Glassell was there with his bootleg Scotch. Rem and his wife had had a family quarrel a few months earlier, and when she left Carmel, Rem drove his car to the Grand Canyon and the Painted Desert of Arizona, to paint pictures. While there he had grown a beard and gone native, and when he returned to Carmel he dressed in Levi's and red flannel shirts, and cowboy boots, and he was drinking heavily.

When we got to Rem's cottage, the place was crowded with celebrating friends, and by midnight the gang was going strong. Someone was playing the piano and couples were dancing. A fire was going in the large fireplace and the order of the festive evening was wine, women and song. With the drinks loaded and the house too warm for comfort, couples were drifting outside to cool off.

In my whisky-fumed intoxication I somehow got paired off during the evening with Blake Beck. She was a pale-faced, aesthetic-looking slim girl with prominent breasts. I had never met her until now and she had hitherto been regarded as one of the so-called intelligentsia, a high-chinned snob of Carmel. She was part owner, with an attractive girl named Connie, of an exclusive women's dress shop near the Cabbages and Kings, and it was rumored that the dress shop was financed by Steve Glassell, who owned a fifty-fifty partnership with the two girls. I knew that Blake modeled the imported dresses, for with her long, thin legs, small waist, the uplift of her bosom, her erect, high-chinned, hipless figure, and her manner of walking, made her a perfect model. Her snobbish manner could have been natural, or learned at some modeling school.

Anyway, you could have knocked me over with a feather when she latched onto me at the punch bowl, her purring voice flattering me about my being destined to attain fame as a western story writer. With her large, violet-gray eyes with mascara eyelashes enormous in the reflected firelight, I was just drunk enough to believe the flattery she poured on like honey. We danced a waltz together, then pushed our way through the crowd out into the fresh air to where my old Cadillac was parked, to drink from the bottle of Scotch in the glove compartment.

On the way out, Blake had picked up her black-and-white skunk fur coat, and at her suggestion we drove out to Point Lobos and parked among the dark, twisted cypress trees on a high cliff. As we sat close together drinking from the bottle we could hear the crashing thunder of the surf below in the rock-bound caves which sent a thin spindrift to where we were.

The house where Barbara Hill and her son, Brad, lived had a separate studio house where I lived and worked. It had its own bathroom, shower, a rock fireplace, and was apart from the main cottage in the pines. I had no recollection of our departure from the eerie Point Lobos, no recollection of driving home, and this was the first and only time I had ever experienced a total blackout.

When I finally came alive from my whisky-fogged stupor, it was broad daylight. I was in my own studio bed and as I lay there motionless trying to get my bearings I was dimly aware that I was not alone. Getting my heavy, sticky eyelids propped open, I saw Blake Beck sitting in a chair fully dressed and smoking a cigarette.

"How the hell," I broke the tense silence in a bone-dry, croaking whisper, "did we get here? The last I remember we were in my car drinking Scotch on Point Lobos."

"You want me to jog your memory?" Blake asked, her red lips smiling mockingly to match the brittle sarcasm of her voice.

"It might help a lot," I managed to put in a lopsided grin. "But at this stage of the game I'd like to sample the hair of the dog that bit me."

There was an opened bottle of Johnnie Walker Black Label on the night stand. The bootleg Scotch I had gotten from the Monterey bootlegger had been White Horse, and I asked Blake how come the Johnnie Walker.

"Compliments of Steve Glassell," she answered. "I had it in the pocket of my fur coat."

"How about joining me in a drink?" I asked.

"Too early in the morning. I can't go to the shop stinking of booze," she said.

Her scarlet lips parted in a rueful smile when she informed me I had taken a virgin to bed last night and now she was probably pregnant.

"The hell you say!" I exploded.

"I never in the world would have given my consent if you hadn't made a promise of marriage," Blake informed. "You can get dressed and pick me and my sister up at the shop and we'll drive to Salinas and get married by a J.P."

"Like hell we will," I said.

"Then I'll accuse you of statutory rape," she informed me.

She brought a small silver box from her large leather handbag and offered me one of her little white pills, telling me it would clear the cobwebs from my brain and restore my loss of memory about last night. Then she left, saying she would be waiting at the shop for me.

That little white hangover pill began to get in its first licks, clearing the whisky fumes from my befuddled brain. I began to look around the room and noticed particularly that the other pillow had not even been dented. Every ashtray in the room was filled with lipstick-stained butts, but none of my hand-rolled cigarettes. Looking at the bed, I was now sure that Blake Beck had not spent the night in my room, that she had come by early that morning to accuse me of rape. I was certain I had never touched the thirty-year-old, self-acclaimed virgin, and that she was playing me for a sucker.

I decided then and there to get the hell long gone from Carmel and leave the untouched Blake waiting at the church, so to speak. I reached for the bottle and took a long drag, wrapped a Bull Durham smoke, and sat down in the old barroom chair where I had dreamed out many a story which had been pecked out on my Corona, to think out a plan for my getaway.

After a few more belts I figured there was not enough booze to make me drunk, and I had the cockeyed clarity of mind which comes to all drunks. The thought that I had played Barbara Hill a dirty, lowdown trick clung in the depths of my mind. I had betrayed the confidence of the finest girl I had ever known, the girl I hoped to someday marry, and I did not have the guts to face up to the worst mess I had ever gotten myself into.

John Barleycorn had put this man on the ropes again.

I packed my suitcase and loaded it in the Cadillac, together with my saddle, typewriter, and the other tools of my trade, ready for a complete getaway. It was a little after noon when I pulled the Cadillac up at Blake's dress shop to tell her I was pulling out. But before I could protest they piled into the car, determined to see that young Lochinvar played his hand out.

In my hungover condition I must have been out of my mind to go along with them instead of stepping on the gas when I spotted them standing there waiting for me. It was a sad farce of the holy bonds of matrimony, that mock-marriage at the J.P.'s house in Salinas, when Blake's sister took the wedding ring off her finger and handed it to me in that dingy parlor.

From the very beginning I had decided that as soon as the knot was tied, no less than a hangman's knot around my neck, I would drive Blake and her sister back to Carmel, dump them at the dress shop and hightail it for parts unknown. But Blake had out-foxed me by telephoning the Del Monte Hotel to reserve the honeymoon cottage for a few days. Now the only thing I could do was to go along with the deal and when the sign was right I would haul freight and leave my bride behind to sue for a divorce.

After we dropped Blake's sister off in Carmel, I stopped at the Monterey bootlegger's and purchased half a dozen bottles of White Horse Scotch, and when we reached the Del Monte Hotel, if Blake entertained the thought of my making the romantic gesture of carrying my bride over the threshold of the honeymoon cottage, she got rid of the notion quickly. I had a far more precious cargo to carry in.

In the cottage living room there were flowers from Connie of the dress shop, from the Cabbages and Kings, and a gift-wrapped bottle of champagne from Steve Glassell. Blake must have spread the news where we could be found.

Thus began for me a drunken two-day sojourn at the hotel. A bewildering zombie nightmare on the part of the whisky-fogged reluctant groom. I had no way of knowing then nor in the following weeks what Blake Beck had in mind when she set her deadfall trap. During those endless days I never drew a sober breath, and no matter how much bootleg Scotch I kept swilling, there was always the feeling of guilt like a ghost which haunted me. I would come alive with a strange zombie effect from the little white pills my bride kept feeding me, then reach for the bottle to clear the cobwebs. It was a damned vicious cycle, booze and pills and no food of any kind, a damned witch's brew entrapment.

Blake spent very little time in the room, leaving me to sleep off the zombie state I was in. Whether she had another room for herself I never knew. Whenever she was in the room she fed me another pill to knock me out. I was awake the morning of the third day when I heard her talking on the telephone. A call had come from her sister telling her to get back to Carmel as soon as possible, that someone had entered the dress shop and squirted fountain pen ink on every dress in the shop, ruining at least two dozen expensive gowns. Blake was using some pretty foul language over the phone, cursing her partner Connie and Steve Glassell, accusing the over-sexed Connie of shacking up with Steve and not taking care of the shop. I couldn't blame her for being mad, because she had expected to make a bundle of money during the pre-Christmas sales, with Christmas about two weeks away.

That telephone call saved the day for me. This was the time to dump Blake at her shop, then get the hell away from Carmel and never more return. I had come alive that morning with an extremely raw throat, making it hard to swallow, and I knew I had to see a doctor soon. So I pulled myself together with the thought that I would be free of Blake, who had been using her witch's spell with expertise over me, keeping me drunk and knocked out with her pills which I learned later were a potent narcotic.

I was a very sick man, running a high fever, but somehow I managed to drive the Cadillac to Carmel. I told Blake I would drop her off at the shop and stay with my friend Radikan for a few days. When I drove to Rad's house he told me I was welcome to their guest room, so I ran the car into the garage, pocketed the keys and closed the door. I told Rad I had a hell of a sore throat and had to see a doctor right away, so he phoned Doctor Swan.

Rad told me his wife, Edie, had left for New England to spend the holidays with her parents, and that he was glad to have me for company. When the doctor arrived, the first thing he did was to put me to bed. He said I had a strep throat which could easily turn into diphtheria. I told him I had been on a prolonged drunk and that Blake had been feeding me some hangover pills which kept me knocked out. Dr. Swan said he knew the potent narcotic pills Blake used and told me if I had any left to flush them down the toilet. I was told to lay off the booze entirely, and he told Rad to feed me a bland liquid diet and a lot of beef broth. He said to be on the safe side he would have to tack a diphtheria quarantine sign on the front door.

I felt like hell in causing Rad's cottage to be quarantined, but he said it would keep the freeloaders away.

"Pull a cork," he quipped, "and every booze hound in Carmel hears it."

I told Rad that Blake had really put me through the wringer, and I was quitting her. I made up my mind I was leaving Carmel as soon as the doctor turned me loose. Rad said he would go with me wherever I wanted to go, that the rent on the cottage was up in a couple of weeks, and that Edie could return to wherever we decided to hole up.

That evening Blake got as far as the front yard when she saw the quarantine sign on the door. Rad and I watched her from below the drawn window blind. She was wearing her fur jacket and when she walked away with her long-legged mannequin stride, I could tell she was mad as a hornet, and if I had one guess coming she was headed for the doctor's office. In about half an hour the phone rang. When Rad answered it was Blake wanting the keys to the car so that she could look at some rental houses her brother-in-law, a real estate agent, had lined up for her to look at. Rad stalled her off saying I had diphtheria and could not be bothered with anything for a week or two, and that she could not have the car keys.

During the next week the inflammation left my swollen tonsils, and my throat was no longer raw. I had been drinking nothing but the soup Rad fixed for me and was beginning to feel like a human again. In another few days Dr. Swan gave me a thorough examination. He said I had barely escaped diphtheria, but said the Scotch I had been drinking straight could have caused my raw throat. I told him I was leaving Carmel, asked him for his bill, and thanked him for what he had done for me.

Rad and I had a long medicine talk. He had been a law student until he went overseas, and he suggested I get a good attorney. He said he had a fraternity brother who was a lawyer in Salinas, and when he got him on the phone he agreed to act as my attorney in any divorce proceedings, suggesting I contact him when I got settled. That night Rad and I got in the Cadillac and headed yonderly. I had my saddle and typewriter in the car so did not have to go back to my studio guest house for anything. Rad had sold his car and packed his and Edie's belongings which he put in storage until they could send for them. My suitcase was already packed with what clothes I had.

As we drove away from Carmel I racked my brain for some remote, quiet place to locate for a while, where I could, by the grace of God, resume my writing career. When we reached the small town of Ojai, inland from the coastal town of Ventura, I knew that back in the mountains there were several resorts, and decided to try Soper's Ranch. It was long past midnight when we stopped in front of the country store and got the tall, genial owner out of bed. Soper showed us several cottages and we chose a two bedroom cabin, with living room, bath, kitchen, and a screened-in porch over a running creek, and I paid a month's rent in advance.

The next morning Soper showed up with a large box of the finest navel oranges I had ever seen, freshly picked from his own orchard. We bought our groceries from his store where there were always freshly-laid eggs, fresh churned butter, and all the oranges we could eat. The cabin was furnished with sheets, pillowcases, blankets and fresh towels every day.

As soon as we were settled I composed a long letter to Barbara Hill, who would be returning from the East right after New Year's. The letter was difficult for me to write. I made no excuses for my despicable drunken behavior at Carmel, nor gave any of the sordid details of my shotgun marriage, except to say I had been skunk drunk and knocked out most of the time, that my farcical marriage had never been consummated and that I was working with a Salinas lawyer to handle my divorce.

I did not ask forgiveness for what I had done and which had ruined everything between us, and due to my misbehavior I realized she could no longer remain in Carmel with all its sordid gossip. I told Barbara that if she and Brad wanted to move to Santa Barbara, where they had many good friends, I would not in any way disturb their privacy. I would remain at Soper's Ranch in Ojai and never go near Santa Barbara until my divorce was settled.

On Christmas Day Rad and I drove to Ventura and ate our Christmas dinner at their best restaurant. For me it was a sad day, and for Rad as well. Back at the cabin we kindled a fire in the sheet iron stove and sat around swapping yarns of other lonesome Christmases we had known, me in remote snowed-in winter line camps in Montana, and one lonely Christmas in Bisbee, Arizona, when I was dead broke. Rad had spent a few lonely Christmases overseas with the Ambulance Corps. When we bedded down for the night all the bitter regrets and the feeling of guilt came to haunt me. Outside, the waters of the flowing creek kept whispering to the granite boulders and grassy banks, telling its secrets.

A week before the holidays ended I began pounding the typewriter, managing to knock out a fifteen thousand word story for Fiction House, and got it in the mail the last day of December. A few days later I received a letter from Barbara Hill. I took a walk up the creek and sat down on a large boulder to read the letter. I had dreaded to open it, but as I read it Barbara placed the blame for what had happened on Blake Beck. By trapping me into marriage, she had sought her revenge on Barbara, whom she had said openly she hated. Barbara said Blake had been sleeping with Steve Glassell for months and was on the make for a man with plenty of money, not a poor author, and the best thing I could do was to get rid of her, and the sooner the better, and that Blake had already latched onto a wealthy Jewish man, a member of a nationally known men's clothing store.

She said she and Brad would return to Santa Barbara and after she became settled she would get in touch with me and talk things over.

I sat there with tears in my eyes. Somehow those tears seemed to purge everything unclean and rotten in the two days I had spent at the Del Monte Hotel, all except the feeling of guilt which would remain in the dark pocket of my mind.

Back at the cabin I told Rad what Barbara had written about Blake Beck, and he advised me to tell it all to my attorney. When I shoved Barbara's letter into the pocket of my pants, a folded newspaper clipping fell out of the envelope which I had overlooked. I opened it and suddenly exploded with:

"Goshamighty, Ira Remsen's dead!"

I handed the clipping to Rad who read it aloud, the gist of which was that Rem had shot himself in the head on Christmas Eve. He had invited his own group of friends in for a holiday party, and just as it got underway, everybody having fun, he placed a long distance phone call to his estranged wife, something he had been doing every night for the past week trying to persuade her to return to him. After a forty-five minute conversation he shot himself, still holding the receiver in one hand. Neither Rad nor I had known Ira Remsen intimately, having only met at parties, and we were not numbered among his very close friends. Neither of us had ever been in his home save that one open party when Blake Beck had latched onto me. But somehow the news of his tragic melodramatic suicide saddened us. We took a last drink out of our almost empty crock of Johnnie Walker in a farewell toast to Rem. I was going on the wagon for a while, at least until I pulled myself out of the messy boghole I had gotten into up to my ears.

CHAPTER 15

Cold Sober and Married

ONE SUNDAY ABOUT NOON, Barbara appeared in her second-hand tin lizzie, and we sat in the cabin and talked while Rad took a walk. She said she had found a rental house on a high bluff overlooking the ocean at Santa Barbara, near Ed Borein's adobe house, and that Brad had started school. Ed Borein, the artist, had offered her the position of curator at a new art gallery in the El Paseo where he had his studio and she had accepted.

    Although we still loved one another, there was that invisible barrier, and I was keenly aware that I had hurt her deeply. Perhaps time would wear down this barrier, but no mention of it was made that day. I had put a drunken torch to the structure which had held our love, burned it to the ground, and it would be up to both of us to slowly erect with the passing of time a new home for whatever remained of our love. Right now it seemed an impossible task unless a modern miracle shaped our destiny. Barbara had her son and the companionship of staunch and loyal friends in Santa Barbara, and I was left alone with my good and understanding friend Radikan, and the task of mending my fences.

    God must have had His hand on my shoulder because during the following months I turned out some of the best stories I had ever pounded out on my typewriter. Edie came back a month later, and I moved into a smaller cabin. I laid off the booze and knocked out two or three thousand words a day, quitting about noon. There was a natural swimming hole above my cabin where I swam on warm, sunny days, letting the sun dry my hide, now a lifeguard layer of dark tan. I worked in Levi's, sweat shirt, and cowboy boots, dressing up only on Sunday when I went to mass at the little Catholic Chapel in Ojai, where there was a fat, jolly Dominican priest named Father Howard. He had at one time been on one of Knute Rockne's football teams at Notre Dame.

Father Howard and I became fast friends. We had long, interesting talks together, and as a result I went to confession and received communion for the first time in years. I was no longer living in sin and was back in my church. I told Father Howard about living with Barbara Hill without benefit of clergy and he said it was better that way than living with a woman I might eventually divorce. I told him all there was to tell about Blake Beck, and I got far more consolation from him than I deserved. He told me it would take a long time, perhaps years, to heal the raw wound in my heart, but that in due time by the grace of God, I would gradually forget. Father Howard was a true healer of bruised souls, as God meant him to be.

A few months later Rad and Edie finally decided to return to New England where Rad would re-enter law school to finish his war-interrupted studies. He would then hang out his attorney-at-law shingle, and they would get married, too. This made me happy for them, but sad that they were leaving. I saw them off at Santa Barbara where Barbara Hill came to bid them goodbye. When Barbara asked me why I did not leave Soper's and move to Santa Barbara, I told her I would stay where I was until I was absolutely certain that Blake Beck would give us no further trouble or embarrassment and my divorce became final. But what I said was part truth and part evasion.

I was aware that Barbara was going out with other men, which was fine with me. She was young, attractive and deserving of a far better man than myself, and I hoped that if she decided to marry again it would be to a real man deserving of her love.

In his studies Father Howard had taken a course in psychology, and in our many long talks he gave me the benefit of his knowledge on the subject. In his thorough understanding of my nature, he told me that somewhere in my subconscious mind there was a hidden desire to be free, unfettered by the bonds of matrimony, that deep in my heart I had no desire to marry the woman I was in love with. If I had I could easily have escaped the trap Blake Beck had set for me by simply leaving Carmel, but instead I deliberately stepped into the trap of a woman I hated, to totally destroy the love which existed for Barbara, leaning heavily on the false crutch of drunkenness to deaden the guilt within me. Thinking it over later, I was forced to admit to myself that Father Howard, in his sage wisdom, had spoken the truth, and I told him so.

"Someday," Father Howard told me, "you will meet a good woman whom you will marry of your own free will, and God will bless that marriage."

Father Howard's prophecy came to pass far sooner than I ever expected.

I stayed at Soper's ranch all that year, then I moved to Santa Barbara where I rented a house on a high cliff overlooking the Pacific Ocean, and my mother came up from San Diego to keep house for me. I saw Barbara only occasionally. She was still driving her beat-up tin lizzie and one day I bought her a brand new Buick sedan I had seen in a display window, more because I could not bear to see her without a decent car while I was driving a brand new Packard convertible. I felt I owed her that much. I was selling every story I wrote by then and was in the chips.

One weekend in Santa Barbara while I was playing touch football with a small group of high school youngsters, in order to catch a long pass I suddenly twisted and heard the sound of a bone crack in my right leg as I caught the spinning ball in mid-air. I thought then of what the Prescott, Arizona, doctor had told me about my bones being brittle, and knew now he was correct. The ambulance came and took me to the Cottage Hospital.

I was lucky to have one of the finest orthopedic surgeons in California set my broken leg so that I would not be crippled for life. I remained in the hospital six or eight weeks and despite the heavy cast I thoroughly enjoyed my lengthy stay, the long hours in bed, the wheelchair and then the crutches. I had my typewriter brought in and sitting propped up in bed I managed to pound out at least one story.

During my stay in the hospital there was a student nurse who wore the light blue uniform instead of the white worn by the graduates. I vowed to myself she was the best looking girl of all the young nurses, an Irish-Canadian colleen named Mina Acheson Evans, who had come down from Calgary, Alberta, Canada, to enter nurse's training at the Santa Barbara Cottage Hospital. She had had a short unhappy marriage which had ended in divorce, a marriage she wanted to forget and seldom talked about to anyone. Mina had been born in Medicine Hat, Alberta, Canada, about a two-day ride on horseback from the Circle C Ranch in Montana where I had spent my youth. She was a soft-spoken girl with wistful gray-green eyes, short brown hair and a perfect profile which, Jack Dempsey told me later when I showed him her picture, was a striking resemblance to the famous actor John Barrymore.

Before many days passed, and after we had become better acquainted, I began calling her Pat because the name Pat suited her Irish background better than Mina, and Pat she was from then on. It was then that I came to realize that Father Howard's prophecy had come to pass, and that I was destined to marry Pat for keeps.

A few weeks later my mother had to return to her home in San Diego, and I gave up the house I had rented and went back to Soper's Ranch where I would wait until Pat was ready to leave her nurse's training course at the hospital. It so happened that she was getting ready to leave anyway because of tubercular glands in her neck which had been removed a few years earlier had been acting up again, and the hospital doctors had ordered her into a sanitarium at Monrovia, California. Instead we decided that when we got married we would go to Prescott, Arizona, where the fresh mountain air would take care of any tubercular trouble she might have.

When I arrived at Soper's Ranch, he told me Jack Dempsey had rented the entire place with all the cottages for a training camp. Dempsey was in training for the heavyweight crown against Jack Sharkey, and when Soper introduced us and told him who I was, the champ told me to move right in, and to take my pick of the cottages except the one he and Jerry the Greek, his trainer, occupied along with a woman cook. Jack told me I was free to take my meals at the training table with his manager, Gus, and his sparring partners. When I offered to pay, the Champ gave me a Gentle Annie poke in the belly and said, "Forget it."

I moved into the same cottage I had been living in before, and the following week the training camp opened full blast. Dempsey told me Jerry the Greek would be glad to massage my game leg and would have me in shape in no time to do road work, jog along with them every morning before breakfast, and that is what I soon did.

Half a dozen sparring partners moved in to occupy the cottages, with a male chef to do the cooking. The training ring on its high platform occupied a fair-sized plot of level ground. Only on weekends was the general public allowed to watch the Champ work out in the ring, but there were always half a dozen sportswriters on hand, together with gamblers from Los Angeles, Las Vegas and Reno.

The Champ occasionally insisted that I have dinner with him at the Ojai Country Club, where his actress-wife, Estelle Taylor, would join us. Whenever I offered to pick up the tab the Champ told me it had been taken care of.

"To hell with you," he would say with a grin. "You don't belong to the Country Club, you sawed-off, hammered-down little bastard. Keep on like that and I'll tell Jerry the Greek to break your game leg by tripping you up while doing road work."

I was awake at six every morning, jogging along with the Champ and his sparring partners, all strung out along the dirt road to Ojai. After a hearty breakfast, I pounded out my yarns on the typewriter. I was sitting pretty at Soper's, all my meals free, and no charge on the cottage I occupied. The Champ had raised me to a new status quo.

Mrs. Walt Coburn — Pat

In the evenings we played pool, but there was one thing I had to watch. That was the Champ's habit of playing practical jokes, such as giving some innocent character the hot foot. This trick took place after supper when we were wont to gather at the store to play pool or pitch horseshoes, or to just sit on the steps of the porch leading to the store. Soper or some previous victim would perch on the top step and engage the prospective sucker Jack had picked out in conversation, with Jack and a few others who were wise sitting on the lower step listening. The Champ was an expert at slipping a paper match between the sole of the victim's shoe and the upper part when he was not watching, then touching a lighted cigarette to the match. In split-seconds the leather shoe became hot and the sucker would let out a startled cry of pain. Before he could get the shoe unlaced and off he had gotten the full benefit of the hot foot, while the group whooped and hollered. I knew the Champ had given the hot foot to all his sparring partners, their managers, sportswriters, gamblers and visitors, but so far I had escaped.

The sparring partners ranged from fast lightweights to welterweights and heavyweights. There were Jimmy McClaren and his manager, Pop Foster, Fidel la Barbara, a golden glove Stanford student, Dave Shade, Mickey Walker, Joe Began, a heavyweight, Armand Emanuel, a practicing lawyer from Los Angeles and his father-manager, as well as others.

Dempsey's middle-aged cook had formerly cooked for royalty in Europe. To the best of my recollection she was Belgian, spoke with a decided accent, and was absolutely trustworthy. Because of the constant danger of someone slipping poison into the Champ's food, to sicken or even kill him, Soper himself, to be on the safe side, bought all the meat, vegetables and other food in Ojai.

Almost every weekend a group of Boy Scouts and their scoutmaster would show up to watch Dempsey work out, and to obtain his autograph. The same held true of all weekend visitors, and the Champ was never too busy to talk with them and sign his name.

On Friday nights we would pile out in our cars and drive to the

Walt, second from the left, and Jack Dempsey, center, at Soper's Training Camp, Ojai, California, 1927

prizefights in Ventura, with ringside tickets bought by Dempsey who would climb through the ropes to introduce the fighters. The rumor that Dempsey would be there always drew a full house.

His training camp at Soper's was scheduled to end on the first of July, and I made my plans accordingly. On the morning of the first I would pick up Pat in Santa Barbara and drive to San Diego to stay at my mother's house, and this is what happened. Six days later Pat and I were married by Judge Griffin with my nephew Coburn Maddox and his wife, Marion, standing up with us. The date was July 7, 1927.

We spent our honeymoon at the then beautiful old Mission Inn at Riverside, California, a renowned spot for traditional honeymooners. My bride Pat neither drank nor smoked, and I was cold sober and intended to stay that way.

We were on our way to Prescott, Arizona, the following week. It was hotter than the hinges of hell when we stopped at the Harvey House at Needles for a midnight snack, with the thermometer reading 102 degrees. When we reached the small mining town of Oatman we decided to call it a day, and rented a room at the little rundown Oatman Hotel where there was no cooling except an overhead revolving fan.

After a long hot drive, we arrived in Prescott the next day. The Hassayampa Hotel had not yet been built, and there were no available rooms at either the St. Michaels or the Head hotels, so we settled for a large front room over the Owl Drug Store, a combination drug store and excellent restaurant where we ate our meals. Pat was a little disappointed with the town as she looked down the famous Whisky Row from our bedroom window and saw only Indians, and men with big hats, but she vowed she would not return to California until the weather cooled.

A few days later we went to McLean's real estate office and rented the first house he showed us. It was at the end of Park Avenue and sat high from the sidewalk in a large rock formation. It was a little white house with a fireplace, and was supposed to be furnished,

Walt Coburn, a budding young writer, 1929

but it was pretty bare and far from luxurious. The rent seemed rather exhorbitant at $125.00 a month. But the prime selling point was the brand new General Electric refrigerator with the motor on top (the first we had ever seen) and a new electric stove.

I was head-over-heels in debt in spite of my free stay at Dempsey's training camp. I still owed my Santa Barbara doctor, Diel's Grocery Store, and back payments on two new cars, besides paying board on my two police dogs, Kurt and Tito, being fed and trained by the man from whom I had purchased them in northern California. So I lost no time in getting to work.

I had my secret reasons for coming back to Prescott. It was here at St. Mary's Hospital that the wise old country doctor had given me the verdict that my cowpunching days were over. The first person I looked up was Dr. Looney, to tell him that his terrible verdict had been a blessing in disguise, that it had eventually launched my career as a writer, and that I had now dedicated my life to writing stories which I considered a God-given priceless treasure.

I had another strong motive for returning to Prescott. I had left here in 1919 on crutches, with a one-way ticket to San Diego where my mother lived. I possessed the miserly sum of fifty bucks given me by my wealthy cattlemen brothers, Will and Bob Coburn, who then operated large ranches in nearby Bloody Basin where I had been injured. These brothers, after my father died, had persuaded my mother into loaning them fifty thousand dollars to invest in cattle. This money was never repaid, and it was up to me to support my mother from 1924 to 1944 when she died, but I was in the chips by then and was happy to do so.

CHAPTER 16

King of the Western Pulps

MY CAREER AS A WRITER was now fully launched. I was sitting pretty, had the world by the tail with a downhill pull, and nothing could stop me. I mentally thumbed my nose at my brothers, Will and Bob, and foolishly never took the time to have my mother sue them for what they owed her.

We spent a year and a half in Prescott. Besides numerous novelettes for the pulp magazines, I wrote a book which ran as a serial in the magazine, and was then published as a book by The Century Company of New York. We paid off all our debts and managed to save over four thousand dollars.

I then had a restless urge to return to the Pacific Coast where I had one more thing to accomplish. I wanted to someday buy a choice piece of land in Del Mar where I had sold my first story, and build a home there, and this is what I did.

It was at this time that I really began to hit my stride as a freelance writer, batting out three thousand words a day, six days a week. J. B. (Jack) Kelly, co-publisher with J. W. Glenister, and editor of their Fiction House chain of pulp magazines, came out to California to visit me. He offered me three cents a word and would feature a twenty-five thousand word novelette of mine each month in *Action Stories Magazine*, with my name topping all others on the covers.

I took a strong liking to Jack Kelly when I first met him, and I think the feeling was mutual, because on that day a strong friendship was formed which lasted until his untimely death in 1932. From our first meeting Jack Kelly took me in tow.

"I'll build you up, cowboy," he promised, "until you'll be the highest paid western writer in the game. Max Brand will never catch up with you. While he's a good writer he knows nothing about the West."

I had been writing under my full name, Walter J. Coburn. It was Kelly who suggested I write under the name of Walt Coburn. And so that I would have no pressing financial worries, Fiction House, at Kelly's suggestion, sent me a check for $100 every week, and at the first of each month I was paid the difference between the $750 I received for the twenty-five thousand word novelette and the weekly checks. Jack Kelly kept his word about giving me the lead story and the cover on every issue of *Action Stories Magazine*.

In 1925 when Fiction House first started publishing *Lariat Story Magazine*, Kelly sent me an original Will James pen and ink sketch with the following inscription:

> This drawing by Will James illustrated "Riders of the Purple" by Walter J. Coburn. The first story in the first issue of *Lariat Story Magazine*. It is presented by the Editor of *Lariat* with his warmest good wishes and in a spirit of respect to a great teller of great stories. (Signed) J. B. Kelly, 9-24-25.

Another of my prized possessions is a telegram I received from Jack Kelly, dated New York, April 1, 1931, which reads:

> Your yarn voted best from your typewriter in a year Stop As Lincoln said of Grant's drinking, I would like to send a barrel of your whisky to a lot of our writers. (Signed) Jack Kelly.

It was soon after I began writing regularly for Fiction House that F. E. Blackwell, of *Western Story Magazine*, turned down the last five or six stories I had sent him. I wrote Jack Kelly about this, and he suggested I send the stories to him. I did this and he bought all of them, sending me the following telegram:

"What can you expect from a pig but a grunt?"

During the years Jack Kelly was editor of the Fiction House group of pulp magazines, he told me that instead of his distributors returning the unsold magazines he had instructed them to return only the covers and send the magazines at the expense of Fiction House to one of the really tough prisons in the state of New York, where only lifers were imprisoned.

During the years from 1925 to 1932 I wrote regularly for *Action Stories*, *Action Novels*, *Lariat Story*, *North-West Stories* and *Frontier Stories*, all Fiction House pulps. In 1931 Fiction House published a magazine called *Walt Coburn's Action Novels*, using reprints of my earlier long novelettes. On the cover was my picture "The Cowboy Author" and opposite it was "I read all of Walt Coburn's stories, Will Rogers." The cover was done by the western artist, Joe DeYong, and the story heads were by Will James, T. A. Tinsley and George E. Wert.

Jack Kelly believed in giving me a lot of publicity and would run feature stories from time to time in the newspapers and magazines such as the following:

> Walt Coburn, one-time Montana cowpuncher, has established a new storywriting record. For sixty consecutive months, representing that many magazine issues, a Walt Coburn adventure story of the old West has been published in *Action Story Magazine*. Fiction House, Inc., publishers of *Action Stories*, announce that this performance shatters all previous records for successful story writing. Walt Coburn, a familiar figure at rodeos, is the son of Robert Coburn, whose Circle C outfit in Montana will be remembered by the oldtimers. Some of them, thinly veiled, play vigorous parts in Walt's true-to-life stories of the old days of the West.

Another publicity blurb put out by Fiction House read as follows:

> Of western story writers there is no end. They are as common as Democrats in Texas. Many of them learned their locale from a Pullman window; some of them just sat down to a typewriter and got it all from a package of cigarettes. You will not have to read many pages of this magazine to

appreciate that Walt Coburn is the Real McCoy. Montana is his home state and old-timers still talk of the Coburn Circle C spread where Walt, boy and man, wrangled horses and punched cows before the days of barb wire. Perhaps you have read Walt Coburn before, but, man, if this is your introduction to his high ridin' cowboy stories, how we envy the thrill of your discovery. Walt Coburn's story people are the hard-living, hard-dying breed who built an empire, who wrote the pages of high courage in American history. Walt Coburn is of them and one of them.

These are but two examples of the publicity Jack Kelly fed with a lavish hand to the reading public. If it had been in the cards and he had lived, his help and encouragement would have carried me on to greater things in the writing game. His sudden untimely death on April 4, 1932, at the age of fifty-three, was a shock. Gone now were our future plans and dreams, cancelled by the Grim Reaper. The bond of friendship between us was stronger than any blood-brother ties, for Jack Kelly's understanding of me had long since become a part of my being. He was the finest friend I ever had, and as grand an Irishman as ever gave a writer a leg up the long ladder of success. Memories still linger of our talks together at Del Mar, California, where Jack visited us with his Irish wife, Laura. It was here Jack learned to roll Bull Durham cigarettes, and where we both planned a trip to Ireland, the birthplace of my grandparents.

After Jack's death I continued to write for the Fiction House chain of magazines, with Jack Byrne and Malcolm Reiss as editors. Both had been with Fiction House many years and remained with it until the death of J. W. Glenister, co-partner with Jack Kelly in the publishing end, and the magazine closed down.

I also continued to write for *Western Story Magazine*, with F. E. Blackwell as editor, and later with Jack Burr. I had only met Blackwell once on my one and only visit to New York as a guest of Jack Kelly in 1931. At this time Blackwell took me for my first and only ride on the subway. After Blackwell retired from the Street and Smith group as editor I never failed to remember him at Christmas.

The cover from the 1931 publication, Walt Coburn's Action Novels, *with the quote from Will Rogers, "I read all of Walt Coburn's stories."*

He wrote me a year or two before he died that he was happy to know one of his old writers still remembered him.

While I wrote continually for *Western Story* during the years from 1923 to 1933, it was not until 1938 that I started writing a story a month for that magazine, and I continued doing this until the 1949 September issue when the magazine was discontinued. As was the case with the Fiction House group of pulps, I was given the lead story and the cover on every issue from 1938 until the last issue in 1949.

In 1933 I started writing steadily for the Popular Publications chain of pulp magazines. These included *Argosy*, *Adventure*, *Dime Western*, *Big Book*, *New Western*, *Ace High*, and a special issue of "Walt Coburn's Western Magazine" during 1949 and 1950. I rated the feature story and top cover billing in *Dime Western* and *Star Western* each and every month for a period of almost twenty years. I also wrote regularly for Popular's other pulps mentioned above. The editor of Popular Publications was Rogers Terrill, and he came west almost every year to visit me and talk shop. He was a great guy and a fine editor as every writer who had worked for him well knew. After he moved to *Argosy Magazine* as editor, Mike Tilden became editor of *Dime* and *Star Western*, with Harry Widner as editor of *Ten Story Magazine*. I never met either Mike Tilden or Harry Widner personally, but I had much interesting correspondence with both of them.

Writing for the Popular Publications, together with Street and Smith's *Western Story Magazine*, and several other pulps such as *Short Stories*, with Dorothy McIllwraith as editor, and *Giant* and *Popular Western*, with Lee Marguilies as editor, I rated the feature story and top billing on the covers of as many as four and five magazines on sale on the newsstands every month over a period of more than twenty years.

During the 1930s and 1940s, I wrote and sold a yearly turnout of an estimated six hundred thousand words, a tremendous stint when you consider that I did this without cessation for all those years. I am sure other writers have equaled this mark, and may have excelled it, but few, if any, kept it up for more than two decades.

During those years my word rate increased until I was being paid four and five cents per word, and at times even seven cents. Perhaps this is why I was referred to as the "King of the Western Pulps." Over a forty-five year period I put more than twenty million words on paper and sold every word I wrote, and I can truthfully say I have the published stories to prove it.

I have worked many times with a bottle of whisky beside my typewriter, but cold sober I got the job done quicker, easier and much more lucidly. The editors were very tolerant in riding me with a hackamore instead of a spade bit, and it worked out better all around because I never missed a deadline.

There is not much room for description in the pulps. The keynote is action. Some yarns needed romance, others were better without it because it might have a tendency to take the strength out of the story. Unless the woman was a strong character, I kept her out of a western. They would have looked silly around a cow outfit. The only time the average cowpuncher ever saw a woman was when he went to town to blow his wages at the saloons and honkeytonks, with only an occasional schoolmarm with whom to fall in love. It is a known fact that white women were scarce in the early West.

My plots came from the stars. I might awaken in the middle of the night with some idea which would keep me awake. Perhaps it was nothing more than a single character, or a catch phrase I had heard, or a horse which reminded me of one I once knew, and the man who rode that forgotten horse. Dreams took shape, the plots just came from nowhere.

I went after the job of pulp writing as if it were a game from which I got a big kick. I had no set plan of work, no idea in my head, just a kind of cockeyed, haphazard way of putting down words on paper. I liked to have a strong dramatic situation pictured in my mind, such as a stage setting with the characters on it. These characters might be based on some cowhand or outlaw, gambler or bartender or lawman whom I had known on the range or around some cowtown. I turned them loose on paper, let them act out their parts and speak their dialogue. I made no notes of any kind but carried the story in my head. I had no plot to start with so let the characters do the work, act out the whole yarn, the plot developing as the story unfolded.

I mixed reality with imaginary characterization. With few exceptions no real character I ever knew remained wholly real to the end. Real characters and real incidents were likely to be too wooden. In fiction they had to be pliable. I often received letters from old cowpunchers I used fictitiously in my yarns who were easily recognized. One of them said he had taken to packing a six-shooter again so he could live up to the tough rep I had given him.

I went to work immediately after breakfast for four or five hours. I worked in a studio away from the main house, and no one came near my workshop unless they horned in uninvited. I allowed no interruptions such as telephones, vacuum cleaners or visitors. I quit work around noon, my day's work over. I then never thought about the story nor even discussed it with anyone. I took my siesta hour, then saddled my horse and rode back into the hills. Or, if living near the ocean, I would go for a swim. I had no night life except Saturday night, my one night to howl. I never worked on Sunday. Monday was the beginning of my work week, with perhaps a day or two off between each story. Seldom did I take more vacation than that.

I could write a book about the reactions of my readers. There were old-time cowpunchers who worked for my father's Circle C outfit in Montana when I was a kid wrangling horses, men doing time in the pen, outlaws writing me under assumed names, a young Irish lad over in County Donegal who made a play out of one of my yarns, a few priests, and a Britisher who planned on coming out West someday and was, so he said, in the course of preparation by milking cows at a dairy near London. There was a tough Irish cop in New York who said "a bit of a prayer for me" because he liked a story I wrote, a down-and-out prize fighter who once ranked among the old-time

Walt on the lawn of his Del Mar, California, home, 1940

champs, and a lunger living on borrowed time. Heavyweight champion Jack Dempsey read all my yarns. I also received letters from senators, bankers, judges, rodeo contestants, cowhands and cattlemen who could spot a flaw in a story. These were the folks I heard from and their letters were more gratifying than the fat checks.

I have had a few writer friends over the years, mostly some of the old pros such as Eugene Manlove Rhodes, polished writers who left their mark and are now gone. But for the most part since I started writing for a living, I have played a lone hand. I have always been a loner, never a joiner.

In all my years of fiction writing I never rewrote a story, never missed a deadline, drunk or sober, never used an agent, but dealt directly with the editors, and never used a pseudonym.

The folding of the pulp magazines in 1950 wrecked the gravy train for the western pulp writers. Why the magazines folded has never been satisfactorily explained, but I doubt, as some have said, that it was the advent of television. I rather think it was the rising cost of production, and the limit reached on the price the publishers could charge for the magazines, plus an over-production of magazines on the newsstands which had much to do with their discontinuance.

The so-called "adult" western paperbacks have replaced the pulp magazines, but time alone will tell if they will endure over three decades as did the pulps, and give as much low-priced entertainment to so many.

I know that somewhere along the trail the Señor Dios laid a hand on my shoulder and shaped my destiny. Such is my belief and will continue to be until I follow the ghost rider on the pale horse on my last circle into the Shadow Hills.

It was while we were living in Del Mar that I learned by the grapevine that Blake Beck had married the wealthy Jewish playboy she was practically engaged to when I first met her in Carmel. Her husband was one of the three owners of a big name-brand men's clothing store in the East. She seemed to have done well for herself.

About a year later I learned of her tragic death. It happened in Carmel at a large formal party at the Point Lobos home of a well-to-do friend of her husband. During the height of the party Blake, in evening gown and high-heeled slippers, left the party unnoticed, and when she was missed from among the festive guests they went out to look for her. Her husband found her slippers on the edge of the cliff and a few days later her mangled body was washed ashore on a nearby sandy beach, an apparent suicide.

A few weeks after her death, I learned that Steve Glassell, owner of the Cabbages and Kings men's clothing store, had committed suicide. I never learned the details of Steve's tragic death, for I never returned to Carmel and its ghosts.

In 1935, because my wife, Pat, was having trouble with asthma due to the dampness of the coast, we closed our Del Mar house and went to Tucson, Arizona. The dry climate seemed to agree with her so we bought a sixteen-acre piece of land in the Santa Catalina Foothills, then being developed by John W. Murphey, of Tucson. Mr. Murphey, together with his architect, Joseph Jossler, built our burnt adobe house right in the middle of our acreage which had a spectacular view of five mountain ranges. The fifty-two hundred-square-foot house under a red-tiled roof had five fireplaces and was completely furnished with handmade, handcarved solid black walnut furniture, handcrafted by Edward G. Anderson, of Los Angeles, over a four-year period. It was a home of which to be very proud, a real showplace beyond description here. My work studio was built of adobe down the hill and away from the main house. It was of one room with a fireplace, and a large picture window overlooking the Santa Catalina Mountains.

For a few years we spent our winters in Tucson and our summers in Del Mar. Then when gas was rationed during World War II, and we were unable to drive back and forth, we sold our Del Mar place in 1944, and lived permanently in Tucson.

In late 1949 and early 1950, when I was riding the gravy train of my lucrative writing for the western pulps, that gravy train was wrecked almost overnight. Without any advance warning most of the pulps were being discontinued, and this was a blow which threatened my livelihood. I had lived all my life in the certain belief that there were no pockets in a shroud, and that you could not take it with you.

We were riding it out when a wealthy Texas oilman wanted to buy our home, the home into which Pat and I had both put all our dreams and hopes for the future. It was a hard decision to make, but we decided to sell our beautiful home, including all the handcrafted furniture, for the fabulous price we were offered. When we moved out we never returned, not even to drive past the place.

For a year or two we lived in rented houses and then moved back to California, and built another attractive home in beautiful, exclusive Rancho Santa Fe, seven miles in the back country from Del Mar. Then one day a couple of years later some prospective buyers came along and fell in love with the place so we sold it for a ten thousand dollar profit.

After selling this home, we moved to Prescott, Arizona, where we built a log house on an acre of ground six miles from town in the Prescott National Forest, and this is where we now live.

I have managed to keep the wolf from the door by selling reprint rights of my old stories being published regularly in pocket book form. I have also written several original book-length novels, plus two Western Americana books — *Stirrup High* and *Pioneer Cattleman in Montana, the Story of the Circle C Ranch* — of which I am very proud. I have also been writing true stories about the old West for the past several years for Western Publications, a Texas publishing outfit owned by Joe Austell Small who has been buying a story a month from me for his group of magazines, *True West, Frontier Times* and *Old West*.

Ever since I could remember I have been proud of my birthright and rightful heritage as being the son of a pioneer cattleman of Montana. My father's Circle C brand was his Coat of Arms according to cow country heraldry, and I felt it my duty to honor him

Front view of the Coburn home in Tucson, 1945

Living room of Tucson home, 1945

when I wrote *Pioneer Cattleman in Montana, the Story of the Circle C Ranch*, published by the University of Oklahoma Press in December, 1968.

During the lean days of rejection slips, long before I sold my first story, I used to go into the little Catholic Church in Del Mar on weekdays as well as on Sundays. There on bended knees I prayed to God that He would bestow upon me the gift of writing, and in the course of time my prayers were answered.

As of now, by the grace of God, having passed my eighty-first birthday, I still retain that God-given gift of writing stories after more than forty-five years of putting words on paper. I am blessed with good health physically, though beginning to feel mentally exhausted at times. Though having grown bald with the passing years, I still have all my own teeth, still retain good eyesight, am still able to hear the songbirds and watch the sunrises and sunsets, and hear the distant yapping of coyotes.

I am now content to live the quiet life of a self-exiled, semi-recluse in our log house on the outskirts of Prescott, surrounded by the Prescott National Forest of tall ponderosa pines. Above all, I am doubly blessed with a good and loving wife who has put up with my tantrums for forty-four years. I have heard it said that any man who brags about being the head of his own house will lie about something else. Pat handles the purse strings, keeps our house in order and types my manuscripts, doing all the squaw work.

If ever a long-suffering wife is well-deserving of a halo, it is my Pat. By the grace of God I am the luckiest man alive as I sum up my many blessings at the end of the long trail. I will quit this earth ahead of the game when I head for the last campground. A man can live too long, that is for sure. When the juices of youth have dried up, when a man who has led an active life, when the athletic body he took pride in begins to lose its muscle tone, and his taut skin begins to wither, when his joints begin to stiffen and the broken bones picked up in reckless youth begin to ache with arthritis, it is time for that man to travel on. When an old cowhand gets too

Walt on Peanuts at Rincon Stock Farm, 1945

stoved-up to sit on a bronc he used to ride just for the hell of it, and he is too short-winded to jog a hundred yards and has the beginning of a pot, let us face it, he has lived too long.

I still have an active mind and the ability to write stories, but I have slowed down. Instead of three thousand words I used to knock out in the four early morning hours, I now knock out a thousand or fifteen hundred and call it a day.

While I am still young at heart, the carcass is getting old and I can not do the things I used to do when I was young and full of hell. It has been years since I made the rounds of the saloons along Prescott's famous Whisky Row, and had a drink with my old friend Shell Dunbar who owns the famous Palace Bar. So now I drink a couple of bottles of Ballantine Ale at home, with a shot of Bushmill's Irish Whisky on occasion. John Barleycorn never had this old country boy licked, but I admit he had me on the ropes on several occasions.

I never cared for the so-called social life. I suppose you could call me anti-social, but the fact is that while I am a dedicated writer and have been for nearly half a century, at heart I am still a forty-dollar-a-month cowhand and will be until I die.

In the sunset of life I am content to remain at home, feed the bushy-tailed squirrels and the many birds, and listen to the wind whispering in the majestic ponderosa pines. I never get lonesome out here in the quietude where I feel close to God.

Thus summing up my entire life along my back trail, I envy no man, I have made my share of mistakes, and regret them bitterly. I have had my share of enemies and fair-weather friends, but it is the true friends who are there when the chips are down that actually count. In summing up these real friends with the end of the trail in sight, I can truthfully say that my wife, Pat, has been and still is the one true friend I have ever known, the only person, with her loyalty and understanding, who actually knows this man whom she married for better or for worse, until death do us part.

I dedicate this, my last book, to my Pat, the finest, most loyal person I have ever known.

Walt Coburn 1889-1971

Walt Coburn died by his own hand at his home in Prescott, Arizona, on May 24, 1971. Among his papers were found the following rambling notes:

>ADIOS!
>May God forgive me
>I want Father Leonard.
>If possible I want to be buried
>at the Ft. Whipple Cemetery
>My friend Budge Ruffner.
>No funeral.
>
>My work on this earth is finished
>I hired out as a tough hand and
>I'm playing my string out.
>If this last word seems confused, Patty
>That is because that is the state of my mind.
>Rather death than suffering in some insane asylum.
>I've had my last shot of Bushmill's.
>
>I can't make a hand anymore.
>Written my last story.
>Forgive me, Pat,
>This is the only way out.
>I leave and bequeath everything to my wife.
>I leave the world with no regrets.
>So let there be no tears shed.

> This is a difficult thing to do, Patty.
> It's not an act of cowardice.
> It takes all the guts I have.
> I love you.
>   Walt

In another note he wrote:

> I've said my rosary
> Selected the rope — a fine reata.
> A cowhand is going out in style.
> Tell Budge I want a wooden coffin.
> I want a wake. An Irish-cowboy wake.
>
> It's high noon and time to meet the Creator.
> That has given me the gift of writing stories.
> Now it is time to meet God!
>
> High Noon on a Beautiful Day
>
> Say a prayer for me
> God knows I'll need it when I
> Check in for the final verdict.
>   Walt

Bibliographical Note

WALT COBURN was one of America's most prolific writers during the almost half-century from 1922 to 1970. During this period he wrote well over one thousand short stories which were published in the popular western pulp magazines of the period. Additionally close to one hundred books by him were printed and reprinted and sold to thousands of his fans. Walt Coburn's stories appeared for years in the leading western pulp magazines including: *Argosy*, *Western Story*, *Action Stories*, *Lariat Story*, *North-West Stories*, *Adventure*, *Dime Western*, *Star Western*, *Ten Story*, *New Western*, *Ace High Western*, *Big Book Western*, *True West* and *Frontier Times*. Some of his better known books include: *The Ringtailed Rannyhans*, 1927; *Mavericks*, 1929; *Barb Wire*, 1939; *Law Rides the Range*, 1935; *Sky Pilot Cowboy*, 1937; *Pardners of the Dim Trails*, 1951; *Beyond the Wild Missouri*, 1956; *Stirrup High*, 1957; and *Pioneer Cattleman in Montana*, 1968.

Even now several of his books are into advanced printings, and the demand for them continues. His contribution to Western fiction was enormous, and the recognition of that contribution is finally being fully realized.